Whiteness, Class and the Legacies of Empire

Also by Katharine Tyler

MAJORITY CULTURES AND THE EVERYDAY POLITICS OF ETHNIC DIFFERENCE: WHOSE HOUSE IS THIS? *(co-edited with Bo Petersson)*

Whiteness, Class and the Legacies of Empire

On Home Ground

By
Katharine Tyler
University of Surrey, UK

© Katharine Tyler 2012

All rights reserved. No reproduction, copy or transmission of this publication may be made without written permission.

No portion of this publication may be reproduced, copied or transmitted save with written permission or in accordance with the provisions of the Copyright, Designs and Patents Act 1988, or under the terms of any licence permitting limited copying issued by the Copyright Licensing Agency, Saffron House, 6–10 Kirby Street, London EC1N 8TS.

Any person who does any unauthorized act in relation to this publication may be liable to criminal prosecution and civil claims for damages.

The author has asserted her right to be identified as the author of this work in accordance with the Copyright, Designs and Patents Act 1988.

First published 2012 by
PALGRAVE MACMILLAN

Palgrave Macmillan in the UK is an imprint of Macmillan Publishers Limited, registered in England, company number 785998, of Houndmills, Basingstoke, Hampshire RG21 6XS.

Palgrave Macmillan in the US is a division of St Martin's Press LLC, 175 Fifth Avenue, New York, NY 10010.

Palgrave Macmillan is the global academic imprint of the above companies and has companies and representatives throughout the world.

Palgrave® and Macmillan® are registered trademarks in the United States, the United Kingdom, Europe and other countries.

ISBN 978–0–230–57849–4

This book is printed on paper suitable for recycling and made from fully managed and sustained forest sources. Logging, pulping and manufacturing processes are expected to conform to the environmental regulations of the country of origin.

A catalogue record for this book is available from the British Library.

A catalog record for this book is available from the Library of Congress.

10 9 8 7 6 5 4 3 2 1
21 20 19 18 17 16 15 14 13 12

Printed and bound in Great Britain by
CPI Antony Rowe, Chippenham and Eastbourne

*This book is dedicated to my mother Janet Tyler,
Nigel Pleasants and Edward Tyler-Pleasants*

Contents

Acknowledgements   viii

1   Frameworks, Fieldworks and Inspirations   1

Part I   White Amnesia: White Middle-Class Ethnicities

2   BrAsian 'Invasion' of White Suburban English Village Life   39

3   The Racialisation of the Country, the City and the Forgetting of Empire   79

Part II   Confronting Coloniality: White Working-Class Ethnicities

4   The Questioning of Racism in a Former Coalmining Town   111

5   Neighbourhood Activism and the Ambiguities of Anti-Racism in the City   146

Part III   Postcolonial Genealogies

6   Slave Ancestries and the Inheritance of Interracial Identities   175

7   The Co-Existence of Whiteness, Social Class and Coloniality in Britain and the USA   206

Notes   223

Bibliography   229

Index   237

Acknowledgements

There are many people over the years who have contributed to this book. I shall not attempt to list everyone here. Suffice to say you know who you are and thank you.

The residential nature of the fieldwork upon which this book is based has ensured that the memories and relationships I formed during my fieldwork in Leicester and Leicestershire are both professional and personal. To say thank you to the people I came to know in Leicester and Leicestershire seems inadequate. Up until recently my mother lived in Leicestershire, which granted me the luxury of returning home whenever I felt like it. In light of her move away from the county, I feel that finishing this book signals a further ending of my relationship with the county, the city and the people who live there, which makes me feel very sad.

In the South East of England where I now live and work, I am grateful to my colleagues at the Department of Sociology, University of Surrey, for supporting my sabbatical year, which has allowed me the time to write this book.

Peter Wade was my supervisor during both my doctoral and postdoctoral studies in the Department of Social Anthropology at the University of Manchester. To this day, he has still probably read and commented on more of my written work than anyone else. At Manchester I also had the very good fortune to be employed as a Postdoctoral Fellow on a project directed by Jeanette Edwards. Together Jeanette and Pete opened my mind to think anthropologically about ethnicity and genealogy. They also gave me the intellectual freedom to develop my work in Leicester in ways that made sense to me.

Cathrine Degnen generously read and commented on a draft of this manuscript while she was completing her own book. The current shape and form of *Whiteness, Class and the Legacies of Empire* owe much to her perceptive, critical and detailed comments. I am extremely grateful for her time and care in helping me improve this book.

At home, Samantha Hyslop and my partner Nigel Pleasants have kept it all going on the domestic front. I have inevitably spent far too many evenings writing this book away from Nigel when I should have been with him. Not only has he soldiered on without too much complaint, he also read and commented on a final draft. His critical comments transformed the manuscript. More than anyone else, Nigel has supported and sustained me both domestically and academically during the writing of this book. And Edward, our young son, has contributed lots of fun and laughter to this year of writing. He has also given me the added impetus to get this book finished.

My twin sister, Elizabeth Ashton-Tyler, has helped in more ways than I can mention. But there is one woman who has always and consistently been rooting for me throughout the years of studying, fieldworking and writing, and that is my mother, Janet Tyler. And so it is to my mother Janet, as well as Nigel and Edward, that I dedicate this book.

The following chapters are based in part upon material that has been published previously, and I thank the publishers and editors for permission to use it here. Chapter 2 draws upon material published in K. Tyler (2006) 'Village People: Race, Nation, Class and the Community Spirit', in *The New Countryside? Ethnicity, Nation and Exclusion in Contemporary Rural Britain* (pp. 129–48), edited by Sarah Neal and Julian Agyeman, reproduced with permission of Policy Press; and K. Tyler (2003) 'The Racialised and Classed Constitution of English Village Life', *Ethnos*, vol. 68, no. 3, pp. 391–412, reproduced with permission of Taylor & Francis. Chapter 3 draws upon material published in K. Tyler (2008) 'Debating the Rural and the Urban: Majority White Racialised Discourses on the Countryside and the City', in *Majority Cultures and the Everyday Politics of Ethnic Difference: Whose House is this?*, edited by Bo Petersson and Katharine Tyler, reproduced with permission of Palgrave Macmillan. Chapter 4 is based upon K. Tyler (2004) 'Racism, Tradition and Reflexivity in a Former Mining Town', *Ethnic and Racial Studies*, vol. 27, no. 2, pp. 290–309, reproduced with permission of Taylor & Francis. Chapter 5 is based upon K. Tyler (2007) '"Streetville Forever": Collective Action, Ethnicity and the State', *Identities: Global Studies in Culture and Power*, vol. 14, no. 5, pp. 579–602, reproduced with permission of Taylor & Francis. Chapter 6 is based upon K. Tyler (2005) 'The Genealogical Imagination: The Inheritance of Interracial Identities', *The Sociological Review*, vol. 53, no. 3, pp. 475–94, reproduced with permission of the editors of *The Sociological Review*. Some parts of the interview with 'Clare' that feature in Chapter 6 also appear in K. Tyler (2011) 'New Ethnicities and Old Classities: Respectability and Diaspora', *Social Identities*, vol. 17, no. 4, pp. 521–40, reproduced with permission of Taylor & Francis. The final part of Chapter 6 draws upon an interview extract with 'Sophie' that appears in part in K. Tyler (2009) 'Whiteness Studies and Laypeople's Engagements with Race and Genetics', *New Genetics and Society*, vol. 28, no. 1, pp. 35–48, reproduced with permission of Taylor & Francis.

Finally I must record my gratitude to the following for their financial support: the Economic and Social Research Council for a Doctoral Studentship 1996–1999; and 'Public Understandings of Genetics: A Cross-Cultural and Ethnographic Study of the "New Genetics" and Social Identity', funded by the European Commission Fifth Framework Programme: Quality of Life and Management of Living Resources. Contract number: QLG7-CT-2001-01668.

1
Frameworks, Fieldworks and Inspirations

What does it mean to be White in contemporary postcolonial societies? I set out in this book to take the reader on a journey through the complex cultural politics of White ethnic identities in everyday English settings, which is a prominent example of a postcolonial society.[1] *Whiteness, Class and the Legacies of Empire* develops a postcolonial perspective drawn from an established body of literature known (not unproblematically) as Whiteness studies. This perspective is both informed by and helps interpret my own multi-sited ethnographic fieldwork conducted in semi-rural, suburban and urban locales in England. One aim of White ethnicity studies has been to develop a critical language to render visible the local, national and global power and privilege that shapes White ethnicities in Western societies. Scholars in the field of postcolonial studies place emphasis upon the importance of contextualising Western hegemony in the West's imperial past, namely, the histories of European slavery and colonialism. I shall endeavour to deepen the theoretical insights of Whiteness studies by drawing upon ethnographic fieldwork to explore the legacies of Empire to the everyday, mundane and contemporary reproduction of White power and dominance within everyday settings in England.[2] My contention is that the role of the colonial in the formation of contemporary White ethnic identities is either explored in brief or simply ignored by scholars working in the field of White ethnicity studies. There are of course some key exceptions to this, which I shall discuss later on in this chapter.

Yet, historians have shown how the social, cultural, economic and political formation and structure of Englishness and Britishness rest upon the nation's histories of Empire, including Britain's involvement in the slave trade (Mackenzie, 1986a; C. Hall, 2000a; Colls, 2002; Thompson, 2005; Hall and Rose, 2006a). In this regard, Britain's contemporary economic and cultural wealth, international political power and global influence is rooted within and dependent upon the nation's historical exploitation of people, land, wealth, culture, landscape and raw materials from its former colonies. By 1820 Britain ruled 26 per cent of the world's total population, including 'colonies of settlement such as Australia, New Zealand and Canada to the protectorates and dependencies – some tiny, such as Ionian Islands, others vast, like India' (C. Hall, 2000b, p. 5). It is often assumed in the contemporary White English imagination that Empire is something that happened 'over there' and 'then', thus does not affect 'us' English people 'over here' and 'now'. Moreover, there is some evidence to suggest that the influence of the British Empire on the formation of the present is fading fast from public memory (Thompson, 2005, Chapter 9). This is in spite of the fact that the brutal, bloody and oppressive histories of Empire are interwoven into the landscape, language, political organisation and everyday social fabric of British society. For example, the historian Robert Colls (2002, p. 164) has written, 'Nothing could be nicer than a cup of tea, but only the water and milk were English.' While this is a sentiment that remains true today, the point here is that the history of English people's daily consumption of tea opens up a pathway to examine the British colonisation of India, including the establishment of tea plantations in Assam and Darjeeling. Sugar, like many other commodities, was dependent upon the exploitation of slave labour in the Caribbean colonies. On a more intimate level, some population geneticists have argued that one consequence of Empire and slavery is that there is no such family as a purely White British or purely Black British African Caribbean family within the UK. Rather, the histories of interracial intercourse, including those of rape and coercion between the coloniser and colonised, render Black British and White British mixed in terms of racial ancestry and descent. One consequence of these histories of Empire is that the Black and South Asian people who migrated to England and other parts of Britain from the former colonies, and their descendants, have intimate complex histories, relationships and genealogical connections to Englishness and Britishness that run very deep.

This book will not provide the reader with a history of the British Empire. Rather, in mobilising a postcolonial perspective it will examine some of the legacies of Empire on the formation of contemporary White and interracial ethnicities (or 'mixed-race' ethnicities, in English vernacular). In so doing, this book explores some of the ways in which the colonial worldview of White Western cultural superiority mediates the formation of White and interracial ethnicities in these contemporary postcolonial times. To do this I shall explore how the colonial worldview of White Western superiority that is premised upon the creation of hierarchical differences that mark the racially unmarked White self off from racialised Others becomes 'inscribed in [everyday] languages and representations ... social relationships and social structures – in what people think ... but also in what they do, and in the structured situations where they do it' (Eley, 2002).[3]

A central argument of this book is that crucial to the reproduction of racial differences and hierarchies in the present is 'the art of forgetting' (Bauman, 1997, p. 53) the significance of the colonial past in shaping contemporary and everyday formations of Whiteness and Englishness. From this standpoint, the book traces and analyses how some White English people tend to screen out, forget, silence and do not know the meaning and significance of the colonial past within everyday racialised discourses and practices. One significant effect of this is for BrAsians' (I shall explain my use of this term below) and Black Britons' ancestral connections and relationships to Englishness/Britishness to be displaced and forgotten.

Whiteness, Class and the Legacies of Empire examines how White middle- and working-class people living in differing racialised and classed locales reflect upon the presence of BrAsian residents in the places that they live. My argument is that in the postcolonial era BrAsians are represented in the White hegemonic imagination as racialised 'immigrants'. In this sense, BrAsians represent 'an undecidable figure ... who stands betwixt and between citizen and foreigner, a colonial past and a national present, West "and non-West", one of us and one of them' (Hesse and Sayyid, 2006, p. 30).

Crucially, this book's examination of White cultural hegemony is analysed in conjunction with an exploration of the situations, contexts and conditions in which representations and worldviews of White Western cultural superiority are contested, challenged, fractured and broken down. Thus, White hegemony is not complete but allows spaces for questioning, challenging and confrontation of dominant norms and ways of thinking about race, ethnicity and difference in the postcolonial present. In this regard, the book explores how the processes of remembering the slave past mediate the formation of the members of interracial families' ethnicities, which opens up a space for the critical questioning of White power and privilege within English society. In short, this study scrutinises, traces and analyses both the forgetting of the colonial past within White discourses that objectify and Other BrAsians, as well as the active mobilisation and evocation of slave pasts and histories by the members of interracial families when they think about the formation of their identities in the present.

Turning to the ethnography upon which it is based, this book draws upon nearly 27 months of multi-sited residential ethnographic fieldwork, carried out during two separate time periods, which examined the everyday maintenance and control of White power and dominance across semi-rural and urban locales in contemporary postcolonial England. My fieldwork was situated in a provincial region in the East Midlands area of England called Leicestershire. The city of Leicester is situated approximately a hundred miles north east of London. Leicester is famous nationally for its BrAsian populations, which settled in the city at the time of decolonisation of the British Empire and its aftermath. In stark contrast to the ethnic diversity of the city, the surrounding countryside of Leicestershire is predominantly White in terms of population profile. This racial segregation between the White countryside of Leicestershire and the multicultural city of Leicester is typical of the racialisation of space between the countryside and the city in England, where minorities have settled in English cities.[4] That is, not all cities in England are ethnically diverse; some cities, like the rural populations that surround them, remain overwhelmingly White.

My work in Leicester and Leicestershire was based on residential fieldwork within and across three separate research locales and included participant observation and in-depth interviews with research participants.[5] From January to July 1997, I conducted six months of residential fieldwork in 'Greenville', a suburban village that is situated on the border of the city of Leicester and the countryside of Leicestershire. From August 1997 to February 1998 I conducted a further six months of residential fieldwork in 'Coalville', a former coalmining town situated in north west Leicestershire.[6] My fieldworks in these locales studied White people's perceptions of BrAsians who lived locally. The first three ethnographic chapters of this book draw upon fieldwork from Greenville (Chapters 2 and 3) and Coalville (Chapter 4) respectively. Two further ethnographic chapters (Chapters 5 and 6) draw upon 15 months of fieldwork (May 2002 to August 2003) that I conducted in 'Streetville', an inner city and ethnically diverse neighbourhood of Leicester. In Streetville, I became actively involved in local community-based politics and interviewed White, Black and interracial members of interracial families.

In the White English imagination, the idea of 'the village' and the 'coalmining town' are national symbols of Englishness that are associated with a distinctively White culture and aesthetic. While the contemporary 'village in the mind' (Pahl, 1964) represents a White, rural and essentially middle-class ideal of Englishness, the image of the coalmining town in post-industrial England signifies a working-class image of nation, which is also associated with Whiteness. In contrast to the Whitened and homogeneous classed images associated with the former coalmining town and the village respectively, the inner city signifies a multicultural image of nation that is fragmented by class and ethnicity. One aim of this book is to complicate these national images of Englishness through an exploration of the contemporary salience of these popular images of place, ethnicity, class and nation. To do this I will trace everyday configurations of the meaning and constitution of racial, national and classed identities within and between the ethnographic fieldsites of the village, the former coalmining town and the inner city in Leicester/shire.

At this juncture it is worth reflecting for a moment on my use of the terms 'White', 'BrAsian' and 'interracial'. Throughout the book I shall call the people who have White skins and who claim a sense of belonging to Leicester and/or Leicestershire, and/or England and/or Britain as 'White'. Most 'White' English and British research participants did not self-identify as 'White', which reflects the ways in which White ethnicity often remains unmarked as an ethnic identity within everyday British society. To some readers my repeated naming of my White research participants as 'White' might look overstated and laboured. However, in identifying my research participants as 'White', my aim is to make Whiteness a racially marked and visible category in the same way that non-White people are always already racially marked by the racial labels that are routinely used to describe them. With regard to my use of the expression 'BrAsian', I follow a trend among some scholars working within the field of race and ethnicity in Britain, for this idiom to refer to people who can trace their ancestries to South Asia, or are the descendants of South Asian settlers (Ali et al., 2006). I deploy this term throughout in order to provide a reminder of the imperial and contemporary relationships that bind South Asian settlers and their descendants to England and Britain. Following S. Sayyid (2006, p. 7), I understand the term 'BrAsian' to entail 'the recognition of the need to replace the colonial *telos* with a vision in which the distinction between West and non-West is no longer privileged'. The term 'BrAsian' cannot easily be divided into 'British' and 'Asian', 'Western' and 'non-Western' parts, and so represents more than a fusion of its parts; it is 'a confusion' of the terms 'Asian' and 'British' (2006, p. 7). However, the idiom 'BrAsian' was not used by any of the research participants themselves, which is not surprising given that it is an academic expression, and not used in everyday talk in England. Thus in my reporting of my White research participants' words, I shall use the popular idiom 'Asian', which they used. In addition, throughout this book I shall also use the terms 'Black' or 'Black Briton' to refer to people who are either themselves settlers to the UK from the African Caribbean or their descendants. While the term 'mixed-race' is the popular term in English vernacular, I shall use the label 'interracial' to refer to the identities of people who claim to be of 'mixed-race' or 'mixed-heritage' identities. I shall refer collectively to the White, Black and interracial members of 'mixed-race' families as members of 'interracial families'. Like the term 'BrAsians', this was not the term employed by my co-conversationalists. In Chapter 6 I provide a detailed justification for my use of the term 'interracial'.

This introduction sets out the key ideas and theoretical frameworks that feature in and structure the book. It also explains my motivation for writing it, provides some thoughts on the ethnographic study of Whiteness and sets out an overview of the contents of the book's chapters. But first, I would like to pause for a moment to reflect upon a recent series of television programmes aired by the British Broadcasting Corporation (BBC). As I began what I knew had to be the last academic year that I was able to spend time working on the material that constitutes *Whiteness, Class and the Legacies of Empire*, the BBC aired a six-part series of programmes (September–October 2010, BBC4) entitled *The Story of England*.[7] A discussion of this series of programmes provides a good starting point to think about some of the ways in which histories of Empire are screened out in the contemporary White English popular imagination.[8] In this way, an analysis of how Englishness and its imperial past is portrayed in these programmes parallels some of the processes of displacing Empire that I found articulated by the White people with whom I worked in Leicester/shire. This television series is also of particular interest to me because, like my study, *The Story of England* is situated in Leicestershire, and a discussion of it helps to set the ethnographic and theoretical scene for the chapters that follow.

The Story of England: Englishness and the silencing of Empire

The programmes chart the history of Kibworth, a rural village in Leicestershire, nine miles south of the city of Leicester. The programmes were researched, written and presented by the popular historian Michael Wood. This series was marketed by the BBC as a 'Who do you think you are?' of the English nation, which refers to another popular television series, entitled *Who Do You Think You Are?*, aired in both the UK and the USA, which follows the journeys of celebrities who trace their family trees. In this sense, this series of programmes can be read as an historical genealogy of the English nation and therefore part of widespread popular interest in genealogy and identity.

The central idea of *The Story of England* was that an examination of the history of the village of Kibworth could reveal the history of the nation. In other words, national history is mirrored in the local, and local history in that of the national. From this point of view, Wood argues that the history of Kibworth is typical of the history of any village or community in England. Thus, the village of Kibworth comes to represent and stand for the nation. It seems to me that Wood's and the BBC's decision to focus on a rural village and not an urban town or city highlights the significance of the image and icon of the village in popular English imaginings of nation and nationhood. A similar point was made nearly forty years ago by Raymond Williams (1973) in his famous book *The Country and the City*. Williams opens his book with the observation that in the English language the '"country" is both a nation and a part of a "land", "the country" can be the whole society or its rural area' (1973, p. 1). Williams poignantly reminds us that the term 'country' in the English language includes and incorporates not just the countryside but also the entire nation.

Wood's series of programmes chart and span the history of Kibworth from the Vikings, Romans and Anglo-Saxon times up to the modern day. It is emphasised throughout that the aim of the programmes is to trace the history of ordinary people and not that of kings and queens. Indeed, the very ordinariness of this narrative is enhanced by the participation of the contemporary residents of Kibworth in the programmes. Throughout the series mostly White residents of Kibworth read letters, diary extracts and other historical sources to bring to life the lived experiences of those who lived in their village.[9] Villagers also played a crucial role in the making of the series by their participation in the 'the Big Dig'.

One weekend in July 2010, villagers were invited to dig archaeological pits in their gardens. With the guidance of professional archaeologists, the aim was for the villagers to uncover relics and objects from the past. Over the course of the weekend, mostly middle-class White villagers found a rich and impressive array of ancient artefacts, including pieces of pottery that had food burnt into them from Anglo-Saxon times, coins and roof tiles from the Roman period.[10]

Drawing upon the villagers' findings, local and national archives, the expertise of archaeologists, archivists, geneticists and social historians, the programmes weave together the history of the village and thus by implication the nation. At times, connections are made between the political and social trauma that shaped and affected the life of the villagers in the past and the current day. Climate change, economic and social recession are depicted as problems that not only shape and influence contemporary English society but also impacted historically upon the lives of past residents of Kibworth. Overall, a picture is painted of an enduring community united by charity, friendship, natural disaster and death, while also divided by wealth, social status and political and religious conviction. For example, some villagers were involved in the Lollard uprisings against Henry V in 1414, and in the Reformation the local vicar was jailed for his opposition to Henry VIII.

Given my interest in how colonial notions of White cultural superiority are articulated in the present, this documentary series is significant. Its importance is not to be found in what the programmes tell 'us' the viewer about the role of the British Empire in the formation of village life and thus Englishness. Rather, for me, it is precisely the relative absence of information on Empire, compared to the emphasis placed on other aspects of English history, that constitutes the programme's real interest and significance. It is the Roman Empire, and thus *England's* experience of *being colonised* and not the process of *colonising*, that features most prominently in these programmes. In this sense, an analysis of how the history of the British Empire is screened out of this particular story of England signposts some of the processes that constitute the forgetting of the more recent colonial past that I found central to my analysis of White racialised discourses in my studies in Leicester/shire. My contention is that the programme's presentation of Empire rests upon what Georgie Wemyss (2008; 2009) refers to as a 'bundle of silences'. To fully understand what Wemyss means by this term it is worth taking a moment to reflect on her work.

Following the anthropologist Trouillot, Wemyss (2008; 2009) argues that 'bundles of silences' enter historical accounts through key moments in the making of history. Wemyss (2008) explores the selective and sanitised picture of the histories of the British Empire articulated in urban regeneration discourses in the Docklands area in the East End of London. The Docklands area of East London was a major imperial port integral to the slave trade, while Bengali seamen crewed ships that sailed between London and the colonies. Wemyss (2009) argues that the public representation of the Docklands displaces and suppresses the dehumanisation of Africans and the colonial violence and economic and cultural exploitation of Bengalis in Bengal and London. Her contention is that one consequence of this version of history is to reproduce and maintain racial hierarchies that can be traced to colonial constructions of difference within dominant White liberal media and political discourses of difference.

Sharing parallels with Wemyss' analysis of the silencing of Empire in everyday constructions of East London's history, my argument is that one effect of Wood's narrative is to produce similar sanitised versions of colonial history with reference to Leicestershire. In this way, Wood's representation of the nation's history rests upon silencing the cultural and political tyranny, economic exploitation and human suffering intrinsic to British colonialism. Wood's history of England makes only fleeting references to the colonial past, because it pertains to the detail of ancient pasts (of being colonised) rather than the more uncomfortable recent past of Britishness and Englishness associated with imperial projects, the legacies of which are interwoven with the history and contemporary social fabric of Kibworth and the neighbouring city of Leicester. Thus the myriad ways in which Britain's colonial history shaped and moulded life at home, in England, in banal, unconscious and routine ways are not given the detailed critical attention that they deserve.

To advance and develop this argument, it is useful to reflect on some of the actual references that the documentary does make to Empire. In the fifth programme in the series, Wood mentioned how in one dig villagers found a brooch from the East India Company, but no mention is made of the ways in which this company was instrumental in Britain's sometimes ruthless colonisation of India for four hundred years. The East India Company established trade routes mainly in cotton, silk, tea and opium between Britain and its Empire. Over time the company came to rule large areas of India, through the deployment of military force and administrative power. It is only in the sixth and final programme in the series, spanning the Victorians to the modern day, that several references are made to Britain's colonial history, and so it is these I shall focus upon here. However, these references are once again not made in any systematic, critical and sustained way. According to the BBC description of this final programme in the series, the focus is on

> the secret history of a Victorian village more colourful than even Dickens could have imagined. Recreating their 'Penny Concerts' of the 1880s, visiting World War I battlefields with the school, and

recalling the Home Guard, local land girls and the bombing of the village in 1940, finally the series moves into the brave new world of 'homes for heroes'.

(http://www.mayavisionint.com/English_Story/ Episode_Guide.html. I [accessed August 2011])

In this programme, it is noted that in the interwar period the villagers, like the rest of the nation, benefited from the social and economic prosperity of the British Empire, without any further explanation of what this might mean, including detailed analysis of where and how it came about. At the same time, it is suggested that sections of the industrial White working class were as poor and downtrodden as slaves in the Caribbean. Yet no commentary is given on the savage treatment of Africans in the Caribbean, nor of the actual history of Britain's role in the Atlantic slave trade. It is also noted in passing that the railway station in Kibworth was opened in 1857, the same year as what is referred to as the 'Indian Mutiny'. The latter is more accurately described as 'the Indian Liberation War', which, as Wemyss (2008, 6.2) notes, 'marked the beginnings and extension of colonial rule and irrefutable oppression were less visible outside minority communities'. However, rather than provide a sustained analysis of the ways in which the nation prospered from the physical, economic, cultural and political suppression of colonial people, emphasis is placed instead upon the sacrifice of British troops in the World Wars, albeit with some reference to the role that armies from the colonies played in the World Wars. At a talk given by Wood, at the Guildford Book Festival, which I attended in October 2010, he explained how he had interviewed two elderly gentlemen from the village who reminisced about their time working for the East India Company.[11] To the best of my knowledge Wood's interviews with the men that worked for this company were not included in the actual series, but had they been, perhaps a more nuanced account of the ways in which Empire shaped the daily lives of villagers would have emerged.

The scant and stylised representation of Empire in this narrative of Englishness and nation becomes even more startling when we remind ourselves of some of the facts discussed by historians of Britain's imperial enterprise. Historians have detailed the impact of Empire upon national politics and the everyday routines and rhythms of life in the metropole. For example, Catherine Hall and Sonya Rose (2006b) write:

> From the 1770s questions about the effects of empire on the metropole were never entirely off the political agenda, whether in

terms of the worries about the impact of forms of Oriental despotism or the practice of slavery abroad on the liberties of Englishmen at home, debates as to the status of British subjects and British law across the empire, or hopes for a 'Greater Britain' that could spread across the world.

(2006b, pp. 1–2)

Hall and Rose (2006b, p. 21) also report that Empire shaped the daily social fabric and intimate family relationships of ordinary White British people's everyday existence, but not always in consciously noticed ways. Thus it did not matter if individuals supported, condemned or held no views at all on Britain's imperial project. The point is that Empire was often an unremarkable feature of everyday life that influenced both White working- and middle-class cultures. In this regard, religion, food, beverages and literature were key conduits for ensuring that Empire formed the backdrop to everyday life in Britain. For example, missionaries brought the Empire home to parishioners of local churches (Hall and Rose, 2006b). Poetry and fiction took stories and fantasies about the Empire into people's living rooms. Moreover, ideologies of racial superiority intrinsic to the imperial project found their way into nineteenth- and twentieth-century popular literature, school textbooks, children's fiction and geography lessons (Mackenzie, 1986b, p. 3). Historians of theatre have also pointed to the images of Empire within late nineteenth-century music halls and working men's clubs (1986b, p. 11). Tea, sugar, coffee and tobacco were produced on colonial lands and harvested by colonial and slave labour and made readily available for consumption in Britain in the nineteenth century. Moreover, the Industrial Revolution in Britain was built on profits from the slave trade, raw materials and labour from the colonies. As the anthropologist Eric Wolf has famously argued, 'both the people who claim history as their own and the people to whom history has been denied emerge as participants in the same historical trajectory' (Wolf, 1982, p. 23, cited in Hall and Rose, 2006b, p. 21). It is precisely the depth of this shared historical trajectory that is displaced in Wood's televised *Story of England*.

The typicality of this portrayal of Empire is in part captured and conveyed by Paul Gilroy's reflections upon the place of Empire in British public life. Gilroy (2005a, p. 2) observes that 'colonial history remains marginal and largely unacknowledged, surfacing only in the service of nostalgia and melancholia'. For Gilroy, this failure within hegemonic White British public culture to reflect directly upon the imperial past illuminates something 'fundamental about the cultural life of a post-colonial country that has never dealt with the consequences of its loss of empire' (2005b). He contends that 'the vanished empire is essentially unmourned' in British culture, which has led to a deep-seated feeling of melancholy among the White British public (2005b). Gilroy advocates further that 'the chronic, nagging pain' of the absence of Empire 'feeds a melancholic attachment' to the past (2005b). This sense of depressed anxiety and belonging to the past is motivated by feelings of ambivalence and confusion about Britain's place in the contemporary world order. Thus, when the White British public does think of the colonial past it more often than not produces an 'air-brushed version of colonial history' (2005b). This version of history produces a sense of moral uplift with a focus upon 'civilizing missions', trains that run on time and the 'native's' appreciation of 'civilization' and stability (2005b). Gilroy (2005a, p. 2) argues further that 'this popular, revisionist output is misleading and dangerous because it feeds the illusion that Britain has been or can be disconnected from its imperial past'.

Disconnecting Britishness from its imperial histories not only denies postcolonial people who live in the UK their place in the history of Englishness and Britishness but also their place within contemporary formations of nation. In other words, settlers to the UK from the former British colonies and their descendants are all too easily depicted by White English people as immigrants, foreigners and outsiders to England. The consequence of this is to reproduce the English nation and its history as White. In this sense Wood's televised *Story of England* is no exception. The displacing of the history of Empire in the nation's story reproduces an image of England as an island nation, whose history is White in spite of its ethnically and racially diverse colonial past. The history of the English countryside becomes associated with mythical wholly White Viking, Roman and Anglo-Saxon ancestries, and the countryside itself comes to stand for the history of the nation. At the local level, this discourse maintains a separation, on the one hand, between the White inhabitants of the village, the countryside, and the nation, and on the other hand, BrAsians and Black people and their descendants who live in the nearby city of Leicester. In other words, the histories of BrAsian and British Black people's colonial relationships to England and Britain are displaced and forgotten. In this sense, multicultural urban Leicester remains a place detached and set apart from the history of the village of Kibworth and thus of the English nation. Interestingly, it is only when envisioning the future that the documentary provides the viewer with an insight into BrAsians' potential role in Kibworth's village life.

At the end of the final programme multicultural Leicester features in the village's history as evidence that identity, places and people are constantly changing and remaking themselves anew. At a Kibworth village meeting with candidates for the local 2010 elections, the camera provides a close-up of a female BrAsian resident and the BrAsian Liberal candidate. Later on in the programme, the Liberal candidate explains to camera that his grandfather came to Leicestershire from the Punjab in 1918. The camera also focuses for a few seconds on the back of a man wearing a turban walking past a development of new family houses in Kibworth. In his role as commentator, Wood tells the viewer that this extensive development of new houses in the village is an indication that Kibworth is rapidly becoming a town, and that there are now new people to face the challenges of the future.

There was an opportunity to address questions to Wood after his lecture at the Guildford Book Festival. I asked him how he thought the histories of Empire connected the White people and landscape of the village with BrAsians that live in multicultural Leicester and the village. It was clear from Wood's response that he had not really thought about this matter in any profound or detailed way. He explained that some 'Asians' had settled in the new houses in Kibworth. Wood also said, much to the amusement of the White middle- and upper-class Guildford-based audience, that there was a very good Indian take-away and restaurant in the village. However, he pointed out that the majority of the population of Kibworth is White. He also described how as an outsider to Leicester, the city appeared to be a good model of 'race-relations' in England. To support this claim he cited as evidence the now commonplace understanding that the city of Leicester is set to become the first city in England with no clear ethnic majority, a point not supported by the most recently published National Census data of 2001. Interestingly, Wood's reflections on the ethnic composition of the city were set apart from his knowledge on the history of the village and thus the nation.

I have drawn here in detail upon the ways in which the legacies of Empire, ideas of race, nation and place are mobilised in the televised version of *The Story of England* because my critical analysis provides a good platform from which to set out and explain the central themes, arguments and ideas that I explore in this book. As should be clear by now, I seek to examine the reproduction of White power and privilege through a postcolonial perspective and through drawing on my ethnographic study in Leicester/shire. I shall examine the myriad ways in which my research participants from Leicester and Leicestershire screen out, displace and do not know the colonial histories that bind BrAsians to the local, the nation and ultimately the West. These themes will be explored in detail in Chapters 2 and 3. In so doing, I shall examine how the forgetting of the colonial past supports and maintains the racialised division of race and place between the White countryside and the multicultural city of Leicester. However, the book will also examine in Chapters 4 and 5 those moments in which White discourses of cultural superiority are confronted by White people themselves, while Chapter 6 discusses how colonial pasts are remembered and evoked by members of interracial families. Before going any further into the actual details of the content of the chapters that follow, it is worth reflecting in greater depth upon the theoretical frameworks underpinning the book's structure and content.

Whiteness studies through a postcolonial perspective

I have already alluded to the ways in which my study of Whiteness in Leicester/shire draws upon and contributes to a body of interdisciplinary literature problematically entitled 'White ethnicity studies' or 'Whiteness studies'.[12] Scholars in this field of inquiry set out to expose the formation of White ethnic and racial identities (see Doane, 2003; McKinney, 2005: Chapter 1 for the state of the art of this field of scholarship in the USA; Byrne 2006: 9–11 for an overview of Whiteness studies that draws upon empirical research conducted in Britain; Twine and Gallagher, 2008; Steyn and Conway, 2010). Historically social science studies in the field of race and ethnicity have focused on the lives of the oppressed, that is, often minorities that are racially and ethnically marked as Other by the White majority culture. However, the aim of Whiteness studies is to turn the tables on this approach by looking head on at the constitution of White ethnic identity and the reproduction of White people's power. The reason for such an exploration is to illuminate 'the impact of racism on those who perpetuate it' (Morrison, 1992, p. 11). White power has always been visible to those people that have been enslaved, colonised, subjugated and discriminated against by Whites. Whiteness studies builds on this perspective to challenge the idea that matters of race and ethnicity are just Black issues.

Proponents of Whiteness studies contend that it is the invisible and unspoken (unspeakable even) constitution of White ethnicities that facilitates the reproduction of White power and dominance in Western societies at the collective and institutional level and in the everyday rhythms of White people's lives (Frankenberg 1993a; Dyer, 1997;

McIntosh, 2003). By contrast, those who are defined by the White majority as not White, or not White enough, speak from particular racialised subject locations that set them apart from the White majority. It follows from this insight that part of the power of Whiteness lies in its ability to displace the very nature of its own construction (Frankenberg, 1993a). Thus this literature sets out to render visible the historical, political, social and cultural construction and constitution of White ethnicities in Western societies. The effect of this is to contribute to ongoing critiques of racism.

It is important to note that White privilege and power is often reproduced unintentionally and without malice (Essed, 1991). Moreover, White power structures often persist independently of the good or bad intentions of White individuals. One consequence of this is that White people are likely to be unaware of their privilege by virtue of being White. In this vein, White people do not explain their success on the grounds of their ethnic identity (Dyer, 1997; McIntosh, 2003). For example, they do not think that they have a nice house, a good job or a positive response from their children's school because they are White. Rather, White people more often than not believe that their good fortune is solely dependent upon their individual achievements and not because they are White.

As already suggested, a key contention of this book is the idea that the very construction of the White Western subject is the legacy of slavery, European expansion and colonialism. While most scholars that study the formation of White ethnicities in the West would agree with this line of argumentation, little critical attention has been given by these scholars to the legacies of Empire upon the formation of contemporary White ethnicities. The effect of this is for the significance of the colonial past on the formation of contemporary White ethnicities to be conceived only superficially or simply ignored.

Notwithstanding this oversight within White ethnicity studies, there are a few notable exceptions. I have already mentioned Wemyss' (2009) work, which situates her anthropological study of dominant White discourses focused upon Bengalis in East London in the context of histories of Empire. Wemyss draws with skill upon histories of East London's imperial past in order to show the connections between histories of Empire and White everyday, media and political discourses of tolerance and multiculturalism in the present. Wemyss thereby brings to the fore connections between colonial notions of racial hierarchy and difference in the past and their influence upon discourses of multiculturalism and difference in East London in the present.

By contrast to Wemyss' city-based work, Caroline Knowles (2007) interviewed older White people who live in the rural county of Devon in the south west of England, who were directly involved and engaged in imperial projects as either administrators themselves or the spouses of colonial officials. This enables her to draw out the connections between colonial constructions of difference and postcolonial engagements with those demarcated as racialised and classed Others in the present. While both these writers' emphasis upon the relationship between the colonial past and the formation of racial hierarchies in the present has shaped and influenced my focus upon the colonial and its articulation in the present, the approach that I take in this book in making these connections most closely follows Ruth Frankenberg's (1993a) work on the role and place of the colonial in the formation of contemporary American social life, and so it is the details of her study that I shall now elaborate.

In her influential and profoundly important book *White Women, Race Matters*, Frankenberg (1993a) sets out to examine how race shapes the lives of White middle-and working-class American women who self-identify as feminists. Frankenberg's study is inspired by her own biography and identity as a White Western feminist. It is against the background of the exclusion of 'women of colour' from Western feminist politics that Frankenberg scrutinises how racial privilege shapes White feminists' lives. She explores how White women collude in the reproduction of White power and privilege within society. But more than this, Frankenberg also examines the conditions in which White women come to question the ways in which racial privilege has shaped their ethnicities. Frankenberg's work is often cited in the field of White ethnicity studies because she crystallised a vocabulary through which to talk about White ethnicity, its dominance, power and invisibility in the West.

Central to Frankenberg's thesis is her argument that there are close ties in the USA between racist and colonial discourses, as well as between colonial and postcolonial constructions of Whiteness and Westernness. At the heart of European imperialism was ways of 'knowing' those colonised that was supported in the nineteenth century by academic disciplines such as anthropology, geography, linguistics and history (1993a, p. 17; Said, 1978). Over time a body of knowledge about the supposed inferiority of those colonised was produced. This so-called knowledge about non-Western Others was crucial to the ideological justification and political, cultural and economic expansion and imposition of European colonialism (Said, 1978). Frankenberg neatly summarises the relations of power and 'epistemic violence' (Spivak, 1984, cited in Frankenberg, 1993a, p. 17) underpinning the production of Western colonial knowledge about the Other as follows:

> Central to this colonial discourse is the notion of the colonized subject as irreducibly Other from the standpoint of the Western self. Equally significant, while discursively generating and marking a range of cultural and racial Others as different from an apparently stable Western or White self, the Western self is itself produced *as an effect of* the Western discursive production of its Others.
>
> (1993a, p. 17, original emphasis)

Clearly, crucial to the colonial project was the maintenance and control of an essential, fixed and immutable sense of racial distinction between those colonised and the coloniser. Moreover, the White Western self came into being and took meaning in relation to this construction of absolute racial difference.

To explore further the co-construction of the Western self and the non-Western Other, it is worth reflecting upon Edward Said's (1978) analysis of White superiority to be found at the centre of the colonial relation. Said (1978, p. 227) illustrates how in the colonial environment being White became a way of 'taking hold of reality, language, and thought', which shaped a specific way of 'being-in-the-world'. Being White thus meant 'speaking in a certain way, behaving according to a code of regulations, and even feeling certain things and not others' (1978, p. 227). Central to this way of being was

> the culturally sanctioned habit of deploying large generalizations by which reality is divided into various collectives: languages, races, types, colors, mentalities, each category being not so much a neutral designation as an evaluative interpretation. Underlying these categories is the rigidly binomial opposition of 'ours' and 'theirs', with the former always encroaching on the latter (even to the point of making 'theirs' exclusively a function of 'ours').
>
> (1978, p. 227)

Frankenberg (1993a) argues that it is this type of dichotomous and hierarchical worldview that is played out in her White female interviewees' descriptions of themselves and those that they identified as racially and culturally Other. Thus sharing parallels with the colonial past, the White women's descriptions of racialised Others were often hierarchical and dualistic. One consequence of this discourse is for Whiteness and Americanness to take meaning with reference to non-White Others who were thereby excluded from these categories. As Frankenberg puts it:

> One effect of colonial discourse is the production of an unmarked, apparently autonomous white/Western self, in contrast with the marked, Other racial and cultural categories with which the racially and culturally dominant category is coconstructed.
>
> (1993a, p. 17)

Furthermore, Frankenberg's White interviewees utilised a concept of culture that is part of the legacy of Western European expansion into the Americas, Africa and Asia. In this vein, she writes:

> Cultures were conceived as discrete, bounded spaces, culture was viewed as separate from material life, and some groups of people were considered more 'cultural' than others.
>
> (1993a, p. 192)

It is against this background that Frankenberg reflects upon the structure and content of colonial notions of cultural difference as follows:

> [A]t times, colonial discourses took the form, straightforwardly of 'essentialist racism'. At other times, travellers, explorers, and later, colonial administrators valorized aspects of the histories and cultures of those they colonized. However, they did so in ways that, for the most part, viewed colonized people as fundamentally different from and 'Other' than Europeans.
>
> (1993a, p. 193)

At this juncture, I want to pause for a moment in order to reflect upon and summarise how Frankenberg's work has helped me to think through what constitutes a postcolonial perspective on Whiteness in Leicester/shire. A postcolonial perspective traces and analyses the reproduction of a colonial worldview in relation to the maintenance and control of White Western superiority in the present. Intrinsic to this worldview is a 'rigidly binominal opposition' separating the racially unmarked White Western self from racially marked non-White, non-Western Others. Thus it is that the racialised figure of the Other is central to the construction of the racially unmarked White Western self. In other words, the White Western self is defined and constituted in part by ideas and images of non-White and non-Western Others. It is this worldview of White Western cultural superiority and the production of irreducible differences separating the White self from the racialised Other that I shall trace, scrutinise and analyse in Parts I and II of this book. To do this, I shall examine White constructions of BrAsian Others across semi-rural and urban ethnoscapes in Leicester and Leicestershire.

In tracing these configurations of White superiority in the present, I have found it useful to draw upon the concept of 'coloniality'. I borrow this term from Hesse and Sayyid (2006, p. 17), who advocate that coloniality provides a conceptual lens through which to think about the articulation in the present of colonial practices, presentations and nuances that accumulated in notions of Western superiority and racial hierarchy. On this view, 'coloniality' comprises and includes the contemporary reproduction of colonial concepts of culture and race, including the racially unmarked White Western self and the racially marked non-Western Other, as discussed by Frankenberg. It is precisely, in this sense that I shall deploy the term 'coloniality' in this book to capture and convey the maintenance and control of a Western worldview of cultural superiority, as outlined by Frankenberg.

However given the very different histories of the USA and Britain in relation to matters of race, nation and colonialism (a point to which I will return and elaborate on in Chapter 7), my work will take a somewhat different direction from Frankenberg's approach to the colonial. *Whiteness, Class and the Legacies of Empire* will build upon and develop Frankenberg's ideas in order to argue that central to White constructions of racialised Others in the English context is the screening out and displacing of the significance and meaning of the colonial past in the formation of the present.

From this standpoint, my contention is that supporting the manifestation of coloniality in the present is what Hesse (1997) has identified as 'White amnesia' of the colonial past, a term that corresponds to Wemyss' (2009) 'bundles of silences' surrounding the 'invisible Empire' within contemporary articulations of multiculturalism in East London. Gilroy's (2005a) discussion of 'postcolonial melancholia' within everyday constructions of Britishness, which was explored earlier, senses a similar purpose. Hesse and Sayyid (2006) argue that BrAsians' relationships to Britain that were formed through centuries of Empire are routinely terminated by White Britons in everyday speech, thought and social practices, and in government policies and administration. Consequently the role of colonial rule, violence and exploitation in the creation of Britain's wealth, history, culture, identity, political power and so on, is displaced. For Sayyid (2004, p. 152) this means that postcolonial people's relationship to Britain is seen to commence only at the moment when they or their ancestors got off the plane or boat in Britain.

The eclipsing of BrAsian people's relationships to the British nation in this way supports what Hesse and Sayyid refer to as the commonsensical, banal and ubiquitous maintenance and control of the 'immigrant imaginary' (2006, pp. 21–4; see also Sayyid, 2004). The latter is constituted by a chain of hierarchical cultural differences that separate postcolonial settlers and their descendants from the White majority. In this way, Whites come to represent 'the host-community', whereas BrAsians become positioned as members of the 'immigrant-community', people whose origins are thought to be found straightforwardly outside of the nation and ultimately the West (2006, p. 21). This depiction of BrAsians as immigrants ensures that the nation and 'the host society' remain unchanged by the BrAsian presence (2006, p. 22). In short, the culture of Britishness becomes conflated with Whiteness, and what gets screened out are the complex layerings of colonial relations, socio-economic geopolitics and cosmopolitan identities that result. It is exactly the representation of BrAsians as immigrants and the processes of White amnesia that underpin this representation that I shall examine in detail in Part I of this book, and then it becomes a theme that I shall trace throughout the remaining chapters of the book.

Notwithstanding the foregoing line of argumentation, Hesse and Sayyid (2006) propose that the current time also includes new possibilities for questioning, challenging and resisting the excesses of coloniality. They point out that feminist, environmentalist and anti-racist social movements have actively worked to challenge the worldview that constitutes coloniality at global, local and national levels (2006, pp. 19–20). It is in this vein that Frankenberg (1993a, p. 17) also explores those circumstances in which the White middle- and working-class women in her study at times 'drew ... on the language of anti-imperialist as well as anti-racist movements as they attempted to think critically about racism in their lives'. This point is also crucial to my exploration of the discourses of coloniality in Leicester/shire. In Part II of the book, I will explore the conditions in which some White people come to confront and challenge the racism of others. I will show that this is a complex and difficult process. In spite of the good intentions of some White individuals, it is not always easy for them to step outside of discourses of coloniality even when they seek to do so. Notwithstanding the significance of these people's attempts to question the racism of others, the most potent example of the actual work of challenging, confronting and dismantling White power and privilege is to be found in interracial families' ancestral accounts, explored in Part III. This aspect of the book examines how members of interracial families draw upon slave ancestries to articulate relationships and identities across colour-lines. Thus an analysis of the subjectivities of members of interracial families reveals how the silences and erasures of the colonial past are inverted, and a vehicle by which to contemplate processes of remembering the colonial does finally emerge. Central to this process is a critical questioning of White privilege, power and dominance in English society.

White classed ethnicities

From my description of the reproduction of White power and privilege thus far, it might appear that having a White skin automatically guarantees equal access and participation in the social privileges that accompany being White. But this is too simplistic. Rather, central to my examination of Whiteness is an exploration of the way in which White ethnicities are entwined and embedded within class distinctions and inequalities. In this way, racial and class distinctions and identities become inscribed within and are co-constituting of each other. Bridget Bryne (2006, p. 105) argues in her study of the interplay of Whiteness, gender and social class in London that 'race and class are not only inter-related, but can be subject to a similar analysis'. From this point of view, Bryne (2006, p. 105) suggests that classed identities, like ethnic identities, are embodied. Thus visible markers of class identity and distinction become inscribed on the body and can be read and interpreted by others. For example, in the UK classed bodies are thought by the White majority to be of different sizes and shapes (Lawler, 1999, p. 83). Moreover, classed bodies in most Western class-stratified societies are marked and defined by differing dispositions, comportment and aesthetic tastes (Bourdieu, 1984). In this sense, the way people dress, walk, talk and so on become markers of their classed identities. But even more than this, social class, like ethnicity, is constituted by ideas of origins, ancestry and geographical belonging (see Tyler, 2011). In addition, the ways in which individuals perceive others in class and ethnic terms impacts upon their sense of who they are, which in turn is bound up with their feelings of social value and self-worth. Ethnicities and classed identities thus shape how individuals interact with and relate to others on professional, personal and intimate levels. In other words, class and ethnic identities frame who it is that individuals feel comfortable and at ease with, who they choose for their friends, with whom they form romantic relationships, where they live and the domestic aesthetic they feel most comfortable with and seek to reproduce. The profound significance of class to the formation of identity is brought sharply into view by the assertion by Kuhn (1995, p. 98, cited in Bryne, 2006, p. 106) that 'class is something beneath your clothes, under your skin, in your psyche, at the very core of your being'. It might also be argued that the same can be said for ethnicity, to the extent that ethnic identity is not only inscribed and marked on the body but is pivotal to an individual's worldview and sense of self.

Following sociologists working in the field of White ethnicity studies in the UK (Bryne, 2006; Watt, 2006; Reary et al., 2007; Twine, 2010), my approach to social class has been influenced by the work of Beverley Skeggs (1997; 2004) and by some of the ways in which her ideas have been used by Whiteness studies scholars to deconstruct the power and privilege of White classed ethnicities in Britain.

Herself influenced by the work and thought of Pierre Bourdieu, Skeggs (1997) shows how over time and across space certain markers of class distinction have been defined by the powerful to signify the appropriation and embodiment of differing forms of capital. Skeggs (1997, p. 8) succinctly summarises Bourdieu's understanding of differing types of capital as follows: economic capital includes 'income, wealth, financial inheritances and monetary assets'; cultural capital consists in embodied qualities such as 'dispositions of the mind and the body' and institutionalised attributes such as education and qualifications – moreover, cultural capital is the acquisition of know-how about the ways in which local systems of distinction are articulated; social capital is 'resources based on connections and group membership'; and symbolic capital is the form that 'different types of capital take once they are perceived and recognised as legitimate'.

Skeggs (1997) argues that class identities are constituted by the acquisition of these various kinds of capital. Class positioning is thus a constant process of creating distinctions between oneself and others on the grounds of physical appearance, social decorum, educational credentials, wealth, aesthetic taste and so on. Classed identities are always gauged, judged and measured in relation to dominant White middle-class values and norms. For Skeggs, the idea of being 'respectable' as opposed to 'rough' provides the central idiom through which to analyse individuals' closeness and distance from White middle-class notions of normality and acceptability. From this standpoint, a mark of respectability and social standing is approval, legitimation and acceptance by the White middle classes.

Recently, sociologists who study the formation of White ethnicities in Britain have shown how the actual constitution of White ethnic identities becomes entwined, embedded and mediated by class distinctions and capital accumulation (Bryne, 2006; Watt, 2006; Reary et al., 2007; Garner, 2009). Reading across these studies, one forms a picture of the heterogeneity of White middle- and working-class identities, cross-cut and constituted by access to differing forms of capital. Moreover, White people's class positioning and classed aspirations for themselves and their families affect and shape how they represent and engage with ethnic minorities. Thus, the ways in which White middle-class mothers living in South London (studied by Bryne, 2006) engage with ethnic minorities is different from the approach taken by White working-class residents living on a council estate in North London (studied by Paul Watt, 2006). That is to say, the White middle-class mothers with whom Bryne (2006) worked were concerned to maintain an appropriate degree of distinction and distance between their children and those people that they identified as raced and classed Others. Meanwhile, for the White working-class men and women that feature in Watt's (2006, p. 792) council estate study, BrAsian and Black residents could prove their respectability over time if they displayed appropriate classed behaviour (see also Garner, 2009, p. 49).

Central to discourses of racial and class distinction in the UK are ideas about the proper and respectable constitution of place. From this perspective certain areas of a village, a town, or a city become associated with particular people identified with 'geographies of roughness' (Watt, 2006) and respectability. In this sense Whites are often in search of comfortable and respectable places of belonging that vary in terms of openness to racial and class differences. In short, racial and class distinctions and identities become inscribed and embedded within people and places.

For example, James Rhodes (2010; 2011) in his recent study of White working- and lower-middle-class British National Party (an extreme right-wing political party) supporters from Burnley, a former mill town in the north west of England, found that his interviewees identified certain areas of the town with 'scruffy' White people, including the unemployed, alcoholics and drug addicts. The latter were said to lack respectability and responsibility and thus entitlement to public resources. In a similar vein, Butler and Robson (2003, p. 1792) pay detailed attention to the importance of space and locality in the formation of White middle-class identities. They suggest that, 'middle-class people identify with neighbourhoods where they perceive "people like us to live"'. So too,

Vincent et al. (2004, p. 233) argue that 'distinctive areas' are 'created with particular ... characteristics', which reflect the internal differences within the White middle classes. For these writers the way that White middle-class people draw intra-class distinctions between each other, as well as the perceived divisions between class groups, enables them to identify 'people like us' (2004, pp. 239–40). Crucial to this process of distinction-making is the fixing of places and people in racial and class hierarchies. In sum, the discourses of race, class and place are entwined with each other. People and places thus become indistinguishable within a hierarchy and geography of race and class distinction.

Drawing together and building upon these sociological perspectives on the embedding of race, class and place, I shall examine in the ethnographic Chapters 2, 3, 4 and 5 how White research participants' ideas and experiences of the place in which they live become entwined with their ideas about the proper racialised and classed constitution of the White self and the BrAsian Other. In this sense, places become sites for the production of social identities through the construction of racialised Others that are always already seen through a lens that is classed. In short, everyday constructions of the White self and the BrAsian Other are simultaneously classed, raced and placed. In addition, there is a point to be made here about the ways in which discourses of Englishness and nation become configured within articulations of race, class and place. Sharing some parallels to my analysis of how the village of Kibworth in Wood's *Story of England* comes to represent the nation, I shall explore how White research participants' ideas about the proper constitution of their place become associated with ideals of Englishness (see Chapters 2 and 3 in particular).

Although scholars in the field of Whiteness studies in Britain have drawn attention to and analysed the classed constitution of White identities and racisms, more often than not the White working classes have been the subject of analysis (see, for example, Back, 1996; Cohen, 1997; Ware, 1997; Nayak, 2003). With this bias in mind, Byrne (2006) has recently pointed out that the White middle classes and their expressions of racism have received much less attention within Whiteness studies. One aim of this book will be to address this imbalance through exploration of the formation of White middle-class ethnicities (in particular see Chapter 2). Furthermore, my focus upon the formation of White working-class racialised discourses in Coalville and Streetville respectively, combined with my study of Greenville, will provide comparative insights into how both middle- and working-class Whites living in distinct places engage with race and difference. In this way, *Whiteness,*

Class and the Legacies of Empire provides a comparative multi-sited ethnographic account of the co-constitution of Whiteness, social class and place within and across semi-rural and urban locales in England.

Indeed, this book's comparative approach to the formation of White classed ethnicities challenges the assumption within both academic and popular circles that the White middle classes in Britain are better at 'doing' multiculturalism, and being multicultural, than the White working class (see Ware, 2008 for this argument). This assumption is based on the idea that White middle-class people have, to some extent, cultivated cosmopolitan, mobile and global lifestyles that embrace cultural differences in a way that White working-class people have not. Some of the complexities and assumptions that constitute this approach to class analysis are provided by Gillian Evans' reflections on her fieldwork with White working-class people living on a council estate in Bermondsey, South London. Evans (2007) writes eloquently, openly and honestly about her reaction to the racist views of Sharon, a White working-class woman with whom she came to form a close relationship. Evans came to know Sharon and her family well through teaching one of Sharon's daughters, Emma, to read. Reflecting on her visit to Sharon's flat (apartment), Evans comments:

> On my way home ... I am reeling ... I am staggered and sickened by how deeply felt her [Sharon's] prejudice is against Emma's [Sharon's daughter's] Bangladeshi Muslim friends and against black and Asian people in general. I wonder how she has become so prejudiced and, as a consequence I wonder too how I have come to be so open-minded. I am reminded, then, that one of the attributes of a middle class upbringing is the cultivation of an open mind and liberal attitude towards difference and I ponder how ironic it is that that same liberal-minded openness doesn't extend towards the working classes. Middle class people are, for example, much more likely to be tolerant of so-called racial, ethnic and cultural variation than they are of the difference between the classes.
>
> (2007, p. 58)

On the one hand, Evans' thoughts on the classed prejudices of the White middle classes towards the White working classes are borne out in much ethnographic research on social class in Britain (see especially Skeggs, 1997). But, on the other hand, her association of class and racial prejudice is not supported in any straightforward way by my ethnographic analysis of White middle- and working-class racialised discourses in

Leicester/shire. While I recognise and empathise with Evans' feelings of anger and disgust and dis-identification at the types of racial prejudice that she heard expressed in Bermondsey, my analysis shows that some White middle-class people are also capable of expressing illiberal and racist views. At times, but not always, White middle-class discourses on racialised Others are expressed in more subtle ways and idioms than those typically articulated by some White working-class people. However, I believe that it is exactly the blunt and crude racist resentments articulated by some White working-class people that can provide the conditions in which others, such as Sharon's daughter in Evans' account, come to question the racist attitudes of family members, acquaintances, work colleagues and neighbours. In short, my comparative approach to White working- and middle-class racialised discourses in Leicestershire interrogates the common assumption held by White middle-class academics (including myself and Evans) that the White middle classes are somehow more tolerant on matters of race, culture, difference and multiculturalism than the White working classes.

At this point, it is appropriate that I turn my attention to some of the issues involved in describing individuals in class terms. Throughout the ethnographic chapters of this book I refer to White and interracial research participants as 'working class' or 'middle class'. But it is important to note that my research participants did not explicitly self-identify with these classed labels. Research participants' apparent lack of identification with a specific class category highlights the slippery and often difficult task of describing individuals in social class terms. Marilyn Strathern (1982, p. 271) suggests that individuals often express dissatisfaction when assigned a social class status by sociologists. One reason for this is that they do not have control over the criteria by which they are being judged. Moreover, by being named and identified in class terms, the possibility that one might move into a different social class in one's lifetime may seem to have been foreclosed. In addition to Strathern's problematising of sociologists' use of class categories from the standpoint of an anthropologist, sociologists themselves have argued that their use of class categories has the capacity to conflate and flatten the heterogeneous identities that constitute self-identifications in contemporary Britain (Savage, 2000).

While I want to avoid these implications, I have nevertheless come to the conclusion that it is crucial to hold on to the sociological reality that classed identities are differentiated by unequal access to capital, including economic, cultural, social and symbolic capital. In this book, I do not set out abstract and fixed criteria for the identities of 'middle-class' and 'working-class' research participants. Rather, I argue that my White and interracial research participants' class identities become transparent in relation to their views on racialised Others that are situated within and filtered through their notions of respectability. These discourses of racialised and classed distinction are also mediated by their sense of belonging (or not) to a particular place. From this perspective, it was possible for me to identify, differentiate and name my White and interracial research participants in class terms, without exhausting their identity by a socio-economic category or denying the possibility of the shifting and mobile constitution of classed identities during the life course.

One final point needs to be made on the classed constitution of White ethnicities. Crucial to the recent analysis of White ethnicities and class distinction is the formation of gendered and sexual identities and inequalities. In this regard, feminist scholars have argued for an 'intersectional' approach to the study of Whiteness that focuses on how gender, sexuality, class and ethnic inequalities interact and reinforce one another in shaping White ethnicities (Ferber, 2007). Bryne's (2006) work on Whiteness and motherhood in London highlights how White subjectivities are not only racialised and classed but also gendered. Her study explores the ways in which the experience of mothering is simultaneously raced, classed and gendered. In contrast to Bryne's study of White middle-class mothers in London, I did not set out to examine the gendered constitution of Whiteness. Rather, my interest has always focused upon the relationship, co-constitution and entwining of racial and classed identities within the context of place. However, given the ethnographic nature of my work, gendered identities, experiences and inequalities became significant at times even when I was not looking for it.[13] The ways in which White middle- and working-class people represented and discussed BrAsians was always already gendered, and I have retained that gender bias in my accounts. Moreover, as I shall discuss in the methodological sections that frame the ethnographic chapters and will introduce below, my identity as a White middle-class woman worked to shape and influence my fieldwork experiences and what I came to know.

On home ground: Inspiration for writing and methodological reflections

The impetus for conducting the ethnographic studies that form the basis for this book is intimately linked to my own biography. When I was 10 years old I moved with my family from Leytonstone, an ethnically diverse suburb in East London, to Saddington, a small, wholly White and predominantly middle-class village situated in the rolling countryside of rural Leicestershire. By coincidence Saddington is the neighbouring village to Kibworth, the place that features in Wood's *Story of England*, and so adding to the personal impact of this television series. While growing up in Leicestershire I travelled each day from Saddington to schools in the ethnically diverse city of Leicester. My childhood experience of moving and living across racially segregated places stayed with me, and became what I later set out to study in my doctoral research.

When I was 16 years old I attended an inner city (post-school) sixth form college in the city of Leicester where I studied 'A' levels (A stands for 'advanced' level), which remain to this day the qualifications necessary for entrance to British Universities. I took an 'A' level in religious studies, which included the study of Buddhism. Studying Buddhism opened my mind to the possibility of another way of thinking about, experiencing and seeing the world. At 18 years old, I set off for the University of Manchester to study comparative religion and social anthropology for two years, and subsequently transferred to a single-honours social anthropology degree in my third and final year of undergraduate study. Thus by the time I was 21 years old I had spent five years writing and thinking about academic scholarship on non-Western peoples and worldviews. My studies provided me with valuable insights into the ways in which Western ways are not the only way of being, thinking, living and believing. Intellectually these insights provided me with a firm belief in the construction of social reality and the implications of this for interpreting the social life of people. It seemed quite evident to me, interested as I was in social anthropology, that I should apply to do a PhD on the comparative study of Bangladeshi women in a region of Bangladesh and Hyde, a town in Greater Manchester. But academics and their ideas intervened to stop me in my tracks.

I met intellectuals working in the Social Anthropology Department at Manchester who taught me to think critically and much more deeply about the enterprise of social anthropology. It was at this time that I first read Edward Said's (1978) *Orientalism*. Suddenly everything appeared – for a short time, anyway – to make sense. I came to conclude in a very personal and deep way that if we want to see the most important things there is no need to keep travelling and searching; they are all around us. As Wittgenstein wrote (1980, p. 50), 'If you want to go down deep you do not need to travel far; indeed, you don't have to leave your most immediate and familiar surroundings.' And so it is, I have conducted my anthropology at 'home' in England and in Leicester/shire. It is precisely with this in mind that I have given this book the subtitle *On Home Ground*.

This book draws upon two research projects that began while I was studying and working in Social Anthropology at the University of Manchester. The first project is my doctoral research conducted between 1996 and 2000, which set out to examine the reproduction of rural Leicestershire as a White space in the context of BrAsian and Black settlement in the city of Leicester.[14] It is for this study that I conducted residential fieldwork in Greenville and Coalville respectively. The second project was my postdoctoral research conducted while I was employed as a Research Associate at the University of Manchester between 2001 and 2004, and it was this research that included fieldwork in Streetville.[15] After leaving Manchester in 2004, I continued to work on and write about the material collected from these two projects. This book thus represents an accumulation of these efforts.

As noted above, the substantive ethnographic chapters of this book include methodological sections on my fieldwork in the specific locale under review in that particular chapter. However, I would like at this point to reflect on the actual process of doing fieldwork 'at home' in Leicester and Leicestershire. My intention here is not to muse self-indulgently upon the imagined burdens of being a White middle-class woman studying Whiteness across class lines on 'home' ground. Rather, my aim is to render explicit some of the ways in which my White racial privilege and ethnicity worked to shape the fieldwork relationships and knowledge upon which this book is based (cf. Steyn and Conway, 2010, p. 286). In so doing, I want to explore the extent to which I was 'at home' studying White privilege and power in Leicestershire. In short, my question is: what does being at home studying racialisation and racism mean?

Les Back (2002) insists that the ethnographic study of Whiteness must not lapse into the production of bourgeois caricatures of White racists. Thinking about this problem, he is reminded of Clifford Geertz's insight that anthropologists should be wary of not only seeing the problem of 'Otherness' in distant cultures but also in their own. From this point of view, Back advocates that it would be misguided to render the racist into another 'Other'. In order to avoid this, he suggests, social scientists must open themselves up to the possibility of identifying with and seeing a part of one self in the racist Other. He writes: 'We should insist on an ethics of interpretation that can identify what is alien and what is other ... and yet at the same time hold on to the possibility of a semblance of a shared likeness' (2002, p. 43). Back calls this interpretative space the 'gray zone'. He concludes that politically engaged intellectuals of Whiteness must endeavour to identify just what is 'familiar' and what is 'alien' (2002, p. 59).

I find this notion of the 'gray zone' useful to explain and characterise my fieldwork relationships in Leicester and Leicestershire. At times during the fieldwork I identified with the people with whom I worked and thus felt a sense of familiarity and connection with them. At other times, I felt that my co-conversationalists were unfamiliar and their views alien to me, much like the sentiments expressed by Evans that I quoted. In fact, the notion, trope and image of 'home' provides a useful way of conveying this sense of familiarity and distance with the people that I came to know and work with. On the one hand, in the popular English imagination 'home' is a warm place of intimacy, love, comfort, identification and belonging. In this regard, home can refer to one's family, the place within which one grew up and/or now lives, the street, town, village, neighbourhood and nation to which one feels a sense of belonging, connection and identification. On the other hand, this warm image of home and belonging is dependent upon the construction of a boundary between those who belong to the home place and those who do not. In this sense, the very idea of home is dependent upon the construction of outsiders that do not belong. Indeed, it is the idea of Britain being a home set apart from its Empire and the people who lived there that informed the imperial project. In this vein, Hall and Rose (2006b, p. 25) write: 'Home kept the "other" peoples of the Empire at a distance, "their" strange climates, fruits and vegetables and peoples of colour were living in places that were incommensurable.' The irony is that the imperial British 'home' was constituted to a great extent by material and economic comforts such as consumables and raw materials, including pineapples, bananas, sugar, tea, coffee, cotton, silk, tobacco, and many other goods, that came from colonial exploits. My point here is that there are parallels between the inclusivity and exclusivity embedded in the notion of 'home' and the familiarity and distance intrinsic to the 'gray zone'. With these ideas in mind, I shall now attempt to provide some details of the ways in which I felt both familiar and alienated, at home and abroad during my fieldwork in Leicester/shire.

As already mentioned, the fieldwork that forms the impetus for the chapters that follow spans nearly two and half years of fieldwork conducted in two blocks in the late 1990s and early 2000s. When I did the fieldwork in 1997–8 in Greenville and Coalville respectively I was 24 years of age, a university postgraduate student and lived on a grant of about £6,000 a year. When I conducted the fieldwork in Streetville in 2002–3 I was 30 years old, employed by the University of Manchester as a Research Associate on a salary of approximately £20,000 a year, and had a PhD. This difference in my age, academic status and income had an effect on my fieldwork relationships and my sense of belonging and not belonging to the places in which I lived and worked. In practical terms, I was able to afford to rent a flat on my own in Streetville, while in Greenville and Coalville I took lodging with White families. My experience of being a lodger in Greenville was lonely and isolating. I lived with a woman and her teenage daughter. For all sorts of reasons, some of which will be discussed in Chapter 2, the mother and the daughter did not make me feel welcome or at 'home'. I therefore spent the time that I was at their home in my room away from the family. In contrast while in Coalville, I lived with two young White women who were sisters and a similar age to me at the time. We quickly became good friends and they made me feel at home in their home. We often socialised together in the evenings in local pubs and clubs. The sisters also introduced me to their friends who lived locally, which provided an impetus for my focus on the views of young White adults in the region, discussed in Chapter 4. In Greenville, my White middle-class identity was the norm and so went unnoticed by the people with whom I lived and who I interviewed. In Coalville, my class identity became marked by my housemates in humorous ways. I had a 'funny' but 'interesting' job, was depicted as a 'clever student', and spoke with a 'posh' accent that was emphasised by my repeated use of the words 'lovely' and 'oh definitely'. Having the ability to afford to live on my own in a flat that I called 'home' in Streetville was necessary for my acquisition of the credentials needed to join a local residents' and tenants' association. My participation in local neighbourhood networks forms the basis for Chapter 5 of this book. In short, my shifting academic status and aspects of my personal identity influenced and shaped my research experiences over time and across place.

Despite these shifting positionalities, central to my relationships with my White and interracial research participants from Coalville, Greenville and Streetville was the building of connections, identification and rapport. This sense of connection was necessary for people to share with me the details of their lives and to open up about their views on issues of race and identity. In other words, I came to believe in and practise one of the central methodological tenets of social anthropology, namely that the building of relationships with people in the context of fieldwork is necessary for anthropologists to enter into the worldviews of their research participants. At times this process could be very rewarding. I became good friends with some research participants, felt at home in their company and formed relationships that continued beyond the fieldwork period. Moreover, I successfully managed to build a good rapport with those White and interracial people I met only once or twice in the context of an interview.

Crucial to this rapport was my identification with my co-conversationalists. On one level this was pretty easy and straightforward. I was able to draw upon aspects of my biography and upbringing in Leicestershire to create a sense of personal identification with the people I interviewed and shared an experience of place. In this way, my White identity means that I have the privilege to claim belonging to Leicestershire and thus call this region of England my home. It was this privilege, dependent upon my White identity, that I exploited in my fieldwork relationships. For example, in Greenville I talked openly and freely about my upbringing in a rural village in Leicestershire to explain why I was interested in the constitution of Greenville's village identity. Similarly in Coalville and Streetville, I drew upon my origins in Leicestershire to explain why I was interested in studying White perceptions of BrAsians in the county of Leicestershire and city of Leicester. During the course of my interviews with research participants, I was able to draw with ease from my knowledge of places, events and happenings in the region to illustrate that I knew the city and the county in which we lived. Moreover, in some instances former neighbours and old school friends put me in contact with research participants. In these cases, we had people and relationships in common. In short, I repeatedly emphasised and demonstrated to White and interracial research participants how I was at 'home' in Leicester and Leicestershire.

Nonetheless, I also found this sense of connection and recognition with some of my White co-conversationalists deeply troubling. At times in the interviews with White research participants, they articulated what I considered to be racist views. In these instances, I knew that my Whiteness was taken as a sign that I would automatically agree with their views on race. Moreover, I was privy to passing off-the-cuff racist comments from White people I had come to know. My unease with these situations was compounded by my repeated failure to confront and challenge racism 'on the spot' (Back, 1996, p. 85). It often was not clear to me what to say to challenge such views effectively, and any such challenges would also have endangered the relationships of trust that I had built up over time. Moreover, I did not want to truncate and silence my White co-conversationalists' ideas on matters of race, ethnicity, belonging and difference because this is what I had set out to study. In this sense, at times, I worked within and condoned the same framework of White cultural superiority and privilege that I have set out to analyse and challenge in this book (see also Frankenberg 1993a, pp. 40–1).

From this standpoint, the ethnographic material that forms the core of this book is dependent upon and exploitative of my White racial identity on two fronts. Firstly, my ability to claim belonging to Leicestershire helped me to build a rapport with the people who participated in this research. This ability was in part dependent upon my privileges as a White woman. Secondly, my access to racist comments was also dependent upon my Whiteness and my failure to confront such comments. It is no exaggeration, then, to say that in this sense, this book rests upon the racial privileges that I experience on a daily basis as a White woman who is familiar with and at home in Leicestershire. For these reasons, I cannot claim any moral high ground for myself within this project.

Notwithstanding this reality, I set out with the intention of studying White people in order to help undo and shift the anthropological gaze away from the study of so-called ethnic and racial Others. Following Frankenberg (1993a), I wanted to make the White self the object of study. The result is that I have come to understand that the reproduction of White power and privilege is not simply an individual and contemporary phenomenon but is dependent upon and embedded within the histories of European colonialism and reproduced at collective, societal, global and institutional levels. In mobilising my White ethnicity and racial privileges to access White and interracial individuals' views on race, ethnicity and difference in Leicester/shire, my aim is to open up a creative and critical scholastic space whereby I can engage with, interpret and analyse the reproduction of White power and dominance pervasive within White postcolonial English society.

Overview and scope of the book

The chapters in this book will trace the constitution of Whiteness, coloniality, place, nation and social class through an examination of the following interconnected themes: (a) the reproduction of White middle-class discourses of coloniality and White amnesia of the colonial past, which is examined in Part I; (b) the ways in which White working-class people attempt to challenge and question White discourses of coloniality, which is explored in Part II; (c) an exploration of postcolonial genealogies in Part III, which examines how slave ancestries are evoked, remembered and articulated within the members of interracial families' ideas on inheritance, ancestry and descent.

Part I is entitled 'White Amnesia: White Middle-Class Ethnicities' and draws upon ethnographic research in the suburban village of Greenville. Chapters 2 and 3 will examine how White middle-class discourses on BrAsians are co-constituted by ideas of place (rurality/villageness), class (middle-classness), race (Whiteness) and nation (Englishness). In order to do this, these chapters analyse the consequences for the present of the reproduction of a colonial worldview of White Western cultural superiority. My argument is that this worldview of White cultural superiority is intersected with the discourse of White amnesia of the colonial past to depict BrAsians as raced and classed urban Others to the racially unmarked White rural/village self and culture. The specific focus of Chapter 2 is upon how White middle-class villagers in Greenville represent and depict BrAsian residents who live in the village as cultural outsiders, through a set of racialised and classed discourses. In Chapter 3, I pay detailed attention to the racialised and classed constitution of the countryside and the city in Leicester/shire. To do this I draw upon both White middle-class Greenville residents' perceptions of the country and the city, as well as the depiction of Leicester/shire within public marketing literature and websites.

Part II is entitled 'Confronting Coloniality: White Working-Class Ethnicities' and shifts gear, so to speak, to move the emphasis away from a discussion of White middle-class discourses of coloniality and White amnesia to the challenges that present to White discourses of coloniality. The focus in Chapters 4 and 5 is on the formation of White working-class racialised discourses. My argument is that the everyday micro-processes of confronting White privilege are contradictory, complex and ambivalent. That is to say, Whites' questioning of racist attitudes often include the articulation and internationalisation of racist discourses and sentiments. The specific focus in Chapter 4 is on the conditions in which White working-class young adults from Coalville come to critically reflect upon and question the racist attitudes of family members, including parents, grandparents and siblings. In Chapter 5 I examine the participation of White working-class residents from Streetville in a multiethnic community-based network that set out to challenge the racist effects of state electoral reform on that community.

Clearly, my emphasis on White working-class racialised discourses in Part II provides a contrast to the examination of White middle-class discourses explored in Part I. The aim of this comparative approach to social class and Whiteness is to render apparent the similarities and variations within and between White working- and middle-class articulations of race, nation and coloniality within differing places, in these postcolonial times. In this regard, my study provides an insight into how Whites from different classes and places engage with race, ethnicity and difference.

The final part of the book, Part III, is entitled 'Postcolonial Genealogies', and Chapter 6's focus is on how an aspect of the colonial past is evoked and made meaningful. To do this Chapter 6 examines how slave ancestries and histories are drawn on by Black, White and interracial members of interracial families when they reflect on ideas of inheritance, ancestry and descent. Clearly, this chapter's emphasis on the processes of remembering the slave past provides a contrast to Part I, which traces how White amnesia of Britain's colonial past supports and maintains a boundary between the White rural self and BrAsian urban Other. Furthermore, this chapter's attention to the thoughts and reflections of members of interracial families takes seriously the notion that the reproduction of White power and dominance has always been self-evident to people who are not White. Indeed, my examination of the meaning of Whiteness from the perspective of people who do not self-identify as 'White' endeavours to counter the criticism that the study of Whiteness is just a further avenue for White middle-class academics like me to research and write about ourselves.

In the final chapter, I shall attempt to bring things to a close through analysis of how the themes of coloniality and the articulation of Whiteness, place, nation and class running throughout the book contribute to the theoretical framework that informs Whiteness studies. To do this, I will situate and contextualise some of the key conclusions and findings of my study in relation to the writings of anthropologists and sociologists who have studied and analysed Whiteness in the USA. Until very recently, the study of Whiteness in the USA has dominated this area of inquiry. There is now a fracturing of the US-focus of Whiteness studies by scholars who have attempted to place the study of Whiteness in a global perspective (see Steyn and Conway, 2010). My hope is that by situating my findings in a comparative framework that I will also contribute to the de-centring of the US-dominated focus of Whiteness studies.

Part I
White Amnesia: White Middle-Class Ethnicities

2
BrAsian 'Invasion' of White Suburban English Village Life

Picture a place that is suburban in terms of its residential landscape and close proximity to the city of Leicester rather than a 'typical' English village set in rural landscape well away from urban areas. It is in the face of Greenville's ambiguous village identity, situated as it is between the city of Leicester on one side, and the rolling countryside of Leicestershire on the other, that the White middle-class residents in my study reflexively defend their area's village status. In the course of so doing, they contend that it is the area's 'community spirit' centred on village activities that sustains Greenville's village identity, in spite of its geographical location and suburban landscape.[1]

A few months into my fieldwork, I also began to perceive and understand this suburban place as a 'village' and came to see the residents of Greenville as 'villagers'. Nonetheless, the ambiguity inherent within this perception of Greenville was reinforced to me when a good friend of mine came to visit while I was conducting fieldwork in Greenville. My friend is French and grew up in an isolated hamlet set in rural France. I stood surrounded by the suburban landscape of Greenville and told my friend that 'this is a village'. She laughed and categorically stated 'this is not a village, Katharine'. My contention is that the ambiguous nature of Greenville's village identity makes this an ideal place to study everyday ideas on what constitutes notions of villageness in England. In other words, my research participants' maintenance and control of Greenville's village identity makes apparent and renders explicit the elements that constitute villageness and village identity.

In this chapter I trace and analyse how White residents attempt to control their locale's village identity, which is interwoven with its reproduction as a White place in terms of its population profile and middle class in terms of socio-economic composition and aesthetics. From this standpoint, a detailed exploration of White middle-class residents' attitudes towards the minority of BrAsians that live in Greenville provides insight into White residents' ideas about the 'proper' ethnic and classed composition of Greenville's village identity, which derives from an idealised notion of English village life. I contend that White residents' perceptions of BrAsians parallel to some extent a colonial worldview of White Western cultural superiority that is intersected by the forgetting of that past. In this way, an analysis of White middle-class racialised discourses in Greenville opens a valuable research avenue through which to think about the elements that constitute the articulation of discourses of coloniality in the present, and the ways in which these discourses mediate the constitution of the White middle-class village identity.

Cultural geographers and sociologists working in the field of race and ethnicity studies have demonstrated how, in postcolonial English vernacular, the myths, scripts and icons that have formed on 'the countryside' refer not only to 'the nation' but also to White middle-class ethnicity and territoriality (see Agyeman and Spooner, 1997; Neal, 2002; Chakroborti and Garland, 2004; Neal and Agyeman, 2006; Neal, 2009). After the Second World War, many middle-class White urbanites moved to the countryside and settled there in increasing numbers, in search of a quieter, more 'respectable' way of life, which they perceived to be 'sanctioned by tradition and grounded in nature' (Wright, 1999, p. 19). The countryside came to be seen as a safe haven of neighbourliness, tranquillity and community, a 'retreat' from what was perceived to be the decline in English cities often associated with postcolonial BrAsian and Black settlement (Agyeman, 1989; Kinsmen, 1997; Neal, 2002). Murdoch and Marsden (1991, p. 47) observe that 'the yearning for the rural corresponds in many ways to "Anglo-centricity". Within this space identities are fixed within a White, family-centred, increasingly middle-class domain.' In this regard, the countryside and the village community is believed to be a healthy and stable environment in which to bring up well-adjusted children (Phillips, 1993).

The most recent public manifestation of the racialised constitution of pastoral images of Englishness came from the co-creator and executive producer of a popular detective programme entitled *Midsomer Murders* aired on the British television channel ITV. The programme is set in Midsomer, a mythical rural Oxfordshire village, and the creator of the programme opined in the spring of 2011 that: 'Implanting a black face in Midsomer would be tokenism' and 'not representative of the true nature of rural England'. He continued: 'We just don't have ethnic minorities involved [in the programmes]. ... Because it wouldn't be the English village with them. It just wouldn't work. Suddenly we might be in Slough [a multiethnic town in the south east of England].' He added: 'We're the last bastion of Englishness and I want to keep it that way.' (http://www.independent.co.uk/opinion/commentators/matthew-norman/matthew-norman-implanting-a-black-face-in-midsomer-would-be-tokenism-2242713.html [accessed April 2011]). This vision of rural England highlights how the idea of racial and cultural difference can be put to work to segregate village life and the countryside from ethnically diverse cities in contemporary postcolonial England. Significantly, according to the programme maker, this racialised portrait of village life is 'the last bastion of Englishness', which explicitly situates the ideas of villageness within an exclusive and bounded notion of Englishness that is categorically White.

Julian Agyeman and Rachel Spooner (1997, p. 202) examine how centuries of Britain's rural history and the success of Britain's rural economy are intimately interwoven with British colonial pasts and imperial expansion. These histories, they suggest, are ignored in popular and everyday representations of the English countryside as a White domain, as illustrated by my analysis of Wood's series in Chapter 1. On this point, Agyeman and Spooner (1997) write:

> Soldiers from North Africa used the Roman environment of the borders. They were garrisoned on Hadrian's Wall. People from Asia were brought, often as whole villages, to Britain to work in the Yorkshire and Lancashire cotton mills. Many of our stately homes were financed, built and exotically landscaped through African-Caribbean slavery and the last Maharaja of Lahore, Duleep Singh, is buried in the church of the village of Elvedon in Suffolk. Has the presence of these and other people been ... quietly and unceremoniously swept under the carpet?
>
> (1997, p. 202)

While BrAsian and Black people are denied a sense of historical attachment to the English countryside, Neal (2002, p. 445) reminds us that potent symbols of Britain's colonial past remain inscribed on the English rural landscape, for example, country pubs in the south west of England have names like 'Jamaica Inn'. Moreover, as Wood found in his archaeological explorations in the Leicestershire village of Kibworth, discussed in Chapter 1, artefacts from the British Empire are buried in the Leicestershire landscape. Furthermore, Wood's conversations with villagers revealed how some older people have memories of working for colonial institutions. However, as Agyeman and Spooner (1997) contend, it is the screening out and displacement of such colonial histories that connect the contemporary English countryside to BrAsians' and Blacks' histories and identities that in part supports the reproduction of the English countryside as a White domain.

In this chapter, I will build upon this argument to examine how White amnesia of the colonial past mediates White middle-class Greenville residents' representations of BrAsian residents as immigrants, that is, cultural Others whose origins are thought to belong outside of the village community, the nation and ultimately the West. Crucial to this representation of BrAsians as immigrants is the perception that 'their' culture, beliefs and habits are irreducibly Other when juxtaposed to the cultural norms and values held by the racially unmarked White middle-class English villagers. My supposition is that this representation of BrAsians' supposed cultural differences to the White majority parallels in part old colonial beliefs, discourses and ideas on the fundamental hierarchical racial and cultural distinctions that were thought to mark off and separate the coloniser from those colonised, as I outlined in my exposition of coloniality in Chapter 1. That is to say, the White residents' construction of the BrAsian residents as Other resonates with the colonial habit of deploying invidious generalisations to divide reality into a 'rigidly binomial opposition' of 'ours' and 'theirs' (Said, 1978, p. 227). Indeed, following Frankenberg, my contention is that one effect of the articulation of this colonial discourse of cultural differentiation in the present is for an 'apparently autonomous and racially unmarked White/Western self' to be produced in contrast to the racially and culturally marked Other (1993a, p. 17). In Greenville the racially unmarked White village self is taken to represent English values that are implicitly marked as middle class and, at times, explicitly marked as Western. One effect of this discourse is for BrAsians to come to, implicitly and sometimes explicitly, signify values that are believed to be not White, not English, not middle class and not Western.

In the ethnographic sections of this chapter, my aim is to examine how the distinctively middle-class and racially unmarked White ideals about the 'neighbourly', 'friendly', 'charitable', 'sociable' and 'tasteful' constitution of Greenville's village identity and community become apparent in relation to discourses on BrAsian residents that live in the area. I explore White middle-class villagers' attitudes towards a BrAsian family that owns a shop in Greenville, and towards wealthy BrAsian residents that live in the most expensive houses in the area. I trace a set of interlocking racialised and classed discourses that fixate on the assumed 'immigrant' status of BrAsian residents and thereby makes them cultural and classed outsiders to the village and its community. I shall examine the discourse of 'service' that comes into my White co-conversationalists descriptions of the BrAsian shopkeepers. While the BrAsian shopkeepers are thought to provide a 'good service' to the village and to display the respectable and valued attributes of neighbourliness and politeness, they are believed to be fundamentally Other compared to the White majority in terms of their cultural beliefs and practices.

Alongside this discourse of service, I will analyse the discourse of wealthy BrAsians' supposed 'social isolation' from the activities and rhythms that are thought to constitute village life. On the one hand, the wealthy BrAsian residents are thought to have achieved economic parity with the more affluent wealthy White residents, an attribute that is at times admired. However, on the other hand, these wealthy BrAsians' cultural differences to the White majority are thought to cut them off and thus isolate them from Greenville's village community. In addition to this discourse of social isolation, I explore a discourse focused on wealthy BrAsians' imagined 'excess' in terms of their cultural practices and acquisition of material wealth, which is taken to be an indication of the BrAsians' supposed lack of respectability and cultural know-how about how to participate in the patterns and activities of village life.

My argument is that these racialised and classed discourses on the BrAsian residents become entwined with, and are in part constituted by, White middle-class notions of respectability and cultural superiority that is a legacy of the colonial past. Moreover, underlying these racialised and classed discourses of Otherness is the process of White amnesia regarding the colonial past, which positions BrAsian residents on the outside of the village, the nation and the West. In short, this chapter explores how the reproduction of White middle-class cultural hegemony is entwined with ideals of villageness and Englishness that are mediated by classed discourses of respectability, coloniality and White amnesia in the present.

While the classed locations of the White middle-class people with whom I interacted in Greenville reflect the internal class distinctions within the middle classes in England, I shall not attempt to define middle-class identities in any straightforward way in this chapter or the next. Rather, my contention is that White residents' discourses on BrAsians makes White middle-class values, norms and notions of respectability apparent in relation to what they are not. The complexities of my White co-conversationalists' classed identities unfold in relation to their ideas about the proper constitution of village life. Everyday White racialised and classed discourses on the self and the BrAsian Other are mediated by ideals and beliefs on what constitutes the 'proper' and respectable composition of English village life and its community spirit.

Fieldwork in Greenville

I lodged with a White family in Greenville for six months between January and July 1997. I took a part-time job washing-up in the local pub and regularly attended local activities, the details of which will be discussed below. My participation in these events forms the basis for my understanding of the relationships and networks that constitute Greenville's village community.

While living and working in the area, I conducted 30 in-depth interviews with White middle-class and working-class men and women who live in the village. The interviews were conducted mostly in people's homes except for one that was conducted in the local pub and another in the Parish Council meeting rooms. The Parish Council is the administrative body of a rural village. The central aim of the interviews was to understand White residents' perceptions of BrAsians in their locale. In this chapter, I draw on interviews with White middle-class inhabitants of Greenville who are middle-aged, that is, 45 years-plus. This class and age cohort constituted the majority of this body of interview material, which in turn reflects the socio-economic constitution of the village.

In introducing my project to the people I came to know in Greenville I explained in general terms that I was interested in the village identity of Greenville and the relationship between 'Asians' and Whites in the village. I spent much time during the interviews discussing my White co-conversationalists' views on the village status and identity of Greenville in the face of its suburbanisation. I wanted to know what made this place a village, if that was how people saw it. It is in this context that I asked my White co-conversationalists about the presence of BrAsians in the village. A central strategy of the interviews was to give people the time to talk in general terms about what was important to them about their relationships in the area. I took extensive handwritten notes throughout all of the interviews and recorded most of them on a tape recorder and transcribed them verbatim. In those instances where my co-conversationalists did not want to be recorded I took handwritten notes only. My co-conversationalists' words reported in this chapter and the next are at times reported verbatim, and at other times they are based on reconstructions of what was actually said based on my detailed notes.

Crucial to the early stages of my networking in the area was my access to the official 'village directory', which listed key activities, clubs and events organised in Greenville, along with the name and telephone number of the organiser. Over time I built up detailed knowledge of the village activities within the area by interviewing residents who were members of particular clubs, and also by attending many such activities and events myself. There were a number of charitable activities in the area run on a voluntary basis. For example, I attended a club for people with learning difficulties who came from a private care home in Greenville. I also attended a luncheon club exclusively for elderly residents that was organised by volunteers who were mostly middle-aged White women. The village also offered a number of activities that were either specifically for women or attended mainly by women, some of which I participated in. These included a debating group for local women, social groups for women with specific hobbies, such as the flower guild and the sewing club. Moreover, the village hosted local branches of national organisations such as the Women's Institute, which was an organisation specifically for rural women, and the British Legion, an organisation concerned with caring for veterans of the armed services. There was also a range of sports clubs in Greenville, for example, the cricket club, bowls club and golf club, whose members came from both inside and outside of the village. Middle-aged and younger White women also attended keep-fit classes, and line dancing sessions were popular with middle-aged and older White people. The Parish Anglican and Baptist Churches ran a playgroup for younger children, and youth clubs for older children. Boys could also join the Scouts, the junior cricket club and football team. To the best of my knowledge, there were no equivalent sporting teams for girls. The final type of organisation in Greenville was the Parish Council. The Council was responsible for the maintenance of public facilities, for example, the upkeep of street lighting, roads and public buildings like the village hall. The Council received its funding from the local District Council.

Once I got talking with and interviewing a few residents who belonged to a specific club or organisation, I found that it was easier to make new contacts and form relationships. I often found myself passed on to the next interviewee. This was mostly on the grounds that people felt that so-and-so would know more about some aspects of Greenville's community and history than themselves. Or that so-and-so would be a good person to talk with because they had lived in the area for a long time or were involved in a particular village activity. This process of networking and snowballing enabled me to meet with relative ease residents who were not involved in a particular village activity, and so go beyond my initial contacts. However, I was never passed on to a BrAsian resident because none of my White co-conversationalists knew the BrAsian residents who lived in the village, or at least did not know them well enough.

I did most of my extended informal interviews in people's homes. During the day, women would often talk with me in their kitchens. If I interviewed men and/or women in the evenings, we would sit in their living rooms. I was always offered a cup of tea or coffee and sometimes a biscuit or piece of cake. After the interview, I often stayed talking with my White co-conversationalists. If the interview was in the evening then sometimes I was offered a glass of wine as a sign that the tape-recorded interview was over. In this time, we continued to explore the themes we had been discussing in the interview.

I introduced myself to people as a PhD student at Manchester University, and told them that I was from a village in south Leicestershire. If people enquired further about my academic credentials I explained that I was working in the discipline of social anthropology. However, I found that the majority of White residents in Greenville knew little about anthropology and were not concerned with it. I got the impression that I was thought to be a kind of social historian. Or at least people assumed that it was the history of Greenville that I would find most interesting.

I was 24 years old when I lived in Greenville. My Whiteness, middle-classness and Englishness are factors that mediated and shaped this fieldwork. My White ethnicity, English nationality and student status meant that I was generally found unintimidating in discussing issues concerned with the racialised nature of Greenville's village life. White residents automatically interpreted my White skin and Englishness as a sign that I would identify with their points of view rather than take a BrAsian, non-White or non-English perspective. Moreover, I did not give my White co-conversationalists any reason to think otherwise (see discussion in Chapter 1). However, this did not mean that I did not engage with my White co-conversationalists' thoughts and reflections. For example, on the occasions when I was asked about my findings, most people agreed with my suggestion that some White residents held negative views about BrAsians in the village. However, my White co-conversationalists felt that it was other White residents who held such negative views towards BrAsian residents and not themselves. As the ethnographic sections of this chapter will illustrate, this was not the case. It was not just others but they themselves who expressed clear racialised stereotypes.

Only one middle-aged White man, who I shall call Simon, was reluctant to speak with me. A White woman from the village told me that Simon had 'strong' opinions about 'Asians' and so would be a good person to talk with for my project. This was the only time during my research in Greenville that it was recommended that I talk with someone for this reason. When I rang Simon to ask him for an interview, he did not want to meet with me. He later told me when I did meet him that he thought I might have been an 'Asian' business client 'winding him up'. Simon said that it was hard to tell on the telephone if I was a 'nice Leicestershire girl or an Asian'. I eventually managed to persuade Simon that I would value his contribution to my project.

In Greenville my middle-class identity also enabled me to build relationships with residents. My middle-classness was evident and confirmed by the fact I was doing a PhD. My academic identity gave me an aura of respectability. Moreover, my middle-class identity was evident in the way that I spoke, the village in Leicestershire that I come from and my comportment. My gender also shaped and influenced my fieldwork relationships and experiences. My female identity facilitated access to women's social clubs and societies in the village. In addition, I was invited on one occasion to organise 'the tea' for a local cricket team.[2] This invitation was a highly gendered form of inclusion in village life that fits with broader norms of respectability appropriate for women, but which might have been insulting to a man.[3]

My gendered identity as a woman also shaped my attempts at finding somewhere to live in the village. The landlord of the pub in which I took a job washing up initially offered me a room to rent in a flat (apartment) above the pub. However, he later retracted this offer on the grounds that he thought it would be an unsuitable place for me to live as a young single woman. When this offer was withdrawn, I posted an advert in the post-office window inviting villagers to contact me if they had a spare room in their house to rent. I received a call from a single divorced man who offered me a room to rent in his house. I mentioned this offer to the woman who worked in the local library, who offered me advice, drawing upon her reading of my class and gendered identity:

> No you wouldn't like it. He's not for you – he has had a string of well female lodgers. He wants someone to pay the bills, and well, he will expect favours if you see what I mean. It wouldn't just end with the

rent. ... No his not what you want, definitely not. I don't mean to put you off, but this is a bit of inside information if you like.

I eventually took up lodgings with a divorced woman in her late forties and her 15-year-old daughter.[4] It is perhaps no coincidence that the offers of lodgings in Greenville were made by divorcees who were single. By contrast to the majority of families that lived in Greenville, these families found themselves in situations whereby they benefited from the extra money that a lodger contributed to the household. As I have already mentioned in Chapter 1, my experience of lodging here was not a happy one. Over time it became clear to me that my landlady was wary of me and concerned that I would tell details of her private life to people in the village, including her son, who lived with his father elsewhere in Greenville, and her mother who also lived nearby. My landlady was also anxious that I might abuse my use of the telephone by making expensive long-distance telephone calls to the university in Manchester and elsewhere. In spite of my willingness to pay for any such expenses, she eventually banned me from using the telephone. This meant that I conducted all telephone conversations necessary for my networking with villagers in a public phone kiosk in the village centre. I soon realised that my landlady was happiest when I was in my room alone and away from the family. In short, I did not feel at home living with this particular family.

Greenville: A sense of place

Greenville lies only five miles west of Leicester and so is just a 15-minute bus journey from the city centre. It is situated between a large mixed BrAsian and White suburb of the city and a predominantly White village of the more stereotypical kind set in rural landscape such as Kibworth and Saddington. Like my friend from France, visitors to Greenville entering from the city would probably not even notice that they have passed from suburban Leicester into a village. This is because it is its activities and community spirit, not its landscape, that makes Greenville a village (as recognised and communicated to me by residents). Indeed, the area's socio-economic composition is that of a suburb rather than an agriculturally based economy traditionally associated with the rural. The last of Greenville's farms disappeared in the 1950s with the extension of a major English motorway (highway). The development of the motorway has attracted a large influx of middle-class commuters who work in Leicester and other cities in the Midlands region of England. Most of the 4,519 people living in the village at the time of 1991 Census were incomers from the city of Leicester, other parts of Leicestershire and more distant parts of Britain.[5]

Greenville has for a long time been the home of commuters. At the end of the nineteenth century there was an influx of wealthy Leicester businessmen and their families into the area. These people, like many of their modern-day counterparts, were keen to live away from the urban hustle and bustle of Leicester, the place in which they worked. At the time of my fieldwork, these Leicester business people were remembered by some as the 'old village' families. However, there were relatively few people who could name these families and even fewer who could claim to be direct descendants. Claims to belong to Greenville based on kinship ties and place of origin do not have the same salience as they do in many towns and villages in rural Britain studied by anthropologists (for example, see Strathern, 1981; Rapport, 1993; Edwards, 2000; Degnen, 2012). Thus residents do not on the whole concern themselves with making sharp and clear-cut distinctions on the basis of lineage and length of residence. As Mary, the White wife of the vicar of Greenville's Anglican Church, told me:

> Really we're all incomers, I guess. People move here for work. I suppose there are a few old people who have lived here all their lives, but on the whole we're all incomers.

As this chapter progresses, it will become apparent that it is those incomers who are White, English and middle class who are perceived to fit into Greenville's village community. By contrast, BrAsians whose origins are thought to lie elsewhere are rendered immigrants – not only to the village but also to the nation, and ultimately the Western way of life.

Greenville's population, like that of the neighbouring village, is mainly White. By official 1991 Census classification, 98.2 per cent of Greenville's population was 'White', 1.4 per cent 'Asian', 0.2 per cent 'Black' and 0.2 per cent 'Other'. There is great wealth in the area. Greenville is home to well-paid professionals, high-earning executives, middle management and public sector workers. The majority of houses are privately owned. At the time of my fieldwork, most families had one or two cars and went on holiday once or twice a year. Thinking along these lines, Maria, a long-term White resident of Greenville, made explicit what she identified as the 'middle-class' composition of the majority of the White residents. This was unusual. Most of my White co-conversationalists did not deploy the idioms 'middle class' and 'working class'. Maria explained:

> Most people here [that is, in the village] are middle class. Yes, and then there is a very high class band, where the man is a bank manager and the woman can stay at home, compared to the middle classes where both of you have to work to maintain a standard.

The area's landscape is subdivided into different suburban style housing estates (that is, a planned area of housing where all the houses are of similar design and type). To an insider like me, this made it easy to identify people's economic capital and to some extent their class status by identifying the estate on which they lived. A White middle-aged couple explained: 'Depending really on the price of the houses. ... There are definite sort of class areas. ... But it doesn't bother us.'

One of the most prosperous and oldest areas of Greenville is what I call Greenville Gardens.[6] This area consists of wide avenues off which sweeping driveways lead to large mansions. The owners of the larger houses are wealthy business and professional people. One particular road in this area is known locally as 'Anaesthetist Drive', because of the medical profession of the majority of the road's residents. Past and present owners of the larger houses have sold plots of their gardens to build new prestigious homes, which include impressive bungalows and large modern houses. At the time of my fieldwork, there were approximately five affluent BrAsian families who lived in the wealthy Greenville Gardens area.

The area beyond Greenville Gardens, known locally as 'the village', consists of an extensive patchwork of suburban-style housing estates including post-1945 semi-detached houses and modern mock-Tudor designer homes. The latter are replicas of a style of house made of timber in the fifteenth century. At the back of Long Street, the central road that runs through the village centre, are two roads of well-kept terraced houses, which are typically working-class dwellings. It is here that I was told the less wealthy White families live, including restaurant managers and young couples starting out in life. There is also a small council estate that leads off Long Street. The council estate includes a combination of houses rented to low-income tenants by the local authority, as well as privately owned houses that tenants have purchased from the council.

The village centre is full of landmarks that signify English village life. In the middle of Long Street, there is the Queen's Head pub, the village hall, a grocery store, a post office and the Baptist Church. The original

Queen's Head building was replaced in 1970 by a modern building and was renamed 'Barcelona'. However, the pub was restored to its traditional name of the 'Queen's Head' by the brewery that owned it, and it was considered to be a more appropriate name by several of my White co-conversationalists. For example, a retired White woman, who had lived in the area for over twenty years, commented on her relief when the pub name was restored to its original: 'I think that the Barcelona does sound like something on a suburban [housing] estate. The Queen's Head sounds more like a village pub.' Similarly, during the 1960s, the 'village hall' was also renamed as a 'community centre', but the Parish Council voted to restore its original name. Several White retired residents told me that this was a more appropriate name for the building. They considered the name 'community centre' to be the name of a suburban or urban meeting place, whereas the village hall hosts community events in Greenville, which is imagined to be a village place. Clearly, these name changes, and people's reactions to them, highlight that there is some anxiety among White residents about the village identity of Greenville.

To summarise, Greenville is not in any straightforward way a rural village situated in a valley surrounded by the rolling gentle landscape of rural England. Indeed, measured against this stereotype of villageness, the size of the area's population, its close proximity to the city of Leicester and the area's suburban residential landscape would suggest that Greenville is just a suburb of Leicester. These circumstances require that residents actively engage in rhetorical strategies to sustain its village status.

The 'village' community spirit and the formation of White middle-class ethnicities

My question, then, is what do White people imagine to be there when they think about their place on the basis of what they see? Moreover, how are ideas and images of 'village-ness' made into realities through social interaction and relatedness? (See Cohen, 2000, p. 166 for similar ethnographic questions in relation to everyday perceptions of national identity.) As I have mentioned, central to the maintenance and control of Greenville's village identity is the reproduction of its community spirit through activities that are associated with the rhythms and patterns of traditional English village life.

Maria, who we met briefly earlier was, at the time of my fieldwork a middle-aged White professional woman who moved to Leicester as a student from London with her family some 20 years previously. She worked as an ecologist and as such expressed an interest in preserving Greenville's 'green' spaces, a potent symbol of villageness in England. Maria had always played an active role in the local Baptist Church. She explained her perception of the area's ambiguous 'village' identity. In the course of so doing, Maria justified and explained why she thinks Greenville is still a 'village' in spite of its 'lack of green'. She said:

> I know that people think that there is a lack of green for a village, but I feel that Greenville captures that country village feeling. People support local things like the Greenville Players [a local amateur dramatics society] and the Church activities. The Churches are very good at organising charitable events for the old people.

Sheila was a White single woman in her sixties, and when we met had lived in a cottage on Long Street for nearly 40 years. She was born in a rural village in the south of Leicestershire. Her father was a farmer and so she spent much of her youth working on his farm. In her early twenties she moved to Greenville to manage a local farm. She was a respected figure in the community in her position as a lay preacher of the Baptist Church. Several people with whom I spoke told me to talk to Shelia. As one woman said: 'She's a lovely lady and has been here a long time. She will be able to give you the history of the place.' Sheila perceives the ambiguous nature of Greenville's 'village' identity as follows:

> Greenville is still rated as a village but really there is very little between Leicester and us. And where we farmed up on the main road, all that is now built on and it was [once] all fields. ... I think that Greenville is still a village but bordering on a suburb, but the community spirit in it is very village-minded. We have got all sorts of things going. There is the Legion, the British Legion. ... It is a good and caring community.

Paul and Janet were a White married couple in their late fifties who had lived in Greenville for about 25 years. When Paul's business became successful he and his wife, Janet, moved, with their two sons, from a semi-detached house on the outskirts of Leicester's city centre to a spacious bungalow in Greenville Gardens. When we met, Paul still worked in Leicester running his business. Janet spent her days helping her sons' wives, who also lived in the village, with their small children. Paul and Janet commented on Greenville's ambiguous village identity and community spirit like this:

PAUL: It's definitely a village, although the village identity is being eroded.
JANET: People here still do villagey things in the summer. ... We have floats [that is, carnival parades] and garden fetes [that is, local festivities organised by residents to raise money for the upkeep of the area].
PAUL: Umm yes, the residents want it to stay a village.
KATHARINE: Why do you think that is?
PAUL: Favouritism for village life. I guess people view a village through rose-tinted glasses. There is the idea that it's quieter. It's inherent within us. The need to get back to our roots and find the rural life, the idyll.

For Maria, Sheila, Paul and Janet the idea of 'villageness' is not simply a matter of geographical location. Rather, they each suggest that Greenville's village identity revolves around the reproduction of the area's 'community spirit'. The latter is associated with White residents' continued participation in local social, leisure and charitable activities. These thoughts resonate with the opinions of other 'village-minded' White residents, who frequently directed me to the numerous social activities as evidence that Greenville is a 'friendly' place, 'caring' with a good 'community spirit'. As Paul suggests, these ideas are 'inherent within us', and they are intimately interwoven with romantic, idyllic and sentimental ideas about the 'proper' constitution of English village life.

As I described earlier, there are a variety of social and sports clubs in Greenville. I have also alluded to the fact that middle-aged White women play an important part in the reproduction of the village community through their participation in leisure and charitable pursuits. The local churches are also key organisations around which White men and women organised charitable activities for elderly residents, youth clubs for adolescents, and a club for people with learning difficulties. Involvement in these activities is entwined with the social and moral values of charity, friendliness and neighbourliness. These same sentiments are woven into nostalgic and national narratives about the structures of feeling that comprise the traditional English village community. Raymond Williams (1973, p. 30) comments on the ways that the images associated with 'the rural' in late seventeenth-century English poetry reflected the wider 'social and moral' values of 'the natural order of responsibility and neighbourliness', a reflection that continues to the present day.

Middle-class White residents are responsible for the hard work that goes into the organisation of local activities. White middle-class status in Greenville is partly dependent upon 'economic capital' (Bourdieu, 1984), the ability to buy an expensive house in a prestigious environment such as Greenville Gardens. However, White middle-class status is also more than this. It is also reliant upon the acquisition and embodiment of 'cultural capital' (Bourdieu, 1984), which includes a set of culturally appropriate desires, tastes and aspirations for oneself and one's family within the local community. Economic capital enhances White individuals' attainment of middle-class status in Greenville. However, money does not substitute for a perceived lack of the tacit cultural knowledge about how to fit into the social networks of community life. This will become apparent in my analysis of my White co-conversationalists' attitudes towards the wealthy BrAsian residents.

White residents' varied participation in the range of local activities reflects differences in age, gender, lifestyle choices and socio-economic location. In this way, White residents' participation in local activities highlights what some sociologists have referred to as the 'intra-class' distinctions within the middle classes (Butler and Savage, 1995). For example, Greenville's thriving and prestigious golf club includes White men and women from the more affluent areas of the village, as well as members from outside of the village. Only the affluent White middle-class residents can afford to join the local golf club because of its high membership fees. A White man from the village who was not a member of the club suggested: 'The golf club crowd seem to think that they are up in the pecking order.' Similarly, a local White resident who held a catering contract with the golf club explained her experience like this:

> I found it really snobby up there – very rude. ... I left because of the attitude of the people. ... It is really another world. It is like the village does not exist, and you do not really hear about it in the village. It is big business.

In contrast to membership of the golf club, White residents do not need to be wealthy in order to dedicate their time and energy to the organisation of local activities. Participation in local charity and recreational events brings a sense of personal satisfaction, social recognition and status in the community. Thus the kinds of social activities that White villagers participate in and the networks of social relations that are formed around these activities become a form of 'cultural capital' in themselves and mediators through which other kinds of capital worked on White people's lives. Nonetheless, participation in charitable activities and events excludes those villagers who do not have time to participate in such events, and those individuals who feel that they do not belong to such networks.

But even for some of these people, Greenville's 'village' status can itself become a marker of cultural capital, necessary for the maintenance of White middle-class social status and a sense of prestige. This is evident in the attitudes of some of those White residents who do not participate in the local activities. A White female veteran of numerous local activities commented on such people as follows: 'I feel that people who have moved into the village don't always integrate. They tend to use it ... like a commuter place.' For some of these White residents, the area's environment becomes an 'aesthetic backdrop' associated with a high-quality dwelling in a prestigious environment (Cloke et al., 1995, p. 237). As a White middle-aged woman who played no part in the local activities remarked: 'There is a certain snob value to living in Greenville – it is a good address.' Such White residents have a financial and psychological investment in the reproduction of Greenville's 'village' identity. This vision of Greenville rests upon an imagined notion of integration and coherence mobilised by some White residents to protect an aura of prestige and entitlement. Risks to Greenville's fragile and idealised village community threaten not only these White middle-class residents' diverse lifestyles but also their sense of self (Cloke et al., 1995, p. 238). One perceived risk to Greenville's village identity is the presence of BrAsian residents in the village. I shall now turn to an examination of White villagers' attitudes towards the BrAsian shopkeepers in Greenville.

BrAsian shopkeepers and the discourse of service

The most 'visible' BrAsian family in Greenville owns and works in a shop in the village centre. Through speaking to my White co-conversationalists I came to see that BrAsian shopkeepers are positioned in a role of service by White residents. I will argue that this positioning of BrAsians shares some parallels with accounts of the colonisers' expectation of deference on the part of those colonised. In developing and advancing this argument, my analysis draws in part on Caroline Knowles' (2007) examination of the racialised discourses of White administrators and their spouses from the former British colonies who have now retired to rural south Devon, a county in the south west of England. Knowles reflects on the way in which her interviewees' sense of classed and racialised entitlement formed in the colonies is brought 'home' to the English countryside. She writes the following about Joyce, an elderly White woman whose husband formed part of the colonial administration in Hong Kong:

> Asked what she most misses from Hong Kong ... Joyce replies without hesitation: 'the servants of course'. Her home help [home care assistant] does a bit of dusting, but doesn't replace the service that formed the social relations of empire. Joyce and Molly [another interviewee] comport themselves in the Devonshire countryside with a sense of entitlement – forged in the alchemy of race, class and colonial residence and repatriated to a place where domestic servants are still part of living memory – a firm but kindly tone of voice reserved for those who now serve them, as home helps, shop assistants, waitresses, bank and post office clerks.
>
> (2007, p. 178)

This extract conveys something of the feeling of racial and class entitlement expressed by some of my White co-conversationalists towards BrAsian shopkeepers in Greenville. These White residents described their pleasure at the 'friendly', 'polite' and efficient service offered by the BrAsian shopkeepers to the village community. In this way, the BrAsian shopkeepers display attributes and characteristics that are considered to be acceptable and respectable in the village. This apparent acceptance of BrAsian shopkeepers dovetails with a discourse about the BrAsians' supposed fundamental cultural differences from the White majority. These attitudes therefore exhibit similarities with the ways in which Empire colonists had ambivalent attitudes towards those colonised. Both Greenville Whites and historical colonisers recognise some core values shared by the Other and the White self, namely, the value of hard work/service rendered. But at the same time the colonised/BrAsians are seen to be culturally alien to the White self. Thus reminiscent of colonial Britain, my co-conversationalists perceive BrAsians through a 'rigidly binominal' worldview that places 'our' culture in opposition to 'theirs' (Said, 1978). In this way, the White Western village self is co-constructed in relation to the racially marked BrAsian Other. One effect of the articulation of these colonial discourses is to position BrAsian shopkeepers as immigrants, that is, people who are assumed to come from and belong to another time and place outside of the village, the nation and the West. Underpinning this imaginary is White amnesia of the colonial past.

Consider how Mike commented on his reaction and other White residents' reaction when a BrAsian family moved into the local grocery shop. At the time of my fieldwork, Mike was in his forties and owned a building and decorating business. He was divorced and lived with his teenage children in a modest family house in the centre of the village. Mike commented on the BrAsian shopkeepers as follows:

> I remember when the Patels moved in. I thought – yeah, great, open all hours. That is what we want. But people said, 'Wogs moving into Greenville. ... We don't want that.' They are the same people, who will do most of their grocery shopping there, you know, and get charged extra for doing it. But they kept saying, 'We don't want wogs in Greenville.' Why? He is an Irishman and he is a Welshman – and so what is wrong with a coloured guy moving in and doing the village a service, and making money in the process?

In order to demonstrate his support for this family, Mike distances himself from some White residents' objections to BrAsians moving into the village. In this way, Mike is letting me, the interviewer, know that he holds more tolerant views on BrAsians compared to other White people that I might meet and interview from the area. It is significant that Mike uses the offensive terms 'Wog' and 'coloured' to paraphrase and so distance himself from other White villagers' objections. The etymology of the idiom 'Wog' can be traced to the colonial period. In this regard, Wog is said to be an acronym for Western Oriental Gentleman. The expression probably derives from 'golliwog', which is a late nineteenth-century caricatured black children's toy.[7] Mike thus unselfconsciously evokes a word that is pregnant with colonial imagery and meaning. In this sense, Mike's casual deployment of the term 'Wog' illuminates how the British imperial past shapes English vernacular in ways that are often taken for granted. The term 'coloured' renders the BrAsian shopkeepers 'hyper-visible'. Mike draws a parallel between a Welshman's and an Irishman's differences, equating them to the cultural differences of 'coloureds'. However, the Welsh and the Irish are not marked by their colour but their national belonging. By contrast, BrAsians are marked by their 'colour', and in turn negating their national and regional differences, which are rendered indifferent, invisible and inconsequential.

However, in spite of Mike's emphasis upon other Whites' racist views, his description of this BrAsian family constructs and maintains a hierarchical distinction between the White self and BrAsian Other. In this regard, he employs two common stereotypes about BrAsian shopkeepers in England, that is: 'they are open all hours' and they 'charge extra'. His belief that the BrAsian shopkeepers 'charge extra' implies that they are disingenuous in their business practices. It is in this vein that Mike continues to explain how he perceives the shop to be run. While he commends aspects of BrAsian culture, he positions 'them' as Other from the standpoint of a racially unmarked White Western self. In so doing, he mobilises large generalisations to separate 'us' from 'them', founded on an essentialist concept of culture that can be traced to colonial discourses of difference:

> The Patels are a typical example. ... They have got the female dominancy situation, five paces behind. ... She's at the till while I go down the cash and carry. The lad finishes school and he stocks a few shelves up, very nice. It wouldn't work in a Western culture, you know. My wife at the till while I went down the cash and carry. ... That is why I am in admiration of their culture, because they are family group orientated. ... They will prosper and ... they do respect their parents and they will study. They will have all the prime jobs in this country, I am convinced of it. ... We are still ringing bloody mops out and wearing knotted handkerchiefs on our heads going down Skegness [a seaside town in England]. ... The Indians, they have had to work hard because they have come to a totally different country, a lot of them poorish. They have got nothing to lose and so the only way for them is up.

Mike's emphasis upon this family's origins outside of England in 'India' – 'a totally different country' – enables him to construct the idea that there is a racialised cultural boundary separating 'us' Western English people from 'those' 'poorish', non-Western 'Indians'. Like many of my White co-conversationalists who feature in this chapter and the next, Mike perceives BrAsians' relationship to England to take meaning at the moment of their supposed settlement to England. It is precisely the emphasis upon BrAsians' migration to England and their origins elsewhere that screens out BrAsians' histories with Englishness and Britishness formed through Empire. Moreover, erasure of the colonial historical context facilitates their construction as Other to the racially unmarked White English self and so opens the way for generalisations about the middle-class White self and BrAsian Others. This, then, constructs a series of distinctions between 'our' and 'their' ways of life.

Mike thinks that the Patels are a 'typical' example of BrAsian immigrants, and so they become an 'ideal bearer' of BrAsian cultural practices and values (Blommaert and Verschueren, 1998, p. 96). He admires, praises and valorises what he perceives to be core BrAsian values and cultural practices. He thinks that 'they' are family orientated in business, 'their' children work hard at school, 'their' kids respect 'their' parents and 'their' wives are subservient to 'their' husbands. These are respectable qualities that ensure BrAsians provide a useful service. In contrast, Mike's single-parent family represents the contradictory Western attitudes and cultural components of individualism, the loss of family values, youthful deviance and liberation from patriarchy. Mike's static and conservative image of BrAsian culture becomes a projection for his idealistic vision of male dominance and respectful children. BrAsians' embodiment of traditional virtues (in contrast to Western decadence) is thought by Mike to be highly conducive to BrAsians' economic success and their social mobility 'up' the class system.

Mike also portrays a stereotypical and quaint image of the White English. The English are perceived as daft and ridiculous in 'wearing knotted handkerchiefs' and 'wringing out mops'. Mike's stereotype of the racially unmarked White English simultaneously commends but also denigrates the commercial and entrepreneurial aspects of BrAsians' economic prosperity and hard work. On the one hand, the Patels are thought to charge their customers 'extra' and their business success is imagined to be dependent upon the exploitation of family labour. On the other hand, the White English are believed to favour the good old-fashioned, solid and respectable White working-class values of steadfastness, honesty and clean living. Mike's self-ridicule of the White English evokes an image of deviant BrAsians stealing the economy from the naïve White English. Thus, the wearing of handkerchiefs and going to Skegness is an extension of White classed English and Western respectability to the point of self-mockery, and not a transformation of it. In other words, Mike's critique of White English culture actually reinforces and reifies the normalcy and respectability of White Englishness that he is seeking to invert and mock.

Paul and Janet, who we met earlier in this chapter, also reflect on the way they think that the BrAsian shopkeepers are an asset to the area. They praise aspects of BrAsians' lifestyles that are perceived as respectable and thus fit into the village. However, BrAsians are also thought to stand out as different from English culture and 'our' ways:

PAUL: The local shops here are wonderful. They have taken over the grocery shop, which is superb.
JANET: Yes, they always remember our names. I only went in there once and then the next time they said hello. They are so polite.
PAUL: The English used to be a nation of shopkeepers. Well, they beat us hands down. They are so polite and friendly. They are brilliant.

As in Mike's account, this particular BrAsian family is referred to by the collective and objectifying description 'they'. From Paul's and Janet's point of view, 'they' are thought to be 'polite and friendly'. In this regard, the family is believed to be gracious in their service to their customers by greeting them nicely and remembering their names. It could be argued that this family is thought to fit into the socially accepted and respectable values of politeness, friendliness and neighbourliness associated with the norms of Greenville's village community. However, the apparent acceptance and praise of this family shows that their goodness is essentially in their role of servants and service providers. While the BrAsians in the shop are accepted and appreciated for their good service to the village, their perceived cultural differences separate and mark them off from the village culture. In this way, in parallel with Mike's account, Paul's and Janet's description of the BrAsian shopkeepers valorises aspects of their culture but in ways that view BrAsians as fundamentally different from White people.

Like Mike, Paul admires BrAsians' supposed financial and business success. However, both Paul and Mike see BrAsians and Whites as pitched in competition with each other over who will flourish in and control the White English economy. For Paul, they are now 'the nation of shopkeepers', whereas 'the English used to be'. For Mike, BrAsians will have 'all the prime jobs in this country'. In this instance, the BrAsian shopkeepers evoke ideas about the wider BrAsian diaspora's supposed 'takeover' and control of the English economy to the detriment of White English people. Thus the adjectives of 'brilliant' (Paul) and 'admirable' (Mike) are ambiguously positive and negative descriptions of BrAsianness. BrAsians are thought to be admirable and even respectable in their economic success, their hard work and their polite service. However, these socially accepted characteristics do not allow 'them' to be incorporated into the invisible social bonds that constitute the imagined White local and national community. That is to say, BrAsians' supposedly different 'origins', cultural practices and potentially threatening business success restricts them to economic pockets of service on the margins of Greenville's village community that is racially unmarked as White. Putting this another way, Mike and Paul would like to restrict BrAsians to the margins of Greenville's village community, but the fear is that BrAsians cannot be restricted and thus kept in their place as simply servants and service providers.

The preceding considerations illuminate the cultural attributes and characteristics that are mobilised by my White middle-class co-conversationalists to explain and describe the BrAsian shopkeepers that live and work in Greenville. One aspect of this narrative is for BrAsians to be accepted into the village community because they are thought to fulfil a useful service. In this regard, they are said to display the socially appropriate and respectable White middle-class attributes of 'politeness', 'friendliness', 'hard work' and economic success. However, this apparent acceptance of the BrAsian shopkeepers is interwoven with a feeling of their supposed cultural distinctiveness and differences from the White middle-class majority. In this way, attributes of respectability that are appreciated, valued and recognised by the White middle classes, such as hard work and business success, are devalued when applied to BrAsians. Thus while aspects of the BrAsian shopkeepers' culture are admired and valorised, they are thought to be from 'a totally different country', which is 'poorish' and deviant in business, and to hold non-Western family values that include the subordination of women and children. It is this process of simultaneously praising and Othering BrAsians' perceived cultural differences that enables my White middle-class co-conversationalists to maintain the belief that they are racially tolerant, while simultaneously rendering this BrAsian family outside the norms that constitute the imagined and respectable middle-class village community.

My contention is that this ambiguous representation of the BrAsian shopkeepers shares some parallels with the colonisers' attitudes of kindliness but yet also sense of cultural superiority towards those who served them, as described by Knowles (2007). As Frankenberg (1993a, p. 193) argues, at times the coloniser valorised aspects of the lives of those people they colonised, but they did so in ways that viewed the culture of the Other as different from that of the racially unmarked White self. One effect of this historical backdrop to my White co-conversationalists' accounts is that the BrAsian shopkeepers are portrayed as immigrants whose origins lie outside of England. Intrinsic to this immigrant imaginary is collective amnesia of BrAsians' colonial and postcolonial relationships with Englishness and Britishness.

Wealthy BrAsian inhabitants and the discourse of 'social isolation'

The second 'immigrant' imaginary that I wish to examine centres on the BrAsians who live in Greenville Gardens, the most prosperous area of the village. These residents have acquired the material trappings associated with an affluent White middle-class lifestyle. However, they are thought by my White co-conversationalists not to possess the socially commended neighbourly and friendly attributes associated with the rhythms of the village community. BrAsians' wealth does not, therefore, simply translate into middle-class social status in Greenville. Rather, BrAsian wealth is devalued and so does not allow 'them' to be seen and included as 'one of us'.

Wealthy BrAsians are thought to isolate themselves and in so doing cut themselves off from important social networks. The discourse of 'social isolation' enables my White middle-class co-conversationalists to once more mobilise a plethora of stereotypical images centred on the wealthy BrAsians' perceived cultural differences from the White majority. Underlying the production of these perceived cultural differences is a 'rigidly binominal' opposition separating the White middle-class village self from those BrAsian Others, which resonates with colonial discourses on race, culture and difference (Said, 1978). In this instance, both White middle-class culture and wealthy BrAsian culture become portrayed as bounded entities that are incompatible and incommensurable. This interpretation of 'our' and 'their' culture as 'discrete', 'bounded' and incompatible can be traced to an essentialist and hierarchical colonial concept of culture. On this point, Frankenberg (1993a, p. 192) suggested that the effect of contemporary manifestations of colonial discourses was for 'cultures' to be 'conceived as discrete, bounded spaces, [while] culture was viewed as separate from material life'. One consequence issuing from this discourse in Greenville is that the qualities, norms and values that constitute White middle-class village life become defined and take meaning in relation to wealthy BrAsian Others.

Simon explains why he thinks the wealthy BrAsians do not participate in local community activities. Like Mike, Simon was a self-employed builder who owned his business. When we met, he had lived in Greenville for over twenty years. Simon lived with his second wife on a suburban-style housing estate in the centre of Greenville. He describes his perception of the wealthy BrAsian residents' relationship to the 'village' community and in so doing constructs a 'we' and 'they' contrast that distinguishes BrAsians from a racially unmarked White village culture. The effect of this discourse of Otherness is to ensure that White and BrAsian cultures are portrayed as discrete, bounded and incompatible. He said:

> They tend to keep themselves to themselves. ... They have tended to build fences and electric gates around the big houses, which is something we never saw in the past. ... I don't think that they do fit into country life. ... Where we would tend to socialise ..., we like to stay

together as a community to belong to groups, to belong to bowls, and we like to enjoy ourselves. You don't seem to find Asians doing that. ... The Asians [i.e. that live in Greenville] don't seem to look for free time – it's work for them. They have got to earn and I am sure that is their upbringing in another country, because they were brought up on a meagre upbringing, on very little money and very little food, whereas we lived better. We have lived in better times and we treasure our spare time to do what we want to do.

Simon constructs a chain of dichotomies separating White and BrAsian cultures: 'We' like to socialise, 'to belong to groups' and 'to enjoy ourselves'. By contrast, 'they' do not look for 'free time', 'they' feel compelled to 'work' and so on. In this regard, he portrays White and BrAsian cultures as discrete and bounded entities. Simon thinks that it is BrAsians' 'meagre' origins elsewhere that motivates them to earn money, a sentiment that resonates with Mike's assertion that BrAsians 'have come to a totally different country, a lot of them poorish', and that, 'they will prosper'. From this perspective, it is 'their' impoverished origins outside of England that is the reason for 'their' cultural differences from 'us'. Once more, these narratives of origin and settlement to England place the BrAsian residents outside of the English nation into a time and place symbolised by a lack of security and economic prosperity. In this way, wealthy BrAsians' colonial and postcolonial claims to Englishness based on ongoing relations with Englishness and Britishness through the histories of Empire are negated, and a sense of racial superiority and classed value is attached to a racially unmarked White middle-class English way of being that is denied to BrAsians.

Simon thinks that what he perceives to be BrAsians' compulsion to work marks their culture as set apart from the village community ethos of friendship and sociality. From this point of view, and sharing some parallels to Mike's portrayal of the relaxed White Englishmen with knotted handkerchiefs, 'we' Whites have achieved the ontological security necessary to enable 'us' to appreciate the value of community and sociality. In contrast, wealthy BrAsians are thought to be more focused upon the material and economic aspects of life because of their 'meagre upbringings'. One effect of this discourse is for BrAsians' economic wealth to become a sign not of their social mobility and classed respectability but their supposed impoverished backgrounds and cultural difference from 'us' – the racially unmarked White village majority. In short, BrAsians' outward displays of prosperity are taken to be an indication of 'their' immigrant status and cultural distinction and classed inferiority to 'us'

Whites. In this way, White and BrAsian cultures become depicted as not only distinct and bounded but also incompatible.

From this standpoint, the electric fences and gates that surround BrAsians' houses disrupt the seemingly timeless and apparently tasteful milieu of Greenville Gardens. They are also symbols of the wealthy BrAsians' apparent 'social isolation', fundamental cultural differences and thus lack of cultural know-how about how to fit into and engage with the village community. Thus BrAsians' economic capital does not attract or facilitate the acquisition of cultural and social capital necessary for acceptance and inclusion into the White middle-class rhythms of village life. Rather, BrAsians' wealth is a sign of the perceived incompatibility between middle-class Whites' and wealthy BrAsians' cultures.

Like Simon, James attempts to account for and explain what he has observed to be the lack of interaction between middle-class Whites and BrAsian residents. In so doing, and in parallel with Simon, he portrays White and BrAsian cultures as bounded and distinct entities that are incompatible with one another. James was an active member of Greenville's Baptist Church, a retired education adviser in Leicester, and had lived in Greenville for 15 years. He used to live in an affluent road in Greenville Gardens, commonly known as 'Millionaire's Road'. In his retirement he moved with his wife to a smaller but nonetheless impressive bungalow on a new housing estate on the outskirts of Greenville. James commented on the culture and social class of BrAsians who live in Greenville like this:

> Asian people in Greenville do tend to be better off and so on. In business terms, men are equal in Greenville. ... They both have their Mercedes. ... There is a tremendous cultural divide and that shows itself mostly with the women. Because the women are of course the flag bearers of the culture and the men like to keep them so. ... There is not really any family-to-family contact. I haven't heard of any and I wouldn't expect any. ... The Asians have their friends and relations who come at weekends and other times. ... There is not any relationship between ethnic groups and cultural groups. ... Really it is very rare. ... It is a two-way thing. ... It is not the Whites excluding the Asians. ... Unless the Asians [i.e. the women] ... are teachers or something [they] are ill at ease with the indigenous population and this is true however much money they have, of course the more educated they are the less true it is. ... Generally I don't think that there is much mixing. ... They are very nice people, but eyebrows are raised when the hordes of friends and relatives come. ... It isn't done in Greenville.

James thinks that BrAsian and 'White' men are equal in terms of business and economic wealth. In this sense, 'they both have their Mercedes'. Yet, for James, BrAsian men's economic equality to middle-class White villagers does not compensate for their perceived lack of integration into the socially accepted norms and values of White middle-class village culture. In this regard James, like Simon, believes that BrAsians' cultural differences render their acquisition of material capital irrelevant in terms of village notions of respectability.

In parallel with Mike's emphasis upon the BrAsian shopkeepers' attitudes to women and gender equality, James suggests that BrAsian women are the 'real flag bearers' of BrAsian culture. This idea that women symbolise the totality of cultural distinctions that demarcate Western and non-Western cultures has been central to colonial and postcolonial Western conceptions of Others for centuries (Said, 1978). For James, BrAsian women symbolise the essence of BrAsian cultural values associated with female subordination. In this way, Whites' and BrAsians' gendered identities and cultures are abstracted from the active and dynamic place that gender and culture have in society. Thus these fundamental components of identity become portrayed as discrete and bounded entities that form the core of racial identity, and so facilitate an ontological distinction separating the White villagers' culture from that of the culture of BrAsians. The effect of this is that White men are positioned as wise and enlightened on issues of gender and equality, whereas BrAsians are the opposite. Thus White men's cultural superiority to BrAsian men is asserted and reproduced despite their economic equality with them.

James' essentialisation of BrAsian and White gendered culture and norms enables him to side-step any implication that Whites in Greenville are excluding BrAsians. In this regard, James suggests that there exists a tacit 'two way' intercultural agreement that 'cultural' and 'ethnic' groups prefer to live separate lives. In other words, James thinks that BrAsians' and Whites' distinct attitudes towards women ensures the ethnic purity and cultural boundaries of their relationships, traditions and identities. In this sense, ethnic and cultural segregation becomes justified and normalised as a natural and agreeable state of affairs. One consequence of this discourse is for the White village community of Greenville to be depicted as tolerant with regard to matters of gender and racial equality.

Notwithstanding the apparent boundedness of Whites' and BrAsians' culture, values and norms, James does offer possible ways of negotiating the perceived incompatibility between wealthy Whites and BrAsians.

He believes that the 'education' of BrAsian women would make cultural 'mixing' easier. Thus education, and not material wealth, is perceived to be a fundamental cultural and class asset and medium through which other forms of capital could be acquired to bridge the perceived 'ethnic', gender, class and 'cultural' divide. In this way, James advocates different treatment for individuals depending upon their degree of adaption to White middle-class gendered and classed aspirations and cultural norms.

There is an analogy here with Marilyn Strathern's (1982) understanding of the dynamic of mobility and closure that comprises everyday perceptions of the English class system. Strathern (1982, p. 270) comments: 'mobility of people between classes alters their personal status, but has no consequences for relations between classes as such'. Similarly, James' acceptance of particular BrAsian women, and their husbands, who become 'educated' and thus more like 'us' in cultural and classed terms, has no consequences for his belief about the fundamentally discrete, bounded and hierarchical cultural and classed relationship separating wealthy BrAsians and Whites in the village.

My argument is that Simon and James draw on a discourse of social isolation to explain BrAsians' absence from the village community. Underlying each man's explanation of wealthy BrAsians' absence from village life is the belief that the culture of the White self and the BrAsian Other are bounded and discrete entities. Frankenberg (1993a, p. 192) argues that the everyday deployment of this concept of culture as set apart from material life represents one legacy of Western European imperial expansion and domination. The articulation of this discourse in Greenville ensures that the racially unmarked White middle-class English village self becomes defined and constructed in relation to wealthy BrAsian Others. In this regard, BrAsians are portrayed as people who lack the White middle-class norms and values of gender equality, educational achievement, neighbourliness, sociability, community-mindedness and a cultural sensibility about the proper aesthetic constitution of the village environment. Thus BrAsians' economic capital is not legitimated and does not allow them inclusion into the White village community. In contrast to the White middle classes, BrAsians' economic success and wealth is not a sign of their social status, respectability and cultural desirability. Rather, the significance of their wealth is devalued because it is an indication of their immigrant status that derives from their economically impoverished 'origins' in another country. Once again, underpinning this idea that BrAsians' origins renders them outsiders to the village, the nation and the West is

White amnesia of the colonial past that connects BrAsians' histories and contemporary identities to the village, England and the West. In short, this discourse of social isolation provides a further avenue through which to analyse the elements that constitute the intersections between discourses of coloniality, White amnesia, class distinction and respectability, villageness and Whiteness.

Wealthy BrAsians and the discourse of excess

A third discourse central to the construction of the wealthy BrAsians as culturally inferior to the White majority is the idea that BrAsians are excessive in their material and cultural lifestyles. From this point of view, BrAsians are considered to be ostentatiously wealthy, as illustrated by their supposedly over-sized houses, combined with their large extended families and extreme religiosity. In other words, BrAsians' perceived wealth becomes associated with ideas about their perceived excess of culture, an excess that is considered to be disruptive to classed notions of village respectability. This portrayal of BrAsians' supposed material and cultural extravagance resonates with what Frankenberg (1993a, p. 192) identified as a legacy of Empire, namely, the belief that 'some groups of people were considered more "cultural" than others'. To put it straightforwardly, Wealthy BrAsians in Greenville are thought by some of my White co-conversationalists to have more religion, bigger houses, bigger extended families, more children, to be more noisy and so on, than White middle-class villagers. One effect of this racialised and classed discourse of excess is for White middle-class culture and lifestyle to be portrayed as normal, modest and lacking in ostentation. For illustration, consider how Paul and Janet described the wealthy BrAsians' presence in the opulent Greenville Gardens area:

PAUL: There are a lot of Asians in the village. There are some just over the road and there are six big houses, which are occupied by Asians – Blackbird Lodge – now Asians have that. Then that house over the road which Asians own is probably the most expensive in the village ... and then they did about £60,000 worth of improvements on the place.

JANET: Yes over a year they have built a big family room, a prayer room and a little temple. Really, it is gi-enormous.

The BrAsians who live opposite Paul and Janet are considered to occupy the most expensive and largest house in Greenville Gardens.

Continuing this line of thought, Paul comments on how there was a petition signed in the Greenville Gardens area to stop the expansion of the BrAsians' house:

> Yes really that has been the only time of dissent in this area, when they moved in. ... There were these rumours that two to three Asian families were sharing a house. The problem was that it was only a four-bedroom house and now it's got six/seven bedrooms and a prayer room. People were worried what would happen once the place was sold because it is far too big for the area. ... It might become a hospice or a rest home for the elderly or something. In reality there has not been any trouble. They are as good as gold. We never see them. You would not know that they were there. They keep themselves very much to themselves. ... You see that there were fears that there would be a couple of hundred people here every Sunday, but there is nothing. When the planning application came it was for an extension from four to ten bedrooms. Everyone signed a petition except for two people, who live on Longley Lane. Everyone was opposed purely because it was too large and the unfounded problems it was thought this would bring. But there have been no such problems.

Paul thought that other residents in this prosperous area shared his fears about BrAsian residents moving into the area and what he feared might happen when they leave: 'that was the only time of dissent in the area, when they moved in'. The rumours that circulated in Greenville Gardens about wealthy BrAsians coming to the village projected onto them essentialist cultural differences that identified the BrAsian incomers with cultural and material excess. Indeed, BrAsians' supposed cultural differences to the White majority correlate and correspond with the perceived physical expansion of their house. For example, Paul thinks that other White residents shared his view that 'they' live in extended families, which is signified for Janet by a 'large family room'. This image is reinforced by the objection that the size of the BrAsians' house would become 'too big for the area'. BrAsians were also taken to express their religiosity in an ostentatious manner that would be disturbing to locals. This concern is illustrated by Janet's belief that the house was extended to include a 'little temple' and 'a prayer room', as well as her wider fear that there would be a 'couple of hundred people here on Sundays', which echoes James' belief that 'hordes of friends and relatives' would visit the village.

Such signifiers of BrAsianness refer to 'codes of discourse' (Solomos and Back, 1995, p. 97), or an 'economy of stereotype' (Morrison, 1992, p. 62), which 'communicate racialised [and in this case classed] information in brief' (Solomos and Back, 1995, p. 97). These codes of discourse enable the construction of a host of cultural and class differences that are thought to distinguish moderate White middle-class lifestyles from the perceived excessiveness of affluent BrAsians' culture. In this way, middle-class Whites become the possessors not of a visible, showy and flamboyant culture but an invisible, moderate, aesthetically tasteful and racially unmarked culture that represents middle-class normalcy and respectability. That is, by contrast to wealthy BrAsians, White middle-class people live in nuclear families, have only moderate numbers of visiting friends and relatives, and do not express and experience their religion in an ostentatious manner. Moreover, Whites do not possess houses that are thought to be out of proportion and unsuited to the area. Thus, BrAsians are considered to have more 'culture' and to be more 'cultural' in the way that they act and behave compared to the normalcy of the White middle classes.

Interestingly, as time has passed, Paul thinks that BrAsians have proved not to be 'any trouble'. Thus, his original view that BrAsians are disruptive converts into the belief that this particular family are as 'good as gold'. Paul's eventual acceptance of this BrAsian family illustrates how for some White residents specific BrAsians can be tolerated: if they 'keep themselves to themselves'. The latter is a phrase that was also invoked by Simon. While Simon attributed negative connotations to BrAsians' supposed isolation from village life, for Paul, BrAsians' absence from the village community is felt to be 'good' because it means they are not rowdy and disruptive. In other words, BrAsians' perceived lack of participation in the village community renders them no 'trouble' to the extent that they do not interrupt the peace, tranquillity and norms of respectability that constitute the rhythms of village life. However, there is always the fear that other BrAsians might not be so well behaved in the future.

Mike reveals further how it is that wealthy BrAsian residents in Greenville Gardens are thought to be culturally excessive in their lifestyle. In the course of so doing, he evokes images from the colonial period to explain what he considered to be the racist views of a customer who lived in Greenville Gardens. Thus by contrast to the majority of my White co-conversationalists, whose depiction of BrAsians as 'immigrants' is supported by colonial concepts of White Western cultural superiority but whose discourses do not refer to the colonial past, Mike recalls images associated with that past. He said:

> I have got a customer up there and they are very nice houses. ... But he is very racist, very British Raj [the British government in

India during the colonial period] and he is an ex-[Royal] Air Force navigator. ... 'Yes dear boy and old chum', and all this you see. All because he was flying a bloody Halifax [a bomber plane] over Germany or something. He has got Indians living to the back and side of him. ... The house with the mosque thingy. ... So you can understand it from their point of view. They have worked hard all their lives to achieve whatever bracket of wealth or status, to enjoy their retirement ..., and all of a sudden you get three families moving into one house and try and run a business from it. Transporter vans coming and going and they probably have a couple of [sewing] machines running in the garage. Women doing a bit of machining [that is the manufacture of hosiery] and then multiples of kids running around the garden, as he is sitting out on a sunny day and it all drives you mad. It is very difficult for them.

Mike's gossip, unlike Paul's, does not derive from direct observation of BrAsians living in Greenville Gardens. Mike really does not know that the people he is talking about have 'a couple of [sewing] machines running in the garage'; he just assumes that is 'probably' the case. Indeed, the extent to which the stories and purported 'knowledge' about BrAsians in Greenville Gardens are transformed and extended through their travels, through repetition and embellishment in different networks of rumours, makes it impossible to know for sure if Mike is talking about the same BrAsian family as Paul and Janet. For example, Janet's reported 'little temple' becomes in Mike's testimony a 'mosque thingy'. The recurring cultural and classed 'codes of discourse' centred on perceived religious, business, family and gendered differences illustrate the limited knowledge that the White villagers that I spoke to possess about BrAsians in Greenville Gardens. Nonetheless the profound social weight that is attached to such limited knowledge is deeply significant.

Mike's distance from the actual source of gossip about this BrAsian family means that he is not ambivalent, as Paul was, in his description of 'them'. Rather, his ambivalence lies in his stereotype of the White 'Raj type'. Mike distances himself from his customer by describing him as 'very racist'. In this way, he is once more letting me know that he does not hold racist attitudes by turning his attention to a person who he thinks does. Mike also recognises the social class distinctions between himself and his customer by mimicking and mocking his upper-class speech, 'yes dear boy, old chum'. This man lives 'up there' in Greenville Gardens, a class apart from the smaller houses in the centre of Greenville where Mike lives. Thus Mike illustrates the way in which middle-class divisions and distinctions within Greenville are made and reproduced spatially, with the more expensive houses 'up there' representing the wealthy White middle classes' higher socio-economic ranking above the White middle and working classes who live elsewhere in the village. In other words, he points to how it is that the acquisition of wealth can enhance and complement middle-class Whites' status in terms of social class. Importantly, Mike acknowledges that BrAsians live 'up there' too; however, once again, a different cultural and classed value is signified by their presence, which is connected to their supposedly excessive behaviour, which becomes interwoven with their perceived lack of history with regard to Englishness and thus the right to claim belonging to the village and the nation.

The older man's racism is signified by his relationship to the British Raj, but Mike simultaneously erases the racism of the Raj by showing empathy with his client's point of view towards the 'Indian' 'invaders'. Mike thinks that the presence of BrAsians in this man's backyard is unjust and a heavy cross to bear, considering the hard work he and others like him dedicated to achieving their present economic and social status, and given the role that they played in the World Wars in defending their country. Thus, in the same breath as speaking of the racism of the Raj, Mike screens out such inequalities, reflecting the ambiguity inherent within White amnesia of colonialism. His simultaneous remembering and forgetting of the racial domination of the British Empire ensures that the past is invoked to justify the White Raj type's right to peace in their retirement.

Mike does not acknowledge BrAsians' relationship to the British Empire and their role in defending the British nation in the World Wars. He does not think that BrAsians' historical contribution to the British nation justifies 'them' a place in Greenville Gardens and in this English village. Thus Whites have a past, history and tradition that represents dynamism and national belonging; in contrast, BrAsians represent 'the absence' of history and national belonging.

Mike's placing of BrAsians outside of the nation's history enables different symbolic capital to be signified by their houses. For the Raj type, a house in Greenville Gardens is a symbol of middle- or upper middle-class status. However, for Mike, the large house of the BrAsians does not signify the same class status. Rather, BrAsians' exaggerated behaviour makes them appear abnormal in their juxtaposition to the racialised and classed normalcy of Mike's White customer. Mike imagines that BrAsians run disruptive and noisy businesses from their house. Such businesses are thought to be dependent upon the labour of female family members. In addition, BrAsians are believed to have 'multiples of kids', and 'three families' are said to 'share one house'. In contrast, the cultural and classed norms of respectability that constitute White middle- and upper middle-class village identity and traditions are implicitly defined by the absence of such culturally marked and excessive ways of behaving.

Mike's perception of the disruptive presence of BrAsians in Greenville Gardens goes beyond his threshold of tolerance. In other words, Mike thinks that what he believes to be the BrAsians' intrusive, loud and disturbing behaviour makes it impossible for him, a non-racist and outsider to Greenville Gardens, and for those White people who live there, to exercise openness and acceptance towards BrAsians. In short, the supposedly excessive, noisy and disruptive culture of the Other is thought to encroach upon White residents' ways. Clearly, for Mike any resignation, indifference, permissiveness or toleration of BrAsians' supposed excesses would lead to a denial of one's own history and traditions, which are the very medium of one's national and racial identity.

It is clear that Mike's initial stereotype of the 'Raj type', like his stereotype of White working-class people who go to Skegness, represents an extension of White classed cultural norms and English tradition to the point of self-mockery, and not an inversion of such norms. Herzfeld (1993, p. 84) comments that 'Self-mockery and humorous understatement are the characteristic forms of British self-stereotyping'. Such self-stereotyping allows Mike to show playfully affected humorous disrespect for the class distinctions between himself and his White customer in Greenville Gardens. However, Mike's and his White customer's class distinctions are overshadowed by the racialised disruptions supposedly caused by BrAsian residents that his narrative inscribes and reproduces.

Before progressing to the final section of this chapter, it is worth taking a moment to summarise the main themes and arguments thus far. From the standpoint of White middle-class villagers of Greenville the following picture of BrAsian residents is seen: they are considered polite, friendly and hard-working but dishonest in business; from a radically different country; compulsive workers who run businesses from their homes that are dependent on female labour; 'poorish' in terms of background; non-Western; their women are subordinated to men but are also the 'flag bearers' of their 'culture'; they have 'multiples of kids', enormous houses that include 'prayer rooms' and mosques, extended families; they keep themselves apart from village life, have vans coming and going from their homes, and so on. My argument is that central to these racialised, classed and gendered representations of BrAsians are discourses of 'service', 'social isolation' and 'cultural excess'. Read collectively, my supposition is that these discourses facilitate the reproduction of the colonial ethos and worldview of White Western cultural superiority in the present. In this sense, my White co-conversationalists draw upon a host of racialised and classed stereotypes to maintain and control fundamental distinctions between the culture of 'our' racially unmarked White, Western, English middle-class village ways of life and non-Western, non-English, non-middle class, BrAsian racially marked Other ways of life. A consequence of this is that those classed attributes that middle-class people value and perceive to be respectable, such as economic wealth, business success, working hard and having a nice house in a decent area, are devalued when acquired by BrAsians. In this sense, the BrAsian shopkeepers and wealthy BrAsian residents' business success and material wealth become a sign not of their classed respectability and equality to the White middle classes but their cultural difference from and racial inferiority to the White majority.

Sharing parallels to colonial discourses, the White middle-class village self is 'produced as an effect of the Western discursive production of Others' (Frankenberg, 1993a, p. 17). My contention is that this racialised and classed discourse springs from the idea that BrAsians are 'immigrants', that is, people whose origins are thought to be outside of the village, the nation and ultimately the West. Thus it is that BrAsians' historical relationships to Englishness and Britishness formed through histories of Empire and centuries of migration to the metropole are displaced and forgotten. In this sense, colonialism is something that 'we' contemporary White English people did to those Others 'over there', 'back then', rather than a historical process that is integral to affordance of the power, privilege, cultural and political standing that constitutes who 'we' White English people are now.

White spaces: The performance of coloniality

To conclude this chapter I shall explore the reproduction and maintenance of White cultural normality in Greenville through people's participation in local social activities. To do this, I turn to a less discursive and more descriptive mode of analysis to present two evenings of entertainment organised by the Women's Institute. By exploring these events in some detail, I shall illustrate how it is not only what people say and think but also what they do that contributes to the reproduction of Greenville as a White middle-class English place. Moreover, these events illustrate further the ways in which discourses of coloniality and White amnesia shape the everyday lives of White middle-class English village people in taken-for-granted and often unconscious ways.

An evening of exotica at the women's institute

The Greenville branch of the Women's Institute consisted of approximately one hundred White female members, the majority of whom were over 50 years old. The members represented a cross-section of White middle-class middle-aged and elderly women from Greenville, which included the wives of wealthy businessmen and retired single women who lived more modestly on their pensions.

What generally happens: The women meet each month. The meetings follow a basic format, with some variation. For example, meetings begin with the women singing in unison the anthem of the Women's Institute, which is the first few verses of Blake's poem 'Jerusalem':

And did those feet in ancient time walk upon England's mountains green?
And was the holy Lamb of God on England's pleasant pastures seen?[8]

The meeting continues with the President welcoming the women, after which the Secretary explains the recent activities of the Greenville branch. Then the main event of the meeting takes place, with a guest speaker or performance by an entertainer.

On this particular evening, the middle-aged White members of the Women's Institute were entertained by a retired White English woman who creatively transformed herself into a Middle Eastern belly dancer, spun from a pastiche of 'Orientalist' (Said, 1978) representations of Otherness. The performance was entitled by the performer 'Not Quite Belly Dancing'. The Secretary called this 'an unusual event' – an exotic Middle Eastern dancer was to perform. Sylvie – the performer's stage name – clapped her way onto the dance floor of the village hall. Sylvie appeared to be a rather large, short woman, but as the audience commented at the end of the event, she was actually quite slim. The trick was that Sylvie unravelled and removed layers of sequinned clothes to reveal shinning leotards, as she wiggled and rotated her hips and belly through one not-quite belly dance after another. Sylvie told the audience that these clothes were her own creation made from shining silk fabrics, bought at the Leicester market and local charity shops. Sylvie removed a layer of shining fabric before commencing a new dance. She used the time between dances to explain the history of each dance.

Sylvie was about 65 years old and was accompanied by a younger helper. Her helper supplied her with cups of water and worked the tape-recorder playing Eastern tunes. At the end of the performance the audience was invited to dance with Sylvie, although everyone declined, including myself. The Women's Institute members were amused by Sylvie's dances; they smiled throughout with surprise and enjoyment at the spectacle.

Sylvie's performance was a unique bricolage of hegemonic representations of the East, which included romantic Hollywood renditions of Middle Eastern dancers and the exotic moves she had learnt at a belly dancing evening class in a Leicester community college, bound together with shining fabrics. Sylvie's spectacle thus made both performer and audience participants in a 'highly artificial enactment of what a non-Oriental has made into a symbol for the whole Orient' (Said, 1978, p. 21). In other words, Sylvie's performance and the audience's gaze upon her unusual display drew upon centuries of Western imperialism reproduced in this contemporary context. Both the audience and Sylvie, however, seemed unaware of the colonial histories implicit within such objectifying and essentialising representations of gendered difference. Rather, the White women were simply 'having fun' in their shared performative moment of exotica. Nonetheless, Sylvie's performance is a reminder to her White audience that cultural differences remain incompatible: one cannot become the Other. Sylvie's attempted appropriation of difference, no matter how imaginary, makes her a problematically amusing spectacle in Greenville's village hall.

An evening of poetry and prose

The second event that I shall explore also took place with the White women of the Women's Institute. This was an annual event at which some of the members put on a show for the entertainment of the villagers. On this particular evening, some of the members were to read and recite poetry and prose for the entertainment of villagers. This event took place in the same village hall as Sylvie's performance. However, on this evening the room was dimly lit and the audience were seated around dining tables. The walls of the hall were decorated with artistic cards that signalled the themes of the poetry and prose that were to be performed. The cards read as follows: 'Landscape'; 'Portraits'; 'Artifacts'; 'Interiors';

'Abstract' and 'Nature'. In what follows I shall describe and analyse the ways in which some of the poetry and prose chosen juxtaposed traditional images of a racially unmarked White English village and rural ways of life with representations of non-English and non-Western Others.

One of the opening poems was entitled 'Dairy of a Church Mouse' by John Betjeman, the British poet Laureate in 1972. It is significant that Betjeman is a national figure and icon of Englishness known for his poetry and campaigns to save historic buildings from demolition, including the façade of St Pancras station in central London. His poem was recited in full, but I cannot reproduce it here for reasons concerning copyright permission. Suffice to say, Betjeman's poem tells the story of a church mouse that lives in an Anglican church and survives by eating the food that parishioners use to decorate the church, especially at the time of religious festivals. Betjeman's poem conjures up images of Englishness associated with its moderate and modest religious traditions and pastoral ways of life. This poem evokes an image of Englishness associated with specific foods, including 'ears of corn', 'a loaf of bread' and 'marrows', that are traditional produce of the English countryside.

This very English reading was read alongside a poem about India that was introduced by Indian-style sitar music. This poem was simply entitled 'India'. By contrast to work by John Betjeman that I knew from my school days in Leicester, I did not know the poem 'India' and have been unable to trace it. It told the story of a busy Indian city filled with the noise and dirt of traffic and the dust from makeshift roads. In this landscape Indian women try to cross busy roads while carrying bricks on their heads that are to be delivered to building sites. Clearly, this urban Indian landscape forms a stark contrast to Betjeman's description of the life of an English country church mouse. But yet within this otherwise chaotic and unfamiliar Indian landscape appear school children wearing traditional English school uniforms that are described as 'neat and tidy'. It seemed to me that the children's uniforms served as symbols of the legacy of British colonialism that were portrayed as bringing some order to this otherwise disordered scene.

A further poem recited begun with the words 'Oh, to be in England', which are the opening lines of Robert Browning's work entitled 'Home Thoughts from Abroad'. This poem suggests that life in England is more civilised, fulfilling and capable of bringing contentment than life abroad in foreign places. Moreover, echoing aspects of Betjeman's poem, Browning's poem conveys this message by drawing on images of the English countryside, in this case, its flora, wildlife, birds, gentle noises and seasons. The poem continues as follows:

> Oh, to be in England
> Now that April's there,
> And whoever wakes in England
> Sees, some morning, unaware,
> That the lowest boughs and the brushwood sheaf
> Round the elm-tree bole are in tiny leaf,
> While the chaffinch sings on the orchard bough
> In England – now!...
>
> That's the wise thrush; he sings each song twice over, ...
> The buttercups, the little children's dower
> – Far brighter than this gaudy melon-flower!

The Indian sitar music was played again to signal to the audience that the next extract is about Others. We were read an extract about the life of a rural poor Indian woman who was described as working very hard in her kitchen. She is making rotis [flat bread] on a hot stove, which the writer notes is a very basic stove, compared to the author's own oven at home in England. This Indian woman is overworked and tired, which is evidenced by her thin frame and scrawny appearance.

Before ending this chapter I want to reflect on the racially unmarked Whitened images of postcolonial Englishness summoned up in these events. What has struck me about both these events is the prominence of the Middle East, in the belly dancing, and India in the evening of poetry and prose. They brought to the fore the significance of the East, particularly India, and a romantic and gendered rendition of the Middle East, within White, Western and English postcolonial constructions of the self and racialised Others. In contrast to Sylvie's evening of exotica, a romantic and nostalgic image of pastoral England was performed in the poetry and prose conveyed through the naturalistic images of flora and wildlife, including the song of delicate tuneful birds and the wit of a clever church mouse, as well as the pleasant and rhythmic passing of the seasons in England. Thus, the countryside, its flora, its wildlife and its natural rhythms become symbols of Englishness illustrating that they are categorically and undeniably racialised as White in and through their juxtaposition to foreign Others and landscapes, including poor Indian women and hot, dirty, 'foreign' and 'gaudy' landscapes.

The latter are positioned as not Western, not English, not White and not home.

My argument is that even within mundane and ordinary evenings of entertainment colonial notions of culture and difference are expressed, articulated and performed, which mark off and distinguish the White, English, Western self from non-English, non-Western, non-White foreign Others. This illustrates how the supposed peacefulness and orderliness of Englishness requires a contrast in order for it to become visible and meaningful. Underlying this series of rigidly binominal oppositions separating 'us' and 'them' is the erasure of the legacies of Empire upon the formation of the present. It is exactly the histories of British colonialism that intimately relate rural Englishness to Indians in Indian, and BrAsian residents in Greenville to village life, its history and traditions. Through these performances of coloniality and White amnesia the idea that the racially unmarked White village of Greenville is home to White middle-class respectable people 'like us' is reaffirmed.

3
The Racialisation of the Country, the City and the Forgetting of Empire

This chapter builds upon and progresses from the last chapter's exploration of the intersection of the discourses of coloniality with the formation of Whiteness, villageness, Englishness and middle-class identities. To do this I focus upon the discourses that support and maintain sharp divisions of race, class and place that mark the White Leicestershire landscape off from the urban BrAsian cityscape in Leicester. In short, I scrutinise the ways in which the tropes of 'the city' and 'the country' provide a route into thinking about the reproduction of discourses of Whiteness, coloniality, Englishness and classed identities.

In the previous chapter, my argument was that central to the routine and mundane beliefs and practices that embed notions of villageness within Whiteness, Englishness and middle classness is the articulation of colonial notions of cultural difference that serve to screen out and displace BrAsian residents' historical colonial and postcolonial relations with Englishness and Britishness. The result of this process is that BrAsians are depicted as immigrants and cultural outsiders to the village, the nation and ultimately the West. The rural thereby becomes associated with seemingly 'timeless and quintessential' national values (see also Chakroborti and Garland, 2004).

In this chapter, I shall develop this aspect of my argument to examine how collective denial of Britain's colonial history not only brings about the Whitening of the village and the countryside but also hardens and fixes negative racialised images of the city (Gilroy, 1987; Hesse, 1993; Keith, 2005). For example, the supposed 'anarchy' caused by BrAsian and Black settlers to British cities was famously dramatised in the 1960s by the nationalist politician Enoch Powell, in his evocation in a speech of 'an old White woman, trapped and alone in the inner city' (Gilroy, 1987, p. 86). Gilroy suggests that the old White woman symbolised the 'bleak inhumanity of urban decay' that Powell and his supporters believed postcolonial settlers to spread. Clearly, this representation of BrAsian and Black settlers to the British city as intruders and cultural outsiders to the nation rested upon the forgetting of the relations of Empire that connected postcolonial settlers to British cities in the first place.

Hesse (1993) maintains that the effect of forgetting BrAsians' and Black Britons' colonial relations to Britain is to denote British inner city neighbourhoods as 'ghettos' in the postcolonial present. The latter are neighbourhoods that are home to BrAsian, Black British and other minorities in the UK; they become depicted as places that represent not only local but also national degeneration and decline. According to Hesse (1993, p. 164), attached to 'the ghetto' are signifiers of racial difference that encapsulate the totality of Black and BrAsian lifestyles, which are juxtaposed to the wholeness of White British identity, history and tradition that lie elsewhere.

In this chapter, I will examine how, on the one hand, the process of White amnesia of the colonial past underpins the idea of the city of Leicester as an exotic place that is the site of BrAsians and their culture, which at times becomes entwined with a working-class aesthetic; and, on the other hand, how the countryside is portrayed as a White middle-class domain that represents the true spirit of Englishness. In making this argument, it is perhaps useful to remind ourselves of some of the history that connects BrAsians and Black Britons to the countryside, the city and the nation. This history is routinely screened out in the racialisation of the country and the city. For example, the building and upkeep of British stately homes was financed and built through the profits of African Caribbean slavery (Agyeman and Spooner, 1997). In addition, whole villages of people from South Asia were brought to Britain to work in the Lancashire and Yorkshire cotton mills (Agyeman and Spooner, 1997). The history of the English nation's stereotypically favourite beverage – tea with sugar – can be traced to colonial histories of slave labour in the African Caribbean and in India, which is also connected to the exploitation of Other people's land (Colls, 2002). Closer to 'home' in Leicestershire, older White people have memories of working for colonial institutions, and relics from Empire remain buried in the landscape. It is precisely the collective amnesia of this history that allows Leicester BrAsians to be depicted as immigrants and cultural outsiders who belong categorically in the city and not the English countryside. One consequence of this discourse is for the countryside to come at times to represent the English nation. In this way, an analysis of the racialised meanings ascribed to the country and the city provides a further window through which to explore the contemporary articulations of a 'rigidly binominal' colonial worldview that puts White English culture in opposition to BrAsian culture (Said, 1978). In other words, the racialisation of the country and the city opens up an avenue through which to examine the articulation of a whole host of cultural stereotypes about the constitution of White English rural culture and identity that is constructed in relation to an idealised, imagined and demonised BrAsian urban culture and identity.

Once more the focus of my account is on White representations of BrAsians. BrAsians constitute the largest minority in the city of Leicester and thus the main focus of White people's attention. However, I shall also consider in this chapter the ways in which Black British minorities are depicted within White representations of the country and the city. To do this, I examine representations of the racialised constitution of the rural and the urban in material published by a marketing firm sponsored by Leicester City Council, and Leicestershire County Council, and in interviews with White middle-class residents of Greenville. The contextualisation of my White co-conversationalists' ideas and reflections in relation to marketing representations of Leicester and Leicestershire highlights how White research participants' thoughts to some extent parallel and resonate with public representations of the racialised constitution of the rural and the urban. In this regard, my supposition is that the full force of my White co-conversationalists' reflections becomes apparent and takes meaning against the background of wider public representations of the city and the countryside.

Promoting Leicestershire: An exotic city and a traditional county

Leicester Promotions' website and brochure provide a window through which to examine the 'official' representation of Leicestershire for consumption by tourists and other outsiders. I have periodically traced Leicester Promotions' marketing of Leicester across a 13-year period from 1997 to 2010. Over the years, these publications have drawn on one-dimensional images of White rural and BrAsian urban cultures. My supposition is that, like my co-conversationalists' depiction of BrAsians in Greenville discussed in the last chapter, these representations of the rural and the urban rest on a worldview of White and BrAsian cultures that is reminiscent of the racialised and rigidly binominal oppositions and generalisations attached to 'ours' and 'theirs' that lie at the heart of the colonial relation (Said, 1978). Sharing some parallels with the colonisers' valorisation of aspects of the cultures of those they colonised, BrAsian identities and culture in the city are at times celebrated as an icon of multicultural Britishness. However, this is achieved in ways that position BrAsians' urban culture as distinct from and Other to rural lifestyles, histories and traditions that are associated with a racially unmarked White Englishness. Portraying BrAsian and White cultures in this way, as bounded and discrete entities, suggests that it is possible for the White middle-class tourist to move between them. However, in moving between White and BrAsian cultures, the culture of the racially unmarked White rural self and BrAsian urban Other remain fundamentally unchanged.

In illustration of the above points, I shall begin by considering the ways in which Leicester Promotions' website in 2006 (entitled 'Explore') constructs a dichotomous relationship between the city and the country. It will become clear that central to Leicester Promotions' depiction of the city is the evocation of an enduring icon of BrAsianness – 'the curry house', that is identified with an area of Leicester known as 'Belgrave'.[1] By contrast, symbols of rurality include fields and villages that are entwined with English history, significance and meaning:

> Leicestershire is a county of enormous diversity. From the buzz of the city to the peaceful English countryside, there is much to see and explore. Leicester itself is vibrant and energetic. ... From award-winning attractions to some of the best curry houses in the UK, discover a dynamic mix of style and culture...
> But just a few minutes away lies a very different world. Beautiful rolling fields, winding waterways, ancient woodland, historic country towns and picturesque villages provide the ultimate rural retreat.
> (http://www.goleicestershire.com/explore/ [accessed January 2006])

The website's section on Belgrave elaborated on Leicester's 'dynamic mix of style and culture' thus:

> Perhaps of all the things that Belgrave is well known for, it is its restaurants that spring to mind. There's no doubt that you can get some of the best curries in the country along Belgrave Road. ... People flock here in their thousands to enjoy the excellent range of spicy, aromatic Asian food. The choice of places to eat includes stylish, contemporary restaurants with light, modern interiors and imaginative

menus, to more traditional curry houses serving authentic Gujarati and Punjabi cuisine.

(http://www.goleicestershire.com/explore/ [accessed January 2006])

From a progressive standpoint, BrAsian restaurants become symbols of the peaceful coexistence of minority BrAsian and White majority cultures in the city. In other words, the restaurants' incorporation of diverse cultural styles and influences points towards the 'glocalisation' of the cityscape – that is, a new localism produced from the fusion of local and global influences (S. Hall, 2000, p. 216). However, another way of reading this image of cultural hybridity is to suggest that it screens out the 'violence of imperialist history that allows for the British love of curry in the first place' (Hutnyk, 1999, p. 101). Furthermore, when juxtaposed to the 'very different world' of the countryside, the curry house is transformed from an icon of contemporary Britishness into a reified and bounded symbol of ethnic and cultural difference. Moreover, the countryside that is racially unmarked becomes implicitly marked as White through its juxtaposition to the 'Asian' city. Thus, unlike the city, which becomes identified with Gujarati and Punjabi traditions, the 'beautiful rolling fields, winding waterways', 'woodland', bricks and mortar of the country towns and villages carry an 'ancient' and 'historic' 'English' past.

Resonating with Wood's *Story of England* (see Chapter 1), this past is associated, in the version of the website published in 2006, with a particular representation of rural English history that emphasises the connections between the local Leicestershire landscape and the Roman Empire, the Norman Conquest of Saxon England and the nation's past monarchs. In spite of the website's multiple references to the nation's histories of being invaded, no mention is made of the violence and atrocities of British colonialism inflicted by the British upon Others and the impact of Empire on the economic and social constitution of the city, the countryside and the nation. The representation of Leicestershire that follows ensures that BrAsians are written out of the countryside's history. In short, BrAsians are depicted as straightforwardly belonging to the city, a place that is contained and set apart from the countryside, which becomes a symbol of Englishness that is racially unmarked as White.

This association of the rural with Englishness and an unmarked White ethnicity is further highlighted by a tourist brochure produced by Leicester Promotions entitled *Dawn to Dusk*. This brochure was first published in 1997 and has since been replaced by the website. Interestingly, the brochure and the differing versions of the websites produced over the years draw on ideas associated with the production and consumption of food to distinguish the rural from the urban. Within the public marketing of Leicester/shire, mundane foods that feature in the websites take on national, racialised and classed significance when put alongside Other foods, most notably 'curry'. Food thus becomes a marker and symbol of the irreducible cultural differences that are thought to separate White and BrAsian, rural and urban, middle-class and working-class landscapes and cultures. While BrAsian food is celebrated, it remains fundamentally different from White English food that is produced in the county. The meanings and significance attached to food illuminate the contemporary reproduction of colonial notions of cultural difference including the valorisation of aspects of the culture of the Other (Frankenberg, 1993a, p. 193), the construction of cultures as 'discrete' and 'bounded spaces', and the binominal opposition of 'ours' from 'theirs' (Said 1978, p. 227, also discussed in detail in Chapters 1 and 2 of this book). The following analysis presents extracts from *Dawn to Dusk* and information that appeared on the websites in 2006 and 2010. I use lengthy quotations in order to reveal the evocation of national, racialised and classed images associated with rural and urban foodscapes across time.

Dawn to Dusk commented on the county's and the city's contrasting cuisines thus:

> Don't forget that Leicester stands in a county famous through the centuries for its great British food. Imagine where we would be without Red Leicester [cheese] or Melton Mowbray pork pies made from some of the finest raw ingredients in the country.[2] That tradition is now echoed in grand style by country house restaurants throughout the county including the magnificent Hambleton Hall ... voted by Lord Lichfield as one of the best hotels in the world...
>
> For anyone foolish enough to still believe that curries consist of tired old tandoori served in a searingly hot sauce of doubtful origins, a trip to Leicester is a must. ... Also in Belgrave Road, another award winning restaurant with surprisingly different décor, Sharmilee serving delicious Gujarati vegetarian food.
>
> Sometimes strangers to Asian food can find the choice a little daunting but please remember, it doesn't cost anything to ask for advice and staff are only too happy to explain the dishes.
>
> (Leicester Promotions, 1997, pp. 66–7)

Echoing similar sentiments, Leicester Promotions' website published in 2006 comments on the county's pork pies as follows:

> Melton itself is famous for its pork pies, which you can find at Ye Olde Pork Pie Shoppe ... you can also sample ... the rich, fruity taste of Melton Hunt Cake [a cake served to fox hunters].
> (http://www.goleicestershire.com/explore/ [accessed January 2006])

Turning to the version of the website 'live' in 2010, the significance of curry in the formation of national identity is emphasised:

> Leicester is known as the Curry Capital of Britain with good reason. Take your taste buds on a journey and visit contemporary restaurants serving a fusion of Indo-Chinese delicacies or head to a more traditional curry house serving the best in Indian cuisine ... it's your choice how hot you dare to go.
> (http://www.goleicestershire.com/food-and-drink/default.aspx/ [accessed December 2010])

And the following is written in 2010 on the county's cheeses:

> **Stilton Cheese**
> The "King of English Cheeses" has been registered as a "Product of Designated Origin" and so is only able to be produced in the counties of Leicestershire, Derbyshire and Nottinghamshire [these are neighbouring counties to Leicestershire].
>
> **Red Leicester**
> This cheese has recently been dubbed the "nation's favourite" – especially on toast.
> (http://www.goleicestershire.com/food-and-drink/ Leicestershire-Produce.aspx/ [accessed December 2010])

And once more in 2010 Melton hunt cake and pork pies are on the menu:

> **Melton Mowbray Pork Pies**
> Recognised internationally as the world's best pork pies ... Leicestershire bakers Dickinson & Morris have been baking pork pies at Ye Olde Pork Pie Shoppe in Melton Mowbray since 1851 ...

Melton Hunt Cake
Dickinson & Morris ... are also the creators of the Melton Hunt Cake. This exclusive fruit cake was originally made in the 1850s for members of the local hunt to eat whilst out fox hunting. The cake is still made using the original recipe combining the finest ingredients: sultanas, currants, muscovado sugar, butter, fresh eggs, cherries and almonds all enhanced with Caribbean Rum. It is available from Ye Olde Pork Pie Shoppe.
(http://www.goleicestershire.com/food-and-drink/ Leicestershire-Produce.aspx/ [accessed December 2010])

Reading across these extended extracts, the British, English, Gujarati, Indian, Indo-Chinese and Caribbean genealogy of rural and urban foods and the aesthetically distinct places in which they are produced and consumed bring together and intersect essentialist ideas of ethnic, class, regional and national difference and belonging. Turning first to the food produced in the county of Leicestershire: Red Leicester and Stilton cheeses as well as Melton Mowbray pork pies are national and international brands sold in supermarkets across the UK and throughout the world. In the above quotations, these commonplace and regionally produced foods are invested with local significance that showcases them as nationally and internationally recognisable symbols of Britishness and Englishness. In this regard, Leicester is situated in 'a county famous through the centuries for its great British food', illustrated by Stilton, which is 'the king of English cheeses' and Red Leicester, which is 'the nation's favourite'. In addition, Melton hunt cake is associated with fox hunting, which has become a controversial symbol of rurality and Englishness. But while fox hunting is unproblematically pictured here as a benign rural pastime, it went on to become bitterly contested in national debate and direct protest, which resulted in a 2004 Act of Parliament to prohibit the practice. The point here is that these foods, including Melton hunt cake, come to represent not only the county of Leicestershire but also Englishness, which at times becomes interchangeable with Britishness.

Furthermore, these locally produced foods are invested with local tradition and history. It is claimed that Melton Mowbray pork pies have been made using the same methods in 'Ye Olde Pork Pie Shoppe' since 1851, and Melton hunt cake is made from the 'original' recipe that was served to members of the local fox hunt in 1850. What is silenced in this celebration of local tradition is that some of the ingredients used to make Melton hunt cake in 1850 would undoubtedly have been produced by slave labour in the British colonies of the African Caribbean. In this vein, 'Caribbean Rum' and 'muscovado sugar', which is also commonly known as 'Barbados sugar', would have been farmed and produced on plantations that were operated by slave labour in the Caribbean. Therefore, the website's emphasis upon the connections between Melton hunt cake and local tradition screens out the historical connections between Leicestershire, the nation and the colonies, 'the power relations between them, and the circuits of production, distribution and consumption in which they lived' (Hall and Rose, 2006, p. 10). One effect of this discourse is for the historical connections between Black people, the English countryside and the nation to be ignored.

Blacks who live in the Leicestershire countryside and the city of Leicester are not mentioned and do not figure in these public representations of the county and the city. Rather, it is 'Asians' who become positive symbols of Leicester's ethnic diversity. BrAsians become associated with the city of Leicester that is 'the curry capital of Britain', and not England. In this sense, BrAsian food is celebrated and an aspect of BrAsian culture is valorised. This slippage in language between 'English' to describe food produced in the countryside, and 'British' mobilised to signify the national appeal of curry, illustrates the racially inclusive constitution of the idea of Britishness within English vernacular – but the racially exclusive, bounded and Whitened constitution of Englishness. In this way, Red Leicester cheese, Melton hunt cake, pork pie and Stilton have appeal to a racially inclusive British public, and yet are produced in a racially exclusive, whitened, purely English setting. This is achieved by invocation of that centuries old, rurally idyllic countryside that stands in stark contrast to the exotica of the city.

While these traditional country foods are depicted as having enduring and constant properties, it would appear that over the course of a decade the visitor to Leicester is thought to have become more cosmopolitan in worldview and tastes. As time passes, the tourist is portrayed as having acquired more expertise and knowledge of BrAsian food. The visitor to Leicester in 1997 is assumed to need help to translate and understand BrAsian menus. But in 2010 BrAsian curries have become 'traditional' 'Indian' food juxtaposed to 'Indo-Chinese delicacies'. Moreover, in 2010 it is assumed that the customer will want to choose 'how hot' they 'dare to go', whereas in 1997 the customer might be 'foolish enough to still believe that curries consist of tired old tandoori served in a searingly hot sauce of doubtful origins'. In 2010, the tourist is expected to be well informed and able to cope with choice and to make choices. Notwithstanding this increasingly cosmopolitan customer, BrAsian food remains 'hot', 'Indian' and its consumption requires 'taking our taste buds on a journey'. Through this narrative BrAsians are depicted as cultural outsiders and are assumed to be immigrants to Leicester, regardless of their colonial relations to Britain, and how many decades of settlement in Leicester have passed. Moreover, the portrayal of BrAsian cuisine as 'hot' and foreign positions the tourist and reader of this literature as unequivocally White. I would go further and suggest that the reader of *Dawn to Dust* is also assumed to be middle class.

The décor and ambiance of the 'magnificent' country house hotel and the traditional 'Ye Olde Pork Pie Shoppe' evoke a contemporary middle-class ideal of the rural that draws on romantic images of 'Ye Olde England'. Hambleton Hall is a prestigious country house hotel where the cost of a double room in 2010 was on average £300 per night. Moreover, the representation of 'ye olde pork pie shoppe' evokes a rustic and nostalgic image of rural England that some White middle-class residents, incomers and the English heritage industry have sought for generations to reproduce, preserve and maintain. In stark contrast, the 'surprisingly different décor' of the Gujarati vegetarian curry house, with its 'daunting menu', draws on orientalist and colonial constructions of BrAsian culture that contribute to the objectification of the stranger and the spectacular consumption of exotica.

It is assumed that the White middle-class tourist has the financial wherewithal to move with ease across rural and urban ethnoscapes, staying in grand hotels, consuming BrAsian food, Melton Mowbray pork pies, Melton hunt cake and English cheeses. In contrast, the BrAsian restaurants' staff are represented as rooted, fixed and tied to the cityscape. In this sense, the White middle-class tourist's movement between these racialised landscapes leaves the culture of the White middle-class self and that of BrAsians who live in the city fundamentally distinct, bounded and discrete entities that are unchanged by social interaction. Significantly, BrAsian Leicester is associated with White working-class culture and tradition rather than that of the White middle and upper classes, which serves to create a further distinction between the decorum of the countryside and the lack of respectability of the city. This is exemplified by Leicester Promotions' marketing of Belgrave's high street as 'The Golden Mile', which refers not to curry but to 'Asian gold'.

The term 'Golden Mile' is a metaphor for cheap hedonism associated with stereotypical representations of contemporary White working-class culture. In English vernacular the term 'Golden Mile' refers to a commercial stretch of road in Blackpool, a seaside town in the north west of England that used to be a popular holiday destination with the White working classes in Britain. The 'Golden Mile' gained its name because of the number of amusement arcades with slot machines located along the stretch of road. But historically, Blackpool evokes a faded grandeur associated with a lost England of the 1940s and 1950s when whole families, including parents, grandparents, aunties, uncles and so on, would visit Blackpool for their summer holidays.[3] However, the association of Blackpool's 'Golden Mile' with Belgrave connects this area of Leicester not to an elegant image of Blackpool associated with an industrial past, but to a one-dimensional image of contemporary post-industrial White working-class culture identified with the flashing bright lights and noise of slot machines and pleasure-seeking consumerism. Now let us consider Leicester Promotions' marketing of Belgrave's 'Golden Mile':

> Blackpool isn't the only place with a Golden Mile. Leicester's Golden Mile may not have the fast food outlets and amusement arcades [which line Blackpool's Golden Mile], but it does have gold, and lots of it. It is said that there is more gold sold across the counters of shops in Belgrave Road ... than anywhere else in Europe.
> (Leicester Promotions, 1997, p. 51)

> Belgrave Road and Melton Road are sometimes collectively referred to as 'The Golden Mile' due to the number of jewellery shops that exist there. Asian gold is usually 22 or 24 carat gold, and very expensive. ... Indian custom demands that gold is bought for special occasions such as birthdays, weddings or to celebrate various festivals. It is usually around Diwali (October/November) that gold is purchased by Hindus and Sikhs, whilst Muslims tend to buy around the festival of Eid.
> (http://www.goleicestershire.com/explore/
> [accessed January 2006])

The juxtaposition of Belgrave to Blackpool's 'Golden Mile' attaches an ostentatious, consumer-orientated and gaudy structure of feeling to the district. Furthermore, the addition of the prefix 'Asian' to the term 'gold' and the attachment of ritual and religious significance to 'Asian gold' supports the idea that this location and its inhabitants are ethnically and culturally Other to the White majority. The implication is that while the BrAsian shopkeepers in Belgrave have achieved a high degree of business success and prosperity, they have failed to cultivate taste, respectability and decorum intrinsic to the county shops, restaurants and hotels. This racialised and classed discourse resonates with some of the ways in which my White co-conversationalists from Greenville portrayed the Wealthy BrAsians who live in the village as possessing material wealth but not the cultural know-how and respectability necessary to fit in with the village and its ways, explored in Chapter 2. In this sense, BrAsians' acquisition of economic capital is not legitimated and thus not converted into cultural and symbolic capital. It seems to me that Leicester Promotions' presentation of the 'Golden Mile' represents a place not where the tourist would want to go to buy gold, but to marvel at the spectacle of the gaudy tastelessness of BrAsian consumers.

It is noteworthy that Streetville, the ethnically diverse area of Leicester that features in Chapters 5 and 6 of this book, is totally ignored in the City Council's marketing of Leicester's attractions to visitors. The landmarks of Streetville, which include the Leicester Mosque and African Caribbean centre, are excluded from official images of Leicester's ethnic diversity. In this way, BrAsians who live in Belgrave represent and symbolise the totality of Leicester's non-White communities, to the exclusion of other racialised minorities who live in the city, including BrAsian Muslims and Black Britons who live in Streetville. In this sense, BrAsians in Belgrave are depicted as respectable migrants and thus the acceptable racialised Other who bring wealth, gold, curry and vibrancy to the city. In short, BrAsian culture is celebrated and valorised but also rendered strange, exotic, culturally Other and exploited when juxtaposed to the histories and traditions of the racially unmarked White rural English culture.

Thus far I have examined the Council-sponsored representation of Leicester/shire periodically over a 13-year period from 1997 to 2010. The juxtaposition of Leicestershire's rural foodscape to the ethnically marked food, religious and vibrant cultural activities in the city provides a glimpse of the racially unmarked White constitution of the traditions of the countryside associated with grand hotels, ancient cheeses and traditional ways of making pork pie and hunt cake. Thus it is that the racialised and classed distinctions between the country and the city are supported by a colonial worldview of White cultural superiority that mediates a whole host of images deployed to convey 'knowledge' about the BrAsian city. Ironically, under critical analysis this actually reveals more about the identity, norms and values of the racially unmarked White middle-class English rural culture.

Sharing resonances with the way that colonial discourses produced knowledge by crude generalisations, the urban culture of the BrAsian Other is valorised but yet depicted as discrete, bounded and fundamentally Other to that of the White middle-class rural self. Thus as in the colonial past, the White Western self is produced as an effect of the Western discursive construction of its Others (Frankenberg, 1993a,

p. 17). Underlying these representations of the White countryside and the BrAsian city is White amnesia of the colonial past that connects and relates these landscapes and its people to each other and to the nation through histories of Empire. I shall now develop this argument further through drawing on my ethnographic study of Greenville.

I will switch to ethnographic mode to analyse the conversations that I shared with White middle-class residents from Greenville. In what follows, I will focus specifically on my White co-conversationalists' thoughts and reflections on the racialised constitution of the village of Greenville and the city of Leicester. I will argue that central to the maintenance and control of Greenville's racially unmarked White village identity is the residents' discursive Othering of the seemingly encroaching ethnically diverse cityscape. In this sense, the tropes of the country and the city, once more, provide a lens through which to view the reproduction of a colonial worldview of White cultural superiority in the present that is rooted within the 'culturally sanctioned habit of deploying large generalizations' by which 'reality is divided into various collectivities' associated with 'us' and 'them' (Said, 1978, p. 227). Where appropriate, I will make parallels between the White villagers' discourses on race, class and place and those portrayed by Leicester Promotions. I will also examine the ways in which my White co-conversationalists' cultural narratives are interwoven with their individual biographies, experiences and worldviews. In this respect, their narratives exemplify how 'people can use the production of places for social identity formation' (Blokland, 2001, p. 269).

The view from Greenville: The BrAsian city and the White country(side)

To trace my co-conversationalists' views and opinions I will identify and scrutinise three interlaced discourses that contribute to the construction of BrAsians as immigrants, an image that is fuelled by amnesia of the colonial past and a worldview of White Western cultural superiority that is a legacy of Empire. The discourses are formed by: (a) the idea that racial segregation between the country and the city is a reasonable and logical outcome of a natural desire and choice to live with people 'just like us'; (b) the belief that the concentration of BrAsians in the city reflects the authorities' failure to manage the flow and numbers of people that migrate to Leicester and the nation; (c) the perception that BrAsian and Black neighbourhoods are 'ghettos' and places beset by urban degeneration.

Choosing to live racially segregated lives

Some of my White middle-class co-conversationalists emphasised that they prefer to live culturally and ethnically homogeneous lives with people like themselves. Racial segregation is then interpreted and understood as a natural state of affairs (see James' account in Chapter 2). In other words, racial segregation is thought to be the outcome of reasonable and personal choice. Following my analysis of wealthy BrAsians' perceived social isolation from the village community in Greenville discussed in Chapter 2, my contention is that this worldview resonates with Frankenberg's (1993a) argument the legacy of colonial concepts of culture is that cultures of the self and Other are conceived as discrete, bounded and incompatible. To exemplify some of the discursive twists and turns that constitute this perspective, I turn to Shelia's views on the country and the city. We met Shelia briefly in Chapter 2. She was a single woman in her sixties who had lived in the centre of Greenville for nearly 40 years. Born in a rural village to the south of Leicestershire, her father was a farmer and she spent much of her youth working on his farm. In her early twenties she moved to Greenville to manage a local farm, but when we met, Shelia had retired, although as a lay preacher she was a respected figure in the community. Sheila draws upon her identity as a farmer to argue that BrAsians belong in the city and not in the village of Greenville. In so doing, she constructs an opposition between 'our' village ways and 'their urban' lifestyles, which resonates with a colonial worldview that defines the Other as different from the racially unmarked and 'apparently autonomous White/Western self' (Frankenberg, 1993a, p. 17)

SHEILA: In Leicester I suppose the odd times I go in can be a bit overpowering with them all. But you know their way of life is different from ours. ... If we were to live in their country, we would have to conform to their way of life, but they don't do that with us. The culture, some of the things, I suppose, I would find hard to accept if I lived in it. ... But I don't live in it. One thing I would find hard to accept is the smell of all the foods that they cook because I am such a traditional eater being a farmer. ... But I guess that if we had a lot in this village, I think that the one thing that would get up my nose literally would be the smell of all their cooking [*she laughs*]. ... I think, I am sure, we in the villages, if we are honest, we don't want them. ... We don't want them encroaching on our nice little village life that we have always been used to, because they are so different. ... Whereas within a city you are not so close to

	your neighbour, are you? You don't know your neighbour so well. Um, I think, I really do think, that we don't particularly want them within the villages. Because there won't be any in Saddington? [the village where I grew up].
KATHARINE:	A few people come and go. ...
SHEILA:	Come and go, yeah. I think that really is okay, while they are in the city, then that is all right. But leave them, down there, down Belgrave way and down that way.
KATHARINE:	So what do you think it is that Asians won't fit into in the village? ...
SHEILA:	I suppose really it is their different way of life. That um, it is difficult to say without really having known much about coloured people. ... As I say, the smell of the food would jigger me – just the smell of the food would be enough for me. And if you got that right through the village I would find that hard.

Sheila associates the city, and Belgrave in particular, with an 'overpowering' presence of BrAsian inhabitants. In striking parallel to Leicester Promotions, she identifies food as a central marker of cultural difference that distinguishes the countryside from the city. Thus Sheila utilises food as a boundary marker of absolute racialised distinction separating 'us' from 'them'. However, by contrast to Leicester Promotions who want to make money from exploiting a particular image of BrAsianness, Shelia emphasises that she does not want to live with 'them'. Moreover, unlike the website, Sheila does not perceive BrAsian food as something to be celebrated, valorised and advertised as tempting to attract tourists. That is to say, Sheila does not entertain the possibility of eating BrAsian food. In fact, she thinks just the smell of it cooking poses a threat not only to the integrity of her identity as a farmer but also to the rhythms and patterns of village life. This motivates Sheila to produce a racialised 'fortress mentality' and 'aesthetic' that represents urban life and BrAsian culture as irreducibly Other to the village, the nation and 'our' ways (Kennedy, 2000, p. 6).

Sheila's lack of familiarity with the city and the people who live there plays a part in the formation of her thoughts and reflections. In this regard, she can only imagine urban life to be the exact opposite to village life. She thus concludes that BrAsians belong in the un-neighbourly cityscape where their culture will not encroach upon others, and definitely not impinge upon 'our' village ways. The village life that Sheila describes is racially unmarked as White and is an 'existence that we have always been used to'. The effect of this discourse is to position and constrain BrAsians to cities that are set apart from the village and its traditions.

In short, BrAsians are thought to be fundamentally Other to the White village self. They are seen as people who do not have any historical claim to the village, the nation and its ways of life.

Like Sheila, June's and Simon's solution to the supposed incompatibility of village and urban ways of life is to perceive social harmony and stability to lie in the creation of racially homogeneous spaces in the country and the city. Once again, underlying this discourse is the idea that BrAsian culture in the city is irreducibly Other to village life and its ways. I introduced Simon previously in Chapter 2. In the following extract from our conversation, Simon's wife participated in the discussion. June and Simon were a middle-aged married couple who had lived in the village for some twenty years. Thinking about the racial division between the village and the city, they are reminded of their daughter's experience of multicultural Leicester:

JUNE: You see, I think that they discriminate more than we do in actual fact ... They discriminate against us. My younger daughter went to St Luke's College [a pseudonym for a Further Education community college in Leicester]. They had someone come to talk to them about ethnic minorities, but she was one of three people who wasn't Asian.
SIMON: Tell her what they said to her ...
JUNE: What about the Melton Road [the central road in Belgrave]?[4]
SIMON: When he [the visitor at the college] said that the Asian population must stick together and work within the group and their businesses must keep themselves to themselves. Well, they were doing what we were told not to do ... and poor old Josie [their daughter] had to listen to that. ...
JUNE: They don't bother me. They might if they live near to me, but it doesn't bother me where it is [in Belgrave] ... I know that is short sighted and selfish ... I mean they probably want to live all together as well. ...
SIMON: If they came as a single person, say, putting them in our street, they must feel slightly threatened being on their own in a community that has been there for many years. ... But their cultural way of life is different from ours. They must find it as difficult to accept our way of life as we find it to accept theirs.

June and Simon reach for a contradictory set of explanations to manage the incongruity between the idea that they are racially tolerant with their belief that racialised groups are happier to live apart. They say that BrAsians at their daughter's college were actively encouraged by a guest speaker to live culturally and racially segregated lives. In this regard, June and Simon conclude that White people are placed at a disadvantage to BrAsians and are discriminated against.

Moreover, June's and Simon's assertion that it is individuals' choice to live segregated lives echoes neo-conservative and colonial ideas that propose that it is 'natural' for 'different kinds of people to live distinct and separate lifestyles' (Smith, 1993, p. 138). Smith (1993, p. 138) eloquently argues that in the postcolonial era this belief rests on the assumption that residential segregation is a 'morally neutral expression of cultural diversity' and so not the outcome of racism. Clearly, a consequence of this logic is White people are tactically conceived as 'the natural occupants' of the countryside, and so conversely BrAsians who live in Greenville and other (suburban) village places are seen as 'space invaders' (Puwar, 2004, p. 8).

Reflecting on matters closer to home, Simon, like Sheila, invokes the past to explain BrAsians' relative absence in Greenville. But he draws on an imagined and purified past that has been stripped of any outsider. For Simon, BrAsians 'must feel slightly threatened being on their own in a community that has been there for many years'. It is helpful here to bring in Christopher Lasch's insight that 'anyone who cannot participate in the collective enterprise of remembering is an outsider' (1991, p. 194). It is collective White amnesia of BrAsians' colonial relationships with the countryside and the nation that enables Simon, and indeed Shelia, to construct this idea of a wholly White and culturally homogeneous village past.

In each of Simon's, June's and Sheila's accounts the village and the city appear as spatial symbols that are inscribed with essential cultural differences that separate the racially unmarked White village self from the BrAsian urban Other. My argument is that this sense of cultural difference is a continuation of colonial discourses of cultural differentiation that positioned colonised subjects as fundamentally Other to the White self. In the present, the White village self is produced as an effect of the discursive constructions of racialised urban Others.

Immigration out of control

In order to account for, and explain further, the racialised division between the country and the city, some of my White co-conversationalists suggested that BrAsians had failed to integrate into the White majority culture. Once more the effect of this discourse is to construct a racially dichotomous worldview separating 'ours' from 'theirs' that is reminiscent of colonial constructions of difference. BrAsians' supposed failure to integrate was felt to be in part dependent upon the inability of authorities to manage and control immigration flows to the UK. In this way, BrAsians become assumed to be and depicted as 'immigrants' to Leicester/shire whose origins lie outside the UK, and their colonial relationships with Englishness are erased. William's thoughts and reflections, which follow below, illustrate some of the elements that constitute this perspective.

When I met William, he was a retired Parish Council Chairman and was a retired businessman. He had lived with his wife in Greenville for over twenty-five years. When thinking about the ethnically diverse cityscape of nearby Leicester, William referred to both the inner city neighbourhoods of Streetville and Belgrave. This reference to both urban neighbourhoods highlights the association of both Streetville and Belgrave with ethnic minorities, and the ways in which these neighbourhoods are thought to possess the same characteristics and thus become conflated and interchangeable with one another in the White imagination. William said the following in response to my question that asked about his thoughts on Belgrave:

> Well, there is a tendency for Asians to live in groups. The basic problem is that we have got too many of them. If we had less they would integrate more. They live in big blocks in Belgrave and Streetville and then the Asian community does not integrate into the wider society in any way. The community [that is, the White community that remains racially unmarked] could accept outsiders if they came in reasonable numbers and integrated into the community. But now they come in large numbers and do not integrate. I've many Asian friends and I was born in India but I have always felt the same way about it. I find that some of them do not want to integrate. They live like they did in India or Pakistan and are not part of the United Kingdom community. And so they do not accept the attitudes of the ways in which we live here. ... They have got to give something back and join in, whereas they don't.

William's explanation for the racialised division separating the countryside from the city rests upon his belief that 'they' have failed to 'integrate' into local society and the UK. Moreover, he implies that the authorities are also at fault for having allowed too many immigrants into the UK and thus Leicester. For William, BrAsians are immigrants whose origins belong in India or Pakistan regardless of their colonial relations to the UK and generations of settlement in Britain. In this sense, William's account highlights the paradox that lies at the heart of the immigrant imaginary and discourse, examined in detail in Chapter 2.

On the one hand, William thinks that BrAsians should 'integrate' into the White majority culture. Nevertheless, on the other hand, his emphasis upon BrAsians' moment of immigration to the UK means that the process of integration is continually deferred (Sayyid, 2004). This is because BrAsians are repeatedly defined by their immigrant status, and so there never will be a time at which they actually are thought to have integrated into national British culture. It is noteworthy that by contrast to Shelia, who explains that she does not know much about BrAsian culture, William mentions that he has 'many Asian friends'. However, these inter-ethnic friendships have not seemingly undermined his belief that BrAsians have failed to integrate into the majority society in the UK. As I argued in Chapter 2, crucial to this depiction of BrAsians as immigrants is the forgetting of BrAsians' colonial relationships to Englishness and Britishness, which in William's case becomes manifest in a very personal way.

During our conversation, William explained to me that his father went to Calcutta in the 1930s to make investments in Calcutta's jute industry. William was born in Calcutta and came to England when he was five years old. His biography is thus intimately interwoven with the histories of British colonialism. However, William does not connect how his family's colonial relationship with India, and his early childhood journey from India to Leicester mirrors BrAsians' varied colonial and postcolonial trajectories of settlement to Leicester and the UK. In this way, William's side-stepping of the consequences of the colonial past for the present blinds him to the significance of the colonial for understanding his own biography, BrAsian presence in Leicester, the governance of immigration and the meaning of contemporary multicultural Englishness and Britishness in the postcolonial present. One effect of this White amnesia is for William to construct the culture of BrAsians who live in the city as immigrants who are thought to be fundamentally distinct not only from village culture but also from White society more generally.

Like William, Flo perceives BrAsians to be immigrants and outsiders to Leicester. At the time of my fieldwork, Flo was in her sixties and had moved with her husband to Greenville from a suburb of Leicester to a bungalow on the outskirts of Greenville seven years before I met her. I came to know Flo through her participation in the local flower guild, a social club that specialised in flower arranging. I asked Flo about the changes she had experienced living in Leicester:

KATHARINE: Can you tell me a bit about the changes you have seen in Leicester?

FLO: Oh I think that is horrible.
KATHARINE: Do you, why is that?
FLO: Well, you see my age group, you see such a different change. I mean there are so many nationalities, aren't there? But it is not so much that, but I don't really know. ... It has all been, well, it is the vandalism and everything. No one seems to have any consideration for anyone nowadays and it has not always been like that in Leicester. ... I do think there ought to be restrictions on them coming into the country, I mean I have nothing against them at all. Some of them are lovely people but, umm, in fact I used to teach ... I used to go to some of the houses and teach English to some of the Asian ladies. And they were lovely and so appreciative, you know. It is not always their fault. I think that so many came in [to the country] and they did just have to make the best of things.

Flo is hesitant to associate the BrAsian presence in Leicester with what she perceives to be negative changes over her lifetime. In this regard, like William, she is keen to emphasise to me that she does not resent individual BrAsians with whom she has met and interacted. Nonetheless, Flo dislikes what she perceives to be the lack of community and hospitality in the city nowadays. In spite of her attempts to do otherwise, Flo cannot but help associate her perception of this social breakdown with immigration to the city. It is from this point of view that Flo renders explicit that which is implied in William's account, that immigration control should be more rigorous and restrictive. Moreover, Flo's reference to 'the vandalism and everything' points towards the everyday association of BrAsians with the 'ghetto'. Once again, Flo's straightforward depiction of BrAsians as immigrants screens out their colonial relationships to the city and the nation formed through the histories of Empire.

Living in the ghetto

As I have already mentioned in this chapter's introduction, Hesse (1993, p. 164) contends that White amnesia has the effect of denoting the inner city as a 'ghetto', a place that represents the site of national degeneration and social decline. Attached to 'the ghetto' are signifiers of racial difference that come to represent the totality of BrAsians' and Blacks' lifestyles. I will now further scrutinise the ways in which some of my White co-conversationalists either referred explicitly to Belgrave and Streetville as the 'ghetto', or associated them with socio-economic decline.

Madge was widowed and retired. She spent the majority of her married life in a large family house in Greenville. When her husband died she moved with a friend to live in a house near Greenville's village centre. Madge was an active participant in Greenville's British Legion and bowls club. In thinking about the changing ethnic landscape of Streetville, Madge suggests that the area has become a 'ghetto':

> Somehow the Streetville area has become a ghetto, hasn't it? And I think there is a fair bit of disillusionment there. ... I mean the people [that is, the White people] who have lived there for many years have literally been taken over. I think it is sad when you get ghettos. But unfortunately they do tend to group together, don't they? Like we are grouping here [that is, in Greenville] and they are grouping there [in the city]. And a lot of them are not integrating. Not from our [Whites] fault. ... And I think that there is a little bit of priority treatment in there. They are taking advantage because they [Leicester City Council] daren't say anything to them. So I don't think there has been as much integration as ghettoism.

Madge's description of Streetville as a 'ghetto' locates this inner city place on the margins of White majority culture and society. Like my other co-conversationalists, Madge articulates a 'power evasive' (Frankenberg, 1993a) discourse that supports the idea that BrAsians choose to 'group together' in the city apart from 'us' Whites who live in the village. In addition, BrAsians and Blacks who live in the inner city are thought to benefit unfairly from the local Council and its disbursement of resources to the detriment of the White majority. Through this discourse Whites position *themselves* as victims – their neighbourhoods that they have laid claim to 'for many years have literally been taken over' by BrAsians and Blacks. Echoing June's, Simon's and Shelia's belief that the village is built out of White people's histories, Madge suggests that White city dwellers also have a claim to belonging to the city based on the longevity of their connection to it, while this criterion of membership is denied to BrAsians.

Maria was some twenty years younger than Madge. She was a professional woman in her forties who moved to Leicester as a student from London with her family when she was in her late teens, and I refer to her briefly in Chapter 2. While Maria does not deploy the idiom of 'ghetto' to define Streetville and Belgrave, these places represent her perception of the negative aspects of Black, White and BrAsian lifestyles. I asked her:

KATHARINE: What do you think to Streetville and Belgrave as places?
MARIA: Well, they are places that are solid Black and then there are Asians but there is a mixture. They are not good to be out in at night, there are lots of break ins [burglaries] and crime that really exists. Then you have got to watch out for drugs. They are full of unsafe and peculiar people, not all are Black. There are a lot of families and a lot of people are on family credits [welfare payments]. Whenever you see schools advertising for teachers, you find that Gujarati is essential. I always feel sorry for the one White child that is in that class. I prefer it when it is mixed cultures and races. But there you find it is solid Black and then you have a few others.

In parallel with Leicester Promotions' depiction of the city, many of my White co-conversationalists from Greenville perceive BrAsians to be the key signifiers of ethnic difference in Leicester. In this way, other ethnic minority people, including Black Britons who live in these inner city areas are rendered invisible. Against this trend, Maria identifies Streetville and Belgrave with Black, White and BrAsian people.

For Maria, the presence of Black and BrAsian people in Streetville and Belgrave is synonymous with the evils of drugs, burglaries and unsafe streets at night. These common everyday descriptions of ethnic minorities come to represent the totality of their lifestyles that threaten to consume urban White culture. Moreover, Maria implies that not all the 'peculiar people' are Black, rather for her being a recipient of welfare payment is also a qualification for peculiarity. Within the shadows of Maria's account is the figure of the non-respectable and poor racially unmarked White working class. In this regard, specific urban places are identified with 'geographies of roughness' identified with both racialised and classed Others (Watt, 2006). For Maria, the ethnic and classed composition of Streetville and Belgrave do not represent a balanced ethnic and class mix. Indeed, Maria's evocation of the 'one White child' in an all-Black classroom echoes Enoch Powell's image of an 'old White woman' alone in the inner city in the face of postcolonial immigration. Like this old White woman alone, the one White child in a 'solid Black' classroom signifies for Maria the vulnerability of respectable Whites who live in the city surrounded by the 'bleak inhumanity of urban decay' (Gilroy, 1987, p. 86).

At this juncture, it is useful to pause for a moment to summarise my White co-conversationalists' ideas and my arguments thus far concerning them. To explain and account for the division in terms of race and place between the countryside and the city, some of my White co-conversationalists suggest that it is individuals' choice to live culturally and racially segregated lives in the countryside and the city. BrAsian and White cultures are thereby depicted as incompatible, self-contained and discrete. Moreover, the onus is repeatedly placed upon BrAsians to overcome their supposed failure to 'integrate' into the White majority culture. Central to this discourse is the representation of BrAsians as immigrants to Leicester – people whose origins are automatically assumed to lie outside of the nation and the West. In addition, BrAsians are portrayed as living in the 'ghetto', a racialised and classed place that is set apart from the norms and values of decent White society and culture. Underpinning these representations of the city is a whole host of racialised distinctions that rigidly categorise and mark 'our' way of life in the village as distinct from 'theirs' in the city. From this perspective, the city is portrayed as the site of smelly food, un-neighbourliness, crime, vandalism, drug abuse, poor Whites, excessive immigration and unfortunate decent White people having been 'taken over' by undesirable racialised and classed Others. So it is that a racially unmarked White village culture takes meaning in relation to what it is not – racialised and classed urban Others.

While some of my White co-conversationalists' attempt to cut themselves off and insulate themselves from the effects of multiculturalism, as alluded to in Chapter 1, it is often assumed in media and political circles that the White middle classes embrace multiculturalism (Ware, 2008). Indeed, as evidenced by my analysis of the representation of the city and the country in the Leicester Promotions literature and websites, the White middle classes are thought to be cosmopolitan in their lifestyles and tastes, and thus good at engaging with and living with ethnic difference. However, in the following section I shall show some of the ways in which White middle-class Greenville residents' attempts to engage with multiculturalism in the city serve only to reinforce the dichotomous racialised divisions between rural and urban ethnoscapes in Leicester/shire. With this in mind, I now turn to an exploration of how White villagers attempted to engage with what they perceived to be the BrAsian culture of the city.

Engaging with the BrAsian city

Mike, who we first met in Chapter 2, believes that Belgrave is a place to visit for the purchase of 'something' BrAsian. In addition, he conveyed his enthusiasm for BrAsian businesses in Belgrave. In so doing, like Leicester Promotions' depiction of the country and the city, Mike valorises and praises aspects of BrAsian culture. However, the effect of this discourse is also for the perceived cultural differences between Whites and BrAsians, the country and the city to be reaffirmed. He said:

> Well, if I wanted something which was Asian I would go down Belgrave Road, like, if I wanted a sari or a deal on jewellery or Indian gold. ... I have been with my friends to a tandoori [restaurant] ..., very nice ... good as gold. ... Yes, smashing, yes, I wouldn't argue with that. The Indians have taken the shops over. They have brought business into the shops which has made the Melton Road [the central road in Belgrave] a very, very busy shopping road. If it would have been left to the Englishman, they would have gone out of business and those shops would have been boarded up.

The resonance between Mike's narrative and Leicester Promotions' portrait of the country and the city illuminates the ready appropriation of stereotypical, 'free-floating' and 'universal' signifiers of BrAsianness (Hutnyk, 1999, p. 101). Indeed, it is not only the association of BrAsians with the ethnicised commodities and brands of 'Indian gold', 'tandoori' and 'saris' that locks them into 'straitjackets' of cultural difference, but also Mike's praise of BrAsians' entrepreneurialism that marks them out as different from the 'Englishman' (see Puwar, 2004, p. 70). It is perhaps no coincidence that Mike's focus upon BrAsians' business success echoes his valorisation and praise but simultaneous Othering of BrAsian shopkeepers in Greenville (see Chapter 2). Mike thus uses the same lens to look at BrAsians in the village and the city.

During our conversation Mike referred to Belgrave as 'Little India'. Belgrave is situated in Leicester and thus inside the English nation, yet it is clear that for Mike its inhabitants' daily rhythms are imagined to lie outside the routines and norms of a racially unmarked Englishness. In short, in spite of Mike's attempts to positively engage with ethnicity and difference in the city, Belgrave is merely a site for 'internal tourism' (Parker, 2000). In a similar vein to Leicester Promotions' portrayal of the city, Belgrave becomes a place that one visits and then leaves for a home that lies elsewhere.

I conclude the ethnographic sections of this chapter with the thoughts and reflections of Mark. His ideas bring together many of the sometimes contradictory themes that are woven into my White co-conversationalists' perceptions of the racialised division in Leicester/shire, including, for example, representations of BrAsian and Black areas of Leicester as 'ghettos', admiration for BrAsians' supposed entrepreneurial success and appreciation of their curries. Significantly, like William, Mark's biography is part of the history of British colonialism. His thoughts and reflections thus provide a particularly acute angle on the ways in which Whites come to negotiate and screen out the consequences of that history in their reflections on ethnic diversity in the present. Mark was the husband of Flo, who we met earlier in this chapter. During my conversation with Flo, Mark joined in thus:

MARK: I suppose the immigrants – or Black or whatever – I mean they went there [to Streetville] because it was perhaps cheap accommodation when they first came. They have been attracted to being more or less among their own kind. And you get a ghetto type situation really, and it is the same with Belgrave.

KATHARINE: You don't see Belgrave as adding anything to the city then with its restaurants and so on?

MARK: Oh, yes very much so. Not for us because we are of a different generation, you know. We don't really go out to particularly foreign type restaurants. ... There are rarely people of our age group that do...

FLO: I do think their shops with all the saris and things are gorgeous. They really are lovely.

MARK: They have widened the scope of the city, no doubt. I think, you can't reverse it and I don't even want to now. I mean Belgrave Road itself is nice along there. I mean during the War (the Second World War), I spent quite a lot of time in India and it certainly is an Indian area. You very rarely see a White face. ... They are hard working and they have taken over all the shops and things now, which everyone [the White English] wanted to give up because of the long hours. And you know, we were too idle to do it. So they came and did it you know. Good luck to them.

KATHARINE: What part of India were you in?

MARK: All over Delhi, Calcutta, Sri Lanka and then in Singapore ...

FLO: Why did they come in the first place?

MARK: They had the right to come. They were British subjects and they had a right to come without passports or anything. ... And because their own country is so poor you know. India

	does very well for those that are working. But you know, there is still a lot of poverty in the countryside.
FLO:	You can't really blame them.
MARK:	Still the ox going round in circles and drawing water, like that you see.
FLO:	But we had a lot of them in the hospitals.
Mark:	That's right for … cleaners and things like that because no one of our lot wanted to do it. … There was really a shortage after the War [that is a shortage of White people prepared to do manual work].
KATHARINE:	Your relationship with India shows how White English people have an ongoing relationship with India.
MARK:	Oh yes a century or so.
KATHARINE:	But yet some people I have spoken with express a sense of surprise that Asians are here in the UK.
MARK:	It is amazing how ignorant some people are, isn't it? My mother used to invite the odd Black service man for Sunday tea you know, mostly RAF [Royal Air Force] people. We went to the local church and a lot of the people in the church they did think the Black came off on the sheets. They really thought that.
FLO:	They really frowned on it, didn't they … I mean they really looked down their noses. … And I used to think it was awful. I often think now have those people [changed]. Well, I suppose they are a bit like us you get used to seeing them, don't you. It is nothing for us to see a coloured person.

Thus it is that Mark constructs a familiar White portrait of BrAsians in Leicester. He thinks that BrAsians prefer to live 'with their own kind' in 'ghettos' set apart from the White majority. BrAsians are depicted as 'hardworking' in relation to their employment in the culturally specific service industries of retail and catering. Moreover, BrAsians' origins are thought to lie in India – a place that is portrayed as economically poor and culturally backward. Again we see that these commonplace, readily available images and stereotypes of cultural difference share parallels with a colonial worldview of White Western cultural superiority that marks and defines the White Western self in relation to non-White non-Western Others. As in the colonial past, aspects of the others' culture is valorised. However, they remain fundamentally Other to the racially unmarked White middle-class self.

Mark acknowledges that his biography is entwined with the history of the British Empire. He served with the British Army in India during the Second World War. Mark knows that settlers to England from India were British subjects and that the same subjects fought in the World Wars on the side of the British. It is from this vantage point that his analysis of BrAsians' migration to England forms a chain of hierarchical differences between the White self and BrAsian settlement. Empire is depicted as something that took place over 'there' – in India, Sri Lanka and Singapore. One consequence of Empire is that BrAsians are subjects of Britain, and so gain the right to migrate to England and other parts of Britain. BrAsians did the jobs 'we' Whites did not want to do. However, this history of Empire connecting 'us' to 'them' is not seen as transformative and co-constitutive of the everyday contemporary rhythms of White local and national society. Rather, BrAsians remain 'coloured', culturally different people who are contained in an 'Indian area' of the city that is denoted as a 'ghetto'. Clearly, Mark does not reveal his amnesia of the colonial past. However, he does show a determined persistence to mark BrAsians as the urban Other, which rests upon screening out and side-stepping the legacies and full implications of Empire for understanding the multicultural present, a point to which I shall return in the conclusion of this chapter.

Central to Mark's and Flo's thoughts on race and the city is their emphasis upon a shift in generational attitudes towards multiculturalism. While Mark and Flo think that BrAsian restaurants and shops have brought economic benefits to the city, they do not frequent such 'foreign' restaurants themselves, and it is not something that they think many others of their generation would do. Thinking of their parents' generation, Mark and Flo distance themselves from the 'ignorance' of those White people who thought that the Blackness of Black skins rubbed off onto sheets. Unlike that generation, Mark and Flo are used to seeing 'coloured' people and know that many of their beliefs and attitudes were mistaken. Generational shifts in attitudes towards ethnicity and difference are the subject of the next chapter, which draws on my fieldwork in a former coalmining town in Leicestershire.

Conclusions: The country, the city and the legacies of Empire

In his book *the Country and the City* (1973), Raymond Williams proposes that the meanings attached to the country and the city provide insight into the constitution of Englishness. In this chapter I have built on this insight to scrutinise the ways in which these metaphors of place furnish an analytical lens through which to consider the racialised and classed constitution of the country and the city in postcolonial England. As with Williams, I am interested in the meanings that are inscribed on and attached to these idioms of place. It is worth reflecting on the disjunction between the image of the countryside of Leicestershire as a White and middle-class space, and the city of Leicester as a BrAsian space and, and compare it to the actual lived realities of the postcolonial people that live in these places. While for some White Greenville residents the areas of Streetville and Belgrave are symbols of BrAsians' cultural and racial differences from White English village life, such stereotypical differences only take their full meaning when detached from the economic realities of BrAsians who live in Leicester/shire. There are wealthy BrAsian families living in Greenville Gardens, the village centre and the neighbouring suburbs of Greenville. BrAsians therefore do move outside the city and its supposed 'ghetto'. Similarly, Belgrave and Streetville are by no means completely BrAsian and Black areas. As we shall see in my study of Streetville in Chapters 5 and 6, working-class and middle-class Whites, as well as new migrants to the city, also live in these neighbourhoods. Racialised and classed stereotypes of place and difference have to be detached from the heterogeneous relationships that constitute people's lived realities, and it is precisely the manifestation of such stereotypes that I have examined in this chapter.

In this chapter I have built upon and progressed my analysis of the everyday articulation of White discourses of coloniality in Greenville in relation to BrAsian residents examined in Chapter 2. I have shown how laced throughout the image of the racialisation of the country and the city is a worldview of White Western cultural superiority that positions the culture of the Other as fundamentally distinct from that of a racially unmarked White English self. Just as aspects of the culture of the colonised were at times valorised by the coloniser, the culture of BrAsians in the city is at times celebrated. Nonetheless, just as the colonised used to dichotomise the metropole/colony, this valorisation of cultural difference is done in ways that ensure that the culture of the countryside and the village remains set apart from the BrAsian city. I have advocated that central to the reproduction of White discourses of coloniality is amnesia of actual colonial histories that connect the social fabric of the English countryside to the BrAsian city. From this standpoint what is screened out in the demarcation and containment of BrAsians (and also Black people) to the city are the intrinsic connections between postcolonial rural and urban cultures formed through the histories and relations of Empire. At times poignant reminders of these relations come to the fore, threatening to fragment the 'bundles of silences' that constitute White amnesia of the colonial past and so almost, but not quite, making visible the invisibility of Empire (Wemyss, 2008, 2009). One such reminder is Leicester Promotions' reference to the traditional ingredients used to make Melton hunt cake, which included Caribbean Rum and muscovado sugar from Barbados. As I observed, at the time of the cake's origins, these ingredients would have been produced by slave labour in the former British colonies of the Caribbean. In addition, the personal biographies of some of my White co-conversationalists from Greenville are intimately connected with the histories of Empire. For example, William was born in Calcutta at the time of British rule and Mark served in the British Army in the former British colonies of India, Sri Lanka and Singapore. I have shown that while William does not relate his early childhood in India directly to BrAsian settlement in the UK, Mark does draw upon his experiences in the colonies to interpret and make sense of BrAsian presence in Leicester. Mark thus knows that postcolonial settlers to Leicester were British subjects and therefore had the right to settle in England. Nonetheless, his thoughts on BrAsians who live in the city remain rooted in a sense of their absolute cultural difference from the White English Western self.

Thus it seems to me that simply *remembering* and *evoking* the histories and connections between BrAsians and Empire does not take us quite far enough. Rather, it matters how the colonial past is remembered, and so it matters *how* we come to know and think about the meaning and legacies of the colonial relations that bind the countryside to the city, and that bind the White English and BrAsian populations who live there. I shall return to a discussion of the significance of how the colonial past is remembered in Chapter 6, and examine there the ways in which members of interracial families draw upon aspects of the slave past to interpret and make sense of the present.

Part II
Confronting Coloniality: White Working-Class Ethnicities

4
The Questioning of Racism in a Former Coalmining Town

Having examined the articulation of discourses of coloniality and White amnesia in Part I, I now turn my attention in this chapter to an exploration of the issues surrounding White people's attempts to challenge and question others' racist attitudes. To do this I draw on my fieldwork in Coalville.[1]

The processes of White hegemony have always been visible to non-White people, that is to say, those people who are routinely excluded by White power and privilege. However, my focus in this chapter is on the conditions in which White people themselves can become reflexive actors on the racist attitudes of other Whites. Ruth Frankenberg (1993b, p. 78) argues in her study of White women's lives in the USA that one way to begin challenging the universality of White dominance is to focus on some White middle- and working-class women's 'moments of questioning' through which they challenge the racist status quo. Frankenberg (1993b, p. 78) comments on the significance of White women's moments of critical reflection thus: 'the moments of questioning are perhaps moments when the door opens on other realms of possibility, other ways of being. Those moments should give us hope [to bring about the end of white superiority].' Frankenberg's emphasis on the way in which White women become reflexive actors on racism is of crucial importance to the study of White racialised discourses. These moments of critical reflection highlight how the often unreflective reproduction of White superiority is in key critical moments destabilised, opened up and confronted.

To trace and analyse the contours of Whites' 'moments of questioning' in this chapter and the next, I again find it helpful to use the concept of 'coloniality'. As set out in this book's Introduction, the term 'coloniality' refers to the reproduction of a colonial worldview of White Western cultural superiority in the present that at times intersects with White amnesia of the colonial past. In Chapters 2 and 3, I have shown that the articulation of discourses of coloniality is intersected with White amnesia of the colonial past in White middle-class racialised discourses on the proper constitution of English village life. I argued that the effect of the articulation of colonial notions of culture and difference in the present is to position BrAsians as immigrants, that is, racialised Others and cultural outsiders to village life. In this chapter and Chapter 5, my aim is to illuminate how, and under what conditions, assumptions of White Western superiority are sometimes confronted.

To explore these processes my attention shifts from the exploration of White middle-class racialised discourses to an examination of the constitution of racialised discourses of White working-class people. My focus is upon White working-class confrontations of racism, as opposed to the White middle classes, because I want to shift the assumption within academic and media discourse that if any Whites are going to be anti-racist then it is going to be the White middle classes. My positioning of White working-class people as reflexive actors on racism, as opposed to the White middle classes, is not to suggest that the White working classes are in some way wise and enlightened on matters of race and ethnicity compared to the White middle classes. Nor is it my argument that White middle-class people cannot also be reflexive actors on racism. In short, I do not want to portray the White working class as anti-racist angels. Rather, my aim is to scrutinise both the reproduction of White working-class racism and also challenges to it. Indeed, my account also illustrates how White individuals who reflect on and set out to reject the racism of others can also unintentionally reproduce racialised stereotypes about BrAsians' supposed cultural differences from the White Western majority. In this way, my study illuminates the difficult task that White individuals face in escaping and avoiding the logic, language and worldview of discourses of coloniality in the present even when it is their intention to challenge others' racist attitudes.

Following my approach to the meaning of social class set out in Chapter 1, I shall not attempt to define what I mean by 'working class' when I refer to the identities of my White co-conversationalists from Coalville. Like the White middle-class research participants from Greenville, my working-class co-conversationalists from Coalville did not identify with a collective classed identity and so did not provide me with any spoken confirmation or criteria through which to classify them in class terms. Rather, the meaning of working-class identity became transparent, I think, in relation to individuals' senses of belonging to Coalville as a place. Moreover, White research participants' perceptions of racialised Others revealed their sense of what constituted respectable ways of living that were interwoven with specifically White working-class values and norms.

Coalville is traditionally a wholly White coalmining town, which lost its major industry in the 1980s and early 1990s during the drastic restructuring of Britain's economic infrastructure from an industrial-based, manufacturing economy to one dominated by hi-tech and service industries. In the post-mining era BrAsians have opened off-licences (liquor stores), newsagents, restaurants and takeaways in Coalville and the surrounding villages. There are also some restaurants and takeaways owned and run by British Chinese people. My purpose in Coalville was to explore working-class Whites' perceptions of the changing ethnic composition of their area in the post-mining era. Following the focus of my ethnographic study of Greenville, my attention in this chapter will also be directed at White people's perceptions of BrAsians, the largest minority that have settled into the area in these post-industrial times.

I came to understand that, in the face of the loss of the area's traditional industry and its associated way of life, some young White adults in their late teens and twenties came to be critically reflexive on what they perceived to be the racism of their parents' and grandparents' generation. In other words, the process of deindustrialisation to some extent opened up a space for young people's critical reflections on the racism of others. These young White people show a diversification of views on race in the post-traditional era, whereas the parental generation represent intolerant attitudes towards race that are associated with the conventions of the industrial past (see Giddens, 1994 for a discussion of reflexivity and tradition in what he refers to as 'post-traditional' society). My contention is that the idioms of 'convention' (traditional White attitudes towards race) and 'innovation' (the non-racist and anti-racist attitudes of some young White adults) provide a framework through which to connect the socio-economic changes in the region to transforming attitudes on race, ethnicity and difference across generations and time.

In this chapter I focus in detail on young White people's critical reflections on the racist attitudes of older and younger White members of their nuclear and extended families, friends and acquaintances. These moments of critical reflection bring to the fore the fragmented intergenerational production and sustenance of racist, non-racist and anti-racist sentiments, and the ways in which gender mediates the formation of attitudes on race. In this regard, my analysis points to the reproduction of both racist, non-racist and anti-racist views across generations, and so identifies the possible conditions in which people, especially younger people, have the potential to produce moderate and more enlightened views on race.

I hope that my analysis of working-class Whites as reflexive actors on racism has wider implications for the sociological analysis of race and class in Britain and elsewhere. My account sets out to disrupt those academic and media representations of working-class Whites that seem to be blind to the possibility that working-class people are reflexive actors in these post-industrial times (see Rhodes, 2011 for a similar approach). The White working classes are more often than not represented by media and academics as the most racist people and thus the most resentful towards ethnic minorities, immigrants and multiculturalism. My attempt to challenge this representation of the White working classes parallels, in some respects, Skeggs' (1997, 2004) study of working-class White women's experiences of class, gender and sexuality in an industrial town in the north west of England. She argues that academic representations of White working-class women too often 'pathologize' these women's experiences of their femininity (1997, p. 21). Skeggs (1997, p. 19) warns of the ease with which the disciplinary practices within the academy, based on 'rational knowing', leads researchers to construct working-class White women as 'objects of knowledge without agency and volition' (1997, p. 19). My analysis seeks to extend this critique of academic and popular representations of White working-class women to include depictions of White working-class people and racism in post-industrial areas of Britain.

Representations of White working-class backlash against multiculturalism

In this section I shall analyse academic and media representations of White working-class racism in Britain in order to set out the ways in which my study in Coalville complicates the arguments of those social science and media commentators who suggest that the White working classes are unreflexive actors and the most racist people in British society.

While Simon Charlesworth (2000) does not suggest that working-class people are racist, he does portray them as unreflexive actors. Charlesworth examines White working-class lives in the former industrial town of Rotherham in South Yorkshire. He describes White and Pakistani working-class people as 'linguistically dispossessed', 'sensorily impoverished' and 'perceptually deprived', and thus unable to achieve any significant form of 'self-realisation' (2000, pp. 138, 284). To take another example, Phil Cohen's (1997) analysis of working-class racism in the London Docklands area denies that working-class White people have the ability to actively question others' racist beliefs and practices. Cohen argues that working-class Whites living in post-industrial communities in Britain unconsciously hanker for a lost past of economic glory, which becomes the driving force for their hatred and envy of BrAsian and Black intruders into their once uniformly White territories. In a further example, Alastair Bonnett (2000) links White working-class racism in Britain to the rise of welfare capitalism. He contends that the British welfare state has historically been seen as a White project, only extended on sufferance to immigrants. Bonnett (2000, p. 132) argues that this has led to the White British working-class belief that extending the welfare state to non-Whites is unfair to White British people. He writes: 'Working class Whiteness in Britain should be approached as a socio-economic achievement of the working-class that is mired in racism' (2000, p. 133).

Bonnett's arguments point us in the direction of recent academic and media accounts that identify the White working classes in Britain with a 'White backlash' against multiculturalism. This discourse of White backlash is based on the supposition that the government unfairly prioritises the rights and socio-economic needs of immigrants and ethnic minorities at the expense of the indigenous White working-class population. The phrase 'White backlash' was coined by Roger Hewitt to capture the response to 'official policies aimed at providing equal rights, opportunities, and protection under the law for minority ethnic groups' (Hewitt, 2005, p. 5; see also Rhodes, 2010, p. 79 for an analysis of White backlash discourses to multiculturalism). While Hewitt identifies this discourse with both the White middle and working classes, within some political and media circles this discourse has been stereotypically associated with just the White working classes.

By way of illustration, consider how the British Broadcasting Corporation (BBC2, 9–11 March 2008) ran a series of programmes entitled *White Season*, which set out to address what the BBC perceived to be the marginality of the White working class in the UK. The producers of this series proposed that 'the White working class had become an endangered ethnic group, its survival threatened by "revolutionary" socio-economic change and its voice muted by politically correct dogma' (Ware, 2008, 2.3). Central to this argument is the question of immigration, which is believed to have fuelled resentment among the poorest sections of the population towards immigrants and ethnic minorities (Ware, 2008, 1.4). The supposed giving of limited public resources to immigrants is thought to have offended White working-class people's sense of 'what is fair', and to leave them feeling that 'their generosity is being abused' (Ware, 2008, 1.4). These negative sentiments towards new immigrants are said to have become entwined with animosity towards established ethnic minorities. In this vein, the Editor of the *White Season*, in an article in *the Daily Mail* newspaper (Klein, 2008, cited in Ware, 2008, 2.5) wrote that White working-class people believe themselves to be 'an oppressed ethnic minority' who are the victims of 'double standards and hypocrisy' whereby 'every other culture ... is revered except the indigenous population'. This alleged sense of abandonment is said to be the cause of White working-class people giving their political support to the far-right British National Party (BNP).

While Ware (2008) acknowledges that some resentment and disillusionment is inevitable in a society that officially espouses equality for all, she argues that this media-driven analysis fails to see that this 'resentment might mean a crisis over the very basis of Whiteness as a basis for identification' (2008, 6.1). In a similar vein, James Rhodes (2010, p. 83) argues that: 'The documentaries, and the tone of the entire *White Season* itself, served to accept this sense of unfairness uncritically.'

As mentioned in this book's Introduction, Rhodes' (2010, 2011) work examines the racialised discourses of White BNP supporters in Burnley, a former mill town in the north west of England. Rhodes analyses how White supporters of the BNP expressed resentment towards local state policies that were thought to unfairly prioritise the needs of BrAsians and Whites, who were believed not to work and illegitimately claimed social welfare payments. In stark contrast to media and some academic representations of White backlash discourses, Rhodes (2011) argues that this discourse of 'entitlement', 'responsibility' and 'respectability' was not just articulated by the poorer White residents of Burnley but also the affluent White working classes and some sections of the White middle classes. Rhodes' emphasis upon the classed heterogeneity of BNP supporters, and their Othering of some sections of the White working class, challenges popular and academic representations of the White working class as an easily identifiable and homogeneous type and category of person. He therefore tries to deconstruct the comfortable White middle-class myth that it is a particular type of post-industrial poor White working-class man that votes for the BNP, and represents the epitome of White backlash discourses to multiculturalism.

One aim of this chapter is to complicate further the logics supporting this kind of media and academic representation of White working-class racism in post-industrial Britain. I will pursue this by attending to certain intergenerational tensions and transformations. I will argue that the idea that White working-class people are resentful of multiculturalism is a one-dimensional viewpoint that tells only half the story. Thus, arguments voiced in the BBC's *White Season* and advanced by Cohen and Bonnett usefully highlight the reproduction of what I refer to in this chapter as 'conventional' racism. In my fieldwork in Coalville, I found that such conventional attitudes on race are associated by some of my White co-conversationalists with the traditional views of the parental generations; such attitudes to race emphasise the supposedly negative impacts of immigration and support the belief that public resources are unfairly distributed to immigrants and BrAsians at the expense of the White majority. An analysis of conventional racism in Coalville provides insight into ideas and attitudes on what constitutes respectable ways of living and behaving. From this point of view, BrAsians and recent immigrants are thought to represent the antithesis of White working-class notions of respectability centred on ideas of work, entitlement and fairness. Moreover, conventional racist attitudes highlight the reproduction of discourses of coloniality in the present premised on the idea that BrAsians are cultural outsiders and irreducibly Other from the standpoint of the racially unmarked White Western self (Frankenberg, 1993a, p. 17).

Even so, my central argument is that a singular focus on conventional racism does not take us far or deep enough. That is to say, social theorists also need to take seriously the ways in which White working-class racist discourses are acknowledged, confronted and challenged by White working-class people themselves. In my fieldwork, I found some young White adults thinking and talking about other White people's racist attitudes in the context of broader socio-economic transformations in their town. In this sense, the loss of the region's coalmining identity has facilitated a space that has enabled young Whites to step back, reflect on and challenge what they perceive to be the racist conventions of their forebears.

Ethnographic inquiry in Coalville

Coalville is the central town of North West Leicestershire and has its own District Council. According to the 1991 Census classification, 79,913 people living in North West Leicestershire (which includes the town of Coalville) were defined as 'White', 279 as 'Asian', 139 as 'Black' and a further 236 as 'Black other'. Other smaller towns in this area of

Leicestershire, besides Coalville, include Ashby-de-la Zouch, a market town, and Castle Donnington. In between these towns are dotted small villages some of which are former pit villages that were the home of working collieries. The town of Coalville is 15 miles north west of Leicester and approximately 13 miles from Greenville.

The centre of the town consists of two main streets and a small shopping centre known locally as 'the precinct'. The central point of the town is Memorial Square, which consists of a clock tower and a war memorial to the World Wars. On the edge of the town is the site of the town's main colliery, now defunct, one of the four collieries in the region, which closed from between the mid-1980s and the early 1990s. Entering the town centre one passes the disused railway line that used to transport coal to other parts of the country and is a relic of the region's once successful coalmining industry. There are several BrAsian-owned restaurants, Chinese takeaways, pizza parlours, fish and chip shops and café shops situated along the streets of the town centre dispersed between banks, clothes shops, newsagents, a large Co-operative store (a supermarket chain traditionally associated with industrial areas), a Co-operative travel agent, several pubs and a bingo hall, where the traditionally White working-class game of bingo is played.

As I have already explained in this book's Introduction, I lived for six months in the Coalville area (August 1997 to February 1998), in a shared house with two people who, like me, were White single women in their twenties. The women were sisters, one of whom owned the house and to whom I and the other sister paid rent. The house was located in a former mining village approximately two miles from Coalville's town centre. I found these lodging by responding to an advert in the town's local newspaper. The women with whom I had the pleasure to live warmly included me into their home and their social group. We quickly became good friends. Each evening we shared the day-to-day happenings and details of our lives. At every weekend we socialised together in the local pubs and clubs. The women introduced me to a network of young White adults in the area, which helped to get my research off the ground. Without a doubt, my good relationships with my housemates, their warm inclusion of me into their lives and their generosity in introducing me to their friends focused my ethnographic attention on the racialised views of young White adults who lived in the area, because these were the people I came to know well.

I spent many days just 'hanging around' Coalville's town centre. I talked to White people sitting in the library, various pubs in the town and the Coalville Café, a popular place for local people to drop in for a coffee, a cigarette and a chat with friends. I found that my habit at that time of smoking cigarettes facilitated and eased my casual networking in the town. Smoking made me feel less conspicuous because it gave me something to do while I sat alone in cafés in the town centre, or on a bench in the local shopping precinct.

This casual networking enabled me to initiate short conversations with White people about their views on BrAsian settlers to the area and also made me privy to passing racist comments that I recorded in my notebook. For example, one elderly woman at a bus stop told me that BrAsians in the local shops 'rip you off' and asserted that 'they should not be in this country'. A young man in his late twenties was convinced that a local BrAsian-owned restaurant used dog meat.

Informal networking was combined with tape-recorded interviews with a cross-section of White people in terms of age (19–70), class and gender in the town. I made specific appointments to interview a wide range of White people, for example, local councillors, schoolteachers, youth workers, members of political parties, journalists, police officers, the Citizen's Advice Bureau, retired miners and workers at the town's Community Voluntary Service. As in Greenville, I sometimes relied on my handwritten notes taken during the interview. Some of these interviews were complemented by informal discussions outside of the interview context. In total, I conducted 30 informal interviews in Coalville. Research participants' words quoted in this chapter are either reported verbatim or are very close reconstructions of their actual words based on my detailed notes.

When I first started fieldwork in the Coalville region, I was initially keen to follow up the relationships between ideas of villageness and rurality, Englishness and Whiteness, which I had explored with the White residents of Greenville. However, I soon stopped asking questions about the rural identity of the area because it became clear that it was the wrong set of questions to ask. My White co-conversationalists either thought that their place was quite obviously 'rural' or were simply not concerned with the concepts of rurality and villageness. Rather, the White people that I came to know were concerned about the socio-economic transformation and future of their town in the post-mining era. I thus started to ask more relevant and locally meaningful questions that grew out of this specific context. In the light of this my interviews focused on two key themes: (1) White people's perceptions of the changing identity of their town in the post-mining era; and (2) their views on BrAsian, Chinese and Black settlers to the town. As I have already stated, this chapter focuses on White people's perceptions of BrAsians, the largest minority of 'non-Whites' living in the area.

Although only one Working Man's club that I contacted refused to speak with me, I received a mixed response from my White interviewees. Some older White people (50 years-plus), for example, retired miners, did not have much to say about the politics of race in the area. They preferred to discuss the history of the town and the socio-economic changes following the closure of the town's collieries, which have had a dramatic impact on their lives. In a similar vein, Frankenberg (1993a, p. 34) found in her interviews with White American feminists that her interviewees often directed the conversation away from race. I repeatedly got the impression that some respected White members of the community, for example, some White local councillors that I interviewed, felt that I might trick them into appearing to be racist. In this context, I sometimes got the sense that my middle-class status, signified by my 'posh' accent, comportment and my association with a university, was interpreted to mean that I would automatically think that White working-class people in Coalville were racist. In this regard, my middle-class identity and academic status worked at times to create a sense of class distance and distinction between myself and my White interviewees. By contrast, in Greenville I found that my middle-class identity worked to create a sense of rapport and connection between myself and my White middle-class co-conversationalists, as discussed in Chapter 2.

Moreover, class was not the only issue in Coalville that worked to silence my White co-conversationalists on matters of race and identity. One White councillor I interviewed quickly changed the subject when I asked about his views on the ethnic composition of the town. I later learnt, in conversation with others, that his son had adopted a child of African Caribbean descent. I realised that my questions were perhaps treading on territory too close to home.

None of my White co-conversationalists expressed the explicitly racist comments that I had encountered during some of my more casual discussions with townspeople in pubs, cafés and at bus stops. However, seven young White adults (between 19 and 30 years of age) that I came to know articulated reflexive views on what they considered to be the conventional racist attitudes of others. It might be thought that these young White people expressed reflexive attitudes simply to conform to what they felt were my middle-class sensibilities or academic judgement on racial issues. However, the time that I spent 'hanging around' with them, for example, Jim and Julie who will appear later, leads me to take their criticisms of others' racist attitudes at face value. I also think that the complexity of other young White adults' accounts, particularly the personal testimony of Vicki, who will also appear in this chapter, indicates the sincerity of their reflections on racism. In short, it became clear to me that I was addressing issues that these young White adults had already thought about. This aspect of my experience is in stark contrast to Charlesworth's (2000, p. 138) conclusion that White working-class people, in his case from Rotherham, were 'linguistically dispossessed' and for whom the interview was 'always an intrusion'.

Tradition and socio-economic innovation: From Coalville to 'Enterpriseville'

I now turn to an exploration of the socio-economic composition of the Coalville region of Leicestershire and how the mining past is remembered and valued by townspeople in the post-industrial present. This aspect of my account provides insight into the dramatic transformations in terms of place and identity that the people of Coalville have experienced, which situates townspeople's attitudes towards BrAsians. Moreover, an understanding of the changing socio-economic composition of Coalville also signposts the transformation in intergenerational attitudes towards race.

There were originally nine pits in the North West Leicestershire coalfield. Three of these were closed in the 1960s. As briefly mentioned earlier, the remaining four pits were closed during the 1980s and 1990s as part of the Thatcher government's policy of 'uneconomic' pit closures across Britain. These pit closures were the cause of the 1984–5 miners' strike. The strike broke new ground in mining history because it was about pit closures and not wages, which had been the reason for previous strikes in the British coalfield. Men were therefore asked by the National Union of Mineworkers (NUM) to strike on behalf of other miners in collieries in different parts of Britain. The majority of men working in the North West Leicestershire coalfield, like their neighbours in Nottingham and South Derbyshire, voted in their local union ballot not to strike and carried on working. The general view in the region was that the pits were running out of coal and would be closed eventually regardless of strike action or not. Moreover, the majority of Leicestershire miners, their wives and families, felt that the leader of the NUM was wrong not to call a national ballot. It was believed that the NUM leader was scared to do so on the grounds that he might have lost the ballot. In Leicestershire, those men and women involved in the strike argued that if a national ballot had been in favour of strike action, then Leicestershire would have gone on strike. However, in the absence of such a ballot Leicestershire's branch of the NUM believed that it had to follow the results of the local union ballot, which overwhelmingly voted to continue working.

The politics of the strike forms an important counter narrative to versions of the miner's strike that circulate in former coalfield towns and villages in other parts of Britain. People in the more militant coalfields of Kent, Yorkshire and South Wales bitterly decried the majority of Leicestershire miners as 'scabs' for continuing to work, and breaking the collective action advocated and supported by the NUM.

At the local level those that did strike were in the minority and were known as the 'dirty thirty'. Tension between those who joined the strike and those who broke the picket lines were reproduced at the time of my fieldwork. I was told that former miners on the District Council, who were on different sides during the 1984–5 strike, would not sit next to each other at Council meetings because each considered the other to be either 'a scab' for continuing to work, or 'a traitor' for following what was thought to be the bullying tactics of the Union.

The last remaining Leicestershire pit was closed in February 1991. Unemployment in the area was high after the closure of the local pits. From 1983 until the closure of the last pit, well over 3000 jobs were lost in the area as a whole, the majority of which were in mining (Diacon, 1990). The miners who found it the hardest to gain new forms of employment were middle-aged men who had about ten years of working life left. Many of these men had no skills other than mining and so resorted to manual work, which was poorly paid and not comparable to the good money earned from the pits. In the light of this reality, many men took early retirement and lived on their redundancy payments, which they managed with caution.

Many miners, however, had to find alternative forms of employment to support their families. Men's career paths often became disjointed, as they moved between jobs until they found work that suited them. Many men retrained into other skills. For example, Jack, a White man, who was 28 years old when I met him, and had lived in the area most of his life, explained how his father moved from mining to work in a local hosiery factory. This subsequently closed and he retrained as an ambulance driver, his current occupation.

Traditionally, miners' wives managed the home, often bringing up children, and took casual paid employment outside the home when extra money was needed. I was told by one retired miner that he was given his wages each week by a woman who worked in the office at the pit and then handed his wages to another woman, his wife, who managed the money at home. When the mines closed more women took unskilled paid work outside of the home to support their families.

At the time of my fieldwork in Coalville in 1997–8, unemployment in the region was less than the national average. For example, in March 1997 the District Council's official figures measured unemployment in the town at 4.9 per cent of the total population. In the region as a whole, unemployment in March 1997 was measured at 4.1 per cent, less than unemployment in the UK as a whole, which was at 6.2 per cent.[2]

While unemployment was low at the time of my fieldwork, most work in the region was of a manual/semi-skilled level and involved long hours for low pay. Many men and women commuted to the easily accessible cities of Leicester, Loughborough, Nottingham, Derby and Burton-on-Trent to work. Moreover, North West Leicestershire's prime position in the middle of the country and its connection to the M1 motorway meant that the District Council was able to attract new businesses to the area from both the private and public sectors (Diacon, 1990). For example, on the outskirts of the town, there were several large business parks, which housed redistribution depots for large companies like Nestlé, Canon and Tarmac. People complained that the wages on these estates were notoriously low. However, the expansion of large retail and business parks on the outskirts of Coalville produced over one thousand new jobs in retailing services and distribution (Diacon, 1990).

Coalville's economic regeneration has been partly due to the fact that people in the area were never solely dependent on mining for their economic well-being. The area also has a long tradition of brick manufacture and granite quarries, which were in operation at the time of my fieldwork. Moreover, the regeneration of the area was also partly dependent on the development of the leisure and tourist industries.

Perhaps the most ambitious project with regard to attracting tourists to the region was the development of the area's rural landscape into a National Forest. The National Forest spans North West Leicestershire and the neighbouring counties of Derbyshire and Staffordshire. In the late 1990s the European Commission and the National Forest Company contributed grants of £900,000 to build a visitors' centre and a 700-seat amphitheatre. This particular project was dependent on mobilising the rural landscape of the region as a resource for future economic development. In this way, the region's rural landscape, like that in other parts of

Leicestershire, has economic and cultural capital built into it that can be marketed to tourists. Economic growth was thus in part dependent on the exploitation of pastoral aspects of the Coalville region's landscape. In Chapters 2 and 3 of this book, I have argued that this aspect of Englishness is intimately associated with a White English middle-class aesthetic.

However, the reality is that the area's mining heritage has also become a resource for the area's economic regeneration. For example, one of the pits located on the edge of Coalville's town centre was converted into a museum. The key attraction of the 'Discovery Park' is a guided tour around the pithead by a retired miner. This tourist attraction received much less public investment and interest than the National Forest. Moreover, another pit, on the outskirts of Coalville, was replaced with a large Morrisons supermarket,[3] which forms part of a complex of superstores, including Aldi (another cheap supermarket) and a McDonald's drive-through. While the building of a retail park on the site of a former colliery is testimony to the legacies of de-industrialisation generally, the preservation and conversation of one of the town's pits into a museum points to the way in which the people that I came to know cared about and cherished their town's mining past.

This local pride in the area's industrial past was exemplified in the 1990s when many councillors, on both the political left and right, were outraged when the Conservative Member of Parliament at the time wanted to rename the town 'Enterpriseville'. It was argued by the MP that this name change would be appropriate for Coalville's post-mining era and was vital to get away from the town's 'muck and brass' image. This proposal was fiercely fought by the majority of people in the region and many local councillors. Jim, who was in his late twenties and was the secretary of the local Labour Party, talked to me about people's reactions to the proposed name change. He explained: 'It hurt people, it actually hurt people. They like the name Coalville because it evokes Coal.' Similar views were expressed by George (the son of a miner), who was in his fifties, and had lived in Coalville all his life. George commented on the proposed name change as follows: 'It was bloody stupid. It is like changing London to Economic City. You can never change the name of Coalville unless the town moves.' Like Jim, George thinks that the name of Coalville is a sign of the town's history, its traditions and foundations.

These sentiments were also conveyed and described in a special edition of the town's local newspaper *The Coalville Times*, which celebrated 100 years of the newspaper's publication. An article entitled 'Golden Days of Coal' sentimentally recalls the economic prosperity that mining brought to the region but also reflects on the dangerous conditions in which men worked:

> Prosperity and industrial growth began, underpinned by the rich coal reserves lying beneath Coalville ... which assured whole families: grandfathers, fathers and sons of a life's work...
>
> Underground work began in extremely dangerous and fearful conditions. The town's mining history is studded with lives lost down the pit.
>
> Roof falls, poison gas (methane or fire-damage) and crippling lung disease went with the territory. Major disaster struck in 1898 when the town lost 35 colliers from a shift of 40, killed when an underground fire broke out at XXX pit [a pit on the outskirts of the town, and the name of the village in which I lived].
>
> But extraction methods progressed until the coalfield boasted the most sophisticated machinery in the country, and broke national records for tonnage per shift...
>
> The 80s saw the last shifts ... the remaining jewel in the coalfield's crown ... ran its last piece of coal out in 1991...
>
> It was indeed, as the reporter at the Times said: 'The end of an era'.
>
> (*The Coalville Times*, 1997)

It is poignant and significant that the article recalls the 1898 pit disaster. As Pitt (1979, p. 35, cited in Richards, 1996, p. 22) argues, such disasters become 'Part of the bloody backcloth against which the miner carries on his working life.' This disaster is commemorated by a brass statue of a life-sized miner wearing his hard hat and lamp, positioned outside Coalville's main library. This memorial was erected by the District Council in April 1998 to mark the hundredth anniversary of the disaster. The newspaper article also reminds its readers of the lung diseases caused by mining. At the time of my fieldwork, many miners had died or were suffering in their retirement from emphysema, bronchitis and pneumoconiosis, commonly referred to as 'black lung'. Significantly, the article concludes that the last shift marked 'the end of an era'. This phrase is important because it points to the way in which the closure of the pits marked the end of a whole way of life for generations of men, women and children centred on the colliery, the town and the surrounding pit villages. It highlights how the people of Coalville perceive the 'Golden era of Coal' to be in the past and so out of reach in the present.

I came to understand that local pride in the past is accompanied by the feeling that the present is a better time for former mining families. The old have retired early and so are able to help their children work by looking after grandchildren. It is also felt that young men have more opportunities because they are no longer compelled to follow their fathers down the pit and can choose alternative careers. Indeed, even prior to the 1980s pit closures, many young men were opting out of mining. In some cases, fathers actively dissuaded their sons from following in their footsteps. From this point of view, the value attached to the actual work of mining became ambivalent.

Pauline explained to me how she thought the present quality of life had improved. When we met, she was in her late fifties and lived with her husband, a former miner, on the edge of Coalville's town centre. Pauline was also the former secretary of the local branch of the National Union of Miners.[4] She said:

> I think that the quality of life is better for those miners who have finished work early. They are now more active. You see more grand-dads collecting their children from school and so the youngsters can go out to work. I think that the quality of life has increased all round. My opinion is that we have left coal behind. We do not want to forget it and we never will. But ... our coal is our history and we want it to be our history.

Rita, a journalist on the town's local newspaper, supported Pauline's view that Coalville's mining past is the area's history and tradition. In contrast, the present and future allows the space for innovation and new ways of being. Rita told me:

> Now you find that there is interest in the future that we have not seen before. People have great pride in Coalville but people have shut the door on the past and are looking forward. People do want to keep the tradition but also move on. I think that changes are coming slowly.

Rita and Pauline agree that former miners and their families want to move on, and not forget their town's mining past and traditions. My contention is that it is exactly the rupturing of traditional ways of life in the region that encourages some young White people to reflect on what they perceive to be traditional views on BrAsians, and this is what I shall now explore.

The changing ethnic composition of Coalville

On the edge of Coalville's town centre is a burnt-out restaurant, its name still clear: The Curry Pot (a pseudonym). This restaurant is a reminder of the racist attacks inflicted on BrAsians who settled into the town. I was told that in this particular restaurant, White customers frequently refused to pay their bills, shouted racist abuse and physically attacked BrAsian waiting staff. During my stay in the area I heard of repeated racist attacks by a White man against a BrAsian takeaway owner and his BrAsian staff in a small market town a few miles north of Coalville. However, to the best of my knowledge, there were no such racially motivated crimes committed against BrAsian and Chinese shops, restaurants and takeaways during the six-month period that I lived in Coalville. In fact, people were keen to point out to me the increased popularity of BrAsian and Chinese restaurants, takeaways and shops in their town. For example, consider the thoughts of Jill and George. We briefly met George above. George and his wife Jill were in their fifties. They ran a social club in the town centre and had lived in Coalville all their lives.[5]

George and Jill comment on the BrAsian restaurants in the area as follows:

GEORGE: Lots of people here will frequent the Asian restaurants. They are always busy because the prices are quite cheap. The one on Main Road is very good. ... They don't have any riff-raff [that is, people who might cause trouble] in there. They have crowds of people; they're doing good business. It used to be filthy down there.

JILL: People's tastes are changing, like the Indian and Chinese places are busy every night. ...

GEORGE: Coalville is changing. People will go out for a meal now. Personally, I don't like going out for a meal. I was brought up in a different society when you ate at home or got fish and chips to take away. The only time we went out for a meal was to go round to your grandma's in your Sunday best. No, it isn't me. It's just the way you're brought up.

Although they clearly believe that BrAsian and Chinese restaurants have brought benefits to the town, Jill and George do not frequent these restaurants. George says that going to any restaurant, be it BrAsian, Chinese or English, is a practice that he has not been 'brought up to do'. In this way, his explanation for not eating in BrAsian and Chinese restaurants is classed and generational rather than racialised. The continuation of his familiar habits gives him 'a structuring medium for the continuity of life across different contexts of action' (Giddens, 1994, p. 101). Thus George's lack of interest in eating out in restaurants becomes mediated through routine practices and traditional ways of being. In this sense, BrAsian restaurants in Coalville partially signify middle-class values, which in this instance is used as a way of creating a separation, a distance, between the traditions and conventions of the working-class Whites in Coalville and the initial arrival of BrAsian and other restaurants into the region. In addition to signalling a shift away from traditional practices, the BrAsian restaurant on the main road is thought to have brought a degree of respectability to the town in that it does not allow 'riff raff', and George implies it is clean. In short, for George and Jill, BrAsian and Chinese restaurants are a sign that 'Coalville is changing': traditional practices are transforming, the area is becoming more respectable, and even more middle class, despite the fact that they do not visit these restaurants.

There is a point of comparison here to Flo's and Mark's interview, discussed at the end of Chapter 3, which serves to highlight and underline the classed and generational constitution of George's account. Mark and Flo were a retired couple in their sixties from Greenville. Mark told me that, like most people of their generation, he and his wife did not eat out in 'foreign' restaurants. Like George, Mark mobilises a generational reason to account for and explain why he does not eat in BrAsian restaurants. However, unlike George's classed reason, Mark's explanation is racialised. That is to say, Mark does eat out in restaurants but he does not frequent so-called 'foreign' ones. Class and generation are thus the key modalities that mediate George's attitudes towards all restaurants including BrAsian ones, whereas race and generation are the dominant modalities that shape Mark's views towards BrAsian restaurants in particular. In this way, George does not specifically discriminate against BrAsian restaurants on racial grounds, whereas Mark does.

Later on in our discussion Jill and George explained why they thought that The Curry Pot was attacked. In his explanation, George combines a discourse of White working-class respectability, normality and convention with reflections on White racists' sentiments and actions:

> GEORGE: I think The Curry Pot came too early. It was a culture shock. The whole idea of sitting down in a restaurant eating meals was too much. They were treated very badly. ... I know who treated them [The Curry Pot] very bad but I daren't name names. But they are still like oh, 'Paki this and that',

	until they are in hospital or they go to the doctors, because they all have Asian doctors.
JILL:	They have so much hatred. They are always making racist jokes.

In accounting for the racism of others, George draws on his classed experiences of BrAsian restaurants, to explain how such restaurants are seen as a 'culture shock' and an affront to White working-class notions of normality. However, neither Jill nor George identify with what they perceive to be some White people's hatred of BrAsians. Their thoughts also highlight that these White racists have BrAsian doctors, an image that reinforces the idea that class distinctions separate and mark off working-class Whites from middle-class BrAsians in Coalville. BrAsians are portrayed as middle class and respectable in contrast to the non-respectable White working-class racists.

Notwithstanding some Whites' racist attitudes towards local BrAsian restaurants, many young White adults are frequent users of the BrAsian and Chinese restaurants and takeaways (the latter are not mentioned by Jill and George). In this regard, these young people represent White working-class people's changing classed and racialised attitudes. For illustration, consider the words of Julie, one of the young White women that I lived with during my stay in Coalville. She explains that for her the presence of BrAsian-owned shops and food outlets is an inevitable part of Coalville's townscape:

> It's a stereotype image, you expect that there will be an Asian shop. I think that you expect it. It's a typical thing that they do, that sounds awful really, don't it? There are balti houses in Coalville and three to four takeaways. ... So the Asians in this area ... are doing that role. They are doing the shop thing and the takeaway thing.

Unlike Jill and George, Julie does not think that BrAsian-owned restaurants are simply a sign that 'Coalville is changing'. Rather, she 'expects' there to be BrAsian-owned restaurants, takeaways and shops because 'it's a typical thing that they do'. This illustrates the ways in which BrAsian food outlets and shops have become routine, banal and unremarkable features of Coalville's landscape for young White adults.

Julie's explanation for BrAsians' presence in Coalville highlights a recurring contradiction and anomaly within Whites' moderately racialised discourses. She reflects on the way in which her association of BrAsians with shops, takeaways and restaurants is a 'stereotype' image that sounds 'awful'. This illustrates her views on the menial nature of such work and her knowledge that these are not the only jobs that BrAsian people do in Leicestershire. However, this self-reflexivity does not completely shift and undermine the reality that her acceptance of BrAsians in Coalville rests in part on an image of BrAsians that screens out the complexity of BrAsians' diverse class locations and lifestyles in Leicestershire.

In this regard, Julie draws on a common stereotype of BrAsian-ness reproduced by my White middle-class co-conversationalists from Greenville, explored in Chapter 2, and within literature and website material produced by Leicester Promotions, examined in Chapter 3. As I have argued, one effect of the association of BrAsians with working in restaurants and shops is to position BrAsians in a position of service to the White majority culture. I have also suggested that this relationship of service parallels to some extent the power inequalities that existed between the coloniser and those colonised, a point discussed in Chapter 2. From this perspective, Julie's evocation of this imagery illustrates one of the ways in which White people may be self-reflexive about their use of racialised stereotypes, while being unable sometimes to escape the insidious nature of racial and cultural stereotypes about Others. The complexity of this process is significant for what it reveals about the articulation of discourses of coloniality in the present. That is to say, Julie's account shows how it becomes difficult for White people to step outside of the discourses of coloniality that structure their lived experience even when it is their intention not to reproduce racialised stereotypes.

During my stay with Julie and her sister, we ate many meals from BrAsian and Chinese takeaways in the area. A curry ordered at home from a balti house in Coalville or a Chinese meal ordered from a takeaway was a must after Saturday or Friday nights drinking in the pubs and clubs in the area. In this respect, we were like many 20- to 30-year-olds in the town. These young White adults' fracturing of other White people's conventional classed practices and racialised attitudes signposts the processes at work in my White co-conversationalists' critical reflections on racism. I turn now to an examination of these moments of critical reflection, which will also bring to the fore the beliefs that constitute conventional views on racism in the area.

Young White adults' critical questioning of others' racist attitudes

Marilyn Strathern (1992) argues that the generational difference between parents and children provides an analogy through which to think about the place of tradition and innovation in English social life. Strathern (1992, pp. 14–15) explains that parents are understood to produce children who are a product of their mutual relationship. The shared relationship between parents comes to signify 'convention' or tradition. Parents implement convention by the passing on of their traditional values through the socialisation of their children (Strathern, 1992, p. 19). Children, in turn, are new individuals who will form separate identities from those of their parents and so have the potential to formulate reflexively innovative and diverse perspectives. Strathern writes:

> Convention, like tradition, seems to be antecedent, to come from the past, while choice, like invention, seems to lie in the future. In kinship idiom, children are future to the parents' past. Increased variation and differentiation invariably lie ahead, a fragmented future as compared with the communal past. ... Time increases complexity; complexity in turn implies a multiplicity and plurality of viewpoints.
>
> (1992, p. 21)

Strathern's analogy of the relationship between parents and children, past convention and future innovation, partly captures the processes at work in young White adults' critical reflections on their relatives' racist beliefs and attitudes. That is, some young White adults come to challenge what they consider to be the racist attitudes of some older members, usually male, of their nuclear and extended family. These young White people's critical reflections on their relatives' racist beliefs enable the potential formation of innovative attitudes on race and reveal the conditions under which this creative space opens up. In this way, these young White adults' critical reflections illuminate the points at which the discourse of coloniality inherited from the parental generation begins to fracture and break down.

My study also shows that in some instances young White people's critical reflections on racism are influenced and shaped by what they perceive to be the more accepting racialised attitudes of a significant relative, for example, the moderate attitudes of a mother. In stark contrast, my co-conversationalists also think that many other young White adults, of both genders, uncritically reproduce their parents' conventional and formulaic racist attitudes. We will now see some of these processes at work in Jim's critical reflections on the racist attitudes of others.

Jim

Jim, whose words I have drawn on briefly above, was 26 years old when we met. He had lived in Coalville all his life apart from his time away at university. I met him several times during my stay in the area; we either arranged to meet up to go out for a drink in the pubs in the town or we simply bumped into each other in Coalville's town centre. At the time we met Jim had been unemployed for about two years, after completing a degree in mechanical engineering at Staffordshire University (situated approximately 40 miles north west of Coalville in the town of Stoke-on-Trent). He was an active member of the local Labour Party and lived with his parents. His mother was a dinner lady in a local comprehensive school and his father worked in one of the town's brickyards. Jim commented on what he considered to be the racist views of his uncles when his grandmother died and BrAsians moved into her house:

> My Gran died and she had a council house and some coloureds [BrAsians] moved in afterwards and my uncle was heartbroken. Mind you, he was drunk at the time and, you know, I thought I'm not like that, both my uncles were. ... I mean the two of them, and now they have a problem and I've never understood it. I think it was the time they were brought up like.

Jim believes that maybe it was the time in which his uncles 'had been brought up' that gave them their racist attitudes. Jim's uncles' generation had experienced dramatic socio-economic transformations in their lives with the loss of the region's mining industry and a shift in the collective sense of identity and belonging associated with that industry and tradition. For Jim's uncles, the presence of BrAsians in the actual home in which they were 'brought up' signifies an intolerable and unacceptable transformation. It is precisely this resentment of, and backlash against, BrAsians that Jim sets out to challenge.

Jim explains how his experience of moving between the ethnically diverse townscape of Stoke-on-Trent and the predominantly White townscape of Coalville has pushed him to reflect on his uncles' and other White people's internalisation of racist stereotypes and attitudes:

> But my uncles are like a lot of people. There's a problem with it [racism], let's put it that way. ... It's like if you open up the *Leicestershire Recorder* [a pseudonym for a local newspaper], someone gets raped and you get a picture of a big Black fella. You are looking at a Black fella and that's the only type of image you get. And then

when you go out round here it becomes noticeable and they fall into the trap. It frightens people half to death that there is some Big Black fella and ... because they are Black people notice it even more because they do stand out from a mass of White faces. I notice it too and you know I hope it's not me, it's not something there [he hopes that he is not racist], because as I say I think it is that Black fellas stand out here. I mean I never noticed it when I was in Stoke-on-Trent. ... A lot of it is to do with the way that people don't question – if there is one thing that I try to persuade people to do and that is question.

The impetus for Jim's explanation and critical reflections on the production and maintenance of racism in Coalville partly draws on his experience of seeing and interpreting the minority of Black men in the 'mass of White faces' through the lens of negative media accounts of Black men. From this point of view, Jim perceives a distinction between White people and Black people within the town of Coalville. Black people become associated and identified with negative media stereotypes and thus become frightening Others, in a way that White people do not. Jim believes that his different experience of not seeing Black people negatively in the more racially diverse townscape of Stoke-on-Trent has pushed him to question and explain his own and other White townspeople's racist emotions and attitudes in the predominantly White townscape of Coalville. In this way, Jim points to the ways in which the experience of feeling racist sentiments and emotions can itself become a factor that enables White people to critically question the conditions that shape, form and maintain others' racist attitudes.

Importantly for my focus on the reproduction of discourses of coloniality and challenges to it, Jim highlights the difficult task that these young White adults experience in resisting and rejecting racialised stereotypes, reactions and emotions that are infused in the structures and processes of everyday life. My argument is that these racialised stereotypes and emotions resonate with colonial discourses that support a rigidly dualistic and hierarchical worldview of Western cultural superiority that defines the White Western self through the construction of non-White Western Others. Thus, sharing some parallels to Julie's stereotypical explanation for the presence of BrAsians in the town, Jim draws on his own feelings about the Otherness of Blacks to question his own and other Whites' attitudes toward Black men. In this way, the actual process of questioning racist attitudes reveals the totalising aspects of discourses of coloniality that assert the fundamental cultural distinction of Whites in relation to those who are classified as not White. Clearly, even reflexively critical White individuals do not always manage to completely escape the racialised stereotypes and emotions that they challenge and confront.

Vicki

Vicki's views on her father's racism provide a different angle on the conditions in which racism can be both challenged and also reproduced within the context of the nuclear and extended family. I met Vicki in a youth club on a council estate on the outskirts of Coalville. She was taking a GCSE class in computing, in a room set aside in the club for such training.[6] When I met her, Vicki was 19 years old and had a two-year-old daughter, who played in the club's crèche while her mother studied. Vicki was a single parent and explained that she wanted to get qualifications in order to get a good job and so break her dependency on welfare payments. Her parents lived not far from her in Coalville. Her father was a builder's labourer and her mother a nursery nurse in a Leicester crèche. Vicki explained the different views of her parents towards BrAsians as follows:

> People are very small-minded and racist here. I mean you should hear my dad – he makes comments and jokes all the time. He thinks that they [BrAsians] come over here and take our benefits [welfare], you know they come just to use the system. But my mum, she's not racist, she works in Leicester in a crèche and she works with a lot of Asian women ... and Asian kids. My mum has to keep her work to herself though because my dad will just make jokes about it.

Like Jim's perception of his White uncles' racist attitudes, Vicki thinks her White father's attitudes on BrAsians are widely held opinions. Vicki's father's claim that BrAsians 'come over here to take our benefits ... to use the system', was a recurring stereotype held by working-class Whites that I encountered. It is the widespread reproduction of this discourse of White backlash to multiculturalism that makes it worth exploring in some detail here.

In a similar vein to Vicki's father, a middle-aged White man I met in a local pub in Coalville told me: 'I think that it will get bad in the future if they keep letting them into the country, what with them taking our jobs and living off the state.' This man adds to Vicki's father's belief that BrAsians are illegitimately dependent on the English taxpayer by arguing that new immigrants who do earn a legitimate living are 'taking our jobs'. The recurrence of these stereotypes about BrAsians and new immigrants to England reflects the commonsense classification of BrAsians (and indeed other established minorities) as 'immigrants', regardless of how many generations of their settlement in England have passed. Once more, this positioning of BrAsians' origins outside of England rests on the forgetting of their colonial and postcolonial relationships with Englishness and Britishness that intimately relates them to the nation, a process that I have explored in detail in Chapters 2 and 3. In addition, as also discussed in Chapters 2 and 3, the construction of BrAsians as immigrants facilitates the contemporary articulation of colonial notions of cultural difference that positions BrAsians as fundamentally Other to a racially unmarked White English self.

As we have seen, at the time of my fieldwork in Coalville unemployment was less than the national average, although available work was often poorly paid. Some Whites felt that their hard-earned wages were unfairly given by the state to immigrants and BrAsians who, unlike themselves, were said to come from outside of England and were thought not to pay taxes and hence not earned the right to claim welfare. As one young White woman told me: 'I work hard for a living ... people's taxes are going sky high because of immigrants.' This discourse illustrates how government policies and media representations that demonise economic immigrants to England and other parts of Britain encourage people to make links between immigrants, ethnic minorities, in this case BrAsians, macroeconomics and personal security (see Gabriel, 1998, pp. 107, 127 for an analysis of the racism implicit in the apparently deracialised politics of immigration in Britain).

In addition, I believe that this local White discourse of racialised resentment and unfairness also reveals something about White working-class notions of 'respectability', 'responsibility' and 'entitlement' (see also Rhodes, 2011; Watt, 2006). So-called problem families that were White but were thought to lack respectability, were believed by some of my co-conversationalists to have replaced miners and their families on the large council estates in the region. These White Others were also often thought to live illegitimately on social welfare payments. For example, I was often told how single young women purposefully get pregnant to gain a council-owned house or flat (apartment) and an address from which to claim welfare payments for themselves and their children. In addition, drug users, the unemployed or the so-called unemployable were thought to claim welfare payments rather than seeking employment. There were even rumours that incest and domestic violence was rife among such 'problem families'. Thus illegitimately claiming social payments was stigmatised by its association with particular categories of White classed Others – namely, the non-respectable and so-called 'rough' working class (see Chapter 1 for discussion of White working-class notions of respectability). The point here is that by accusing BrAsians and immigrants of illegitimately claiming welfare payments, White working-class people in Coalville were distancing themselves not only from immigrants and BrAsians but also the stigma and lack of social worth and value associated with those White classed Others thought to be illegitimately claiming welfare. These classed and racialised discourses of respectability highlight the importance of work to the formation of notions of respectability (see also Rhodes, 2011). In other words, working for a living to support and provide for oneself and one's family was considered by many to be necessary for respectability.

To this extent, my analysis concurs with that of scholars who contend that the White working classes in Britain articulate a discourse of White backlash to multiculturalism motivated by a feeling that ethnic minorities and immigrants unfairly benefit from official state policies, as set out earlier. My account confirms Bonnett's (2000) and other social commentators' claims that working-class Whites' perception of the extension of the welfare state to immigrants and ethnic minorities is expressed in a discourse of socio-economic unfairness. But to end the analysis here would result in blindness to the complexities of White working-class racisms and challenges to it. In other words, these accounts of working-class racism are stereotypical and superficial. We should be alert to the ways in which conventional popular racist beliefs are contested, criticised and rejected by reflexive working-class White people, and also the intergenerational inflection of this process.

Returning to Vicki's account, it is clear that she challenges the idea that all BrAsians illegitimately claim welfare benefits by stating that this belief is 'racist'. Vicki continued to explain and account for her White mother's and father's different attitudes on race and the ways in which her mother's more accepting racialised views had conditioned, formed and shaped her own:

> My mum finds it hard with my dad because these people are her friends, she knows lots of them and so it is different for her. Also my mum is from London and so I think that she is used to it. Whereas my dad is from round here. He has lived in Coalville all of his life and he's very small minded. He's 53 now and he'll probably die that way. Nothing will change him because he doesn't want to change. He sees them as alien and so different and he can't see that there is anything wrong with his views.

But my mum she reads about their religion and everything. She tells me about them, that Indians are very family orientated and that they look after their old people because they all live together. Not like us. Also she tells me about their arranged marriages and they seem to work; they stick with them. Whereas we just run off at the first sign of trouble. I think that they have their family's support in a way that we don't. I mean my dad will fall out with his brothers, and then won't talk to them for ages. I mean he will bear a real grudge. I don't think that would ever happen in an Asian family.

Like Jim's view of his uncles, Vicki thinks that her father is not interested in changing his racist views because they adequately reflect the way the world is. Vicki explains that when one gets older it becomes harder to change, question and challenge one's racist beliefs and habits – they become ingrained, fixed, non-negotiable and static. In contrast, Vicki believes that her mother's upbringing in London means that she does not see BrAsians as a disruption to her notion of normality, convention and sense of 'ontological security' (Giddens, 1994, p. 101). Vicki's explanation for her mother's racialised attitudes rests partly on the idea that familiarity and relationships across the colour-lines reduces racial hostility and enhances understanding. But it is well documented that living close to minorities and recent immigrants can promote rather than reduce racism. However, Ellis Cashmore (1987, p. 27) makes the observation in his study of the logic of White working-class racism in the West Midlands that: 'personal contact ... may be a necessary condition in the breaking down of racist barriers, although it is not in itself a sufficient condition. But when it combines with some personal grasp of the practical problems that face ethnic minorities, then a certain sympathy can result.' In a similar vein, Vicki's explanation for her mother's racialised attitudes rests not only on her upbringing in London but also her mother's relationships with BrAsians at work and her concern to learn about BrAsian people's cultures.

Following her mother, Vicki produces a somewhat stereotypical account of BrAsians' culture grounded on bounded and discrete notions of BrAsians' supposed cultural differences from Whites. In so doing, Vicki inadvertently essentialises cultural differences between Whites and BrAsians in the construction of an 'us' and 'them' binary opposition (Said, 1978, p. 227). Vicki therefore thinks in the same framework as other Whites that she might consider racist. As we have seen in my analysis of White racialised discourses in Greenville in Chapters 2 and 3, another manifestation of this discourse is for the culture of the

White self and BrAsian Other to be conceived as 'discrete' and 'bounded spaces' (Frankenberg, 1993a, p. 192). BrAsians are thus depicted as outsiders to English and White Western culture and so their ways of being are thought to be distinct from those of the White English majority.

However, Vicki considers herself not to be racist precisely because she has learnt from her mother to perceive such cultural differences – that is, arranged marriages and so on – to be positive. Even so, as also explored in some detail in Chapters 2 and 3, the valorisation of BrAsians' perceived cultural differences to Whites works to reaffirm the notion that fundamental differences separate Whites from BrAsians. Vicki thus illustrates the ways in which colonially rooted and essentialist representations of BrAsians' supposed cultural differences to the White majority can be incorporated into discourses that set out to challenge others' racist attitudes. This discourse highlights once more the complex and difficult task that individuals face in avoiding and deconstructing the language and logic that constitutes discourses of coloniality.

Later on in our discussion, Vicki pointed to the ways in which gender is a factor in shaping the fragmented intergenerational manifestation of racist and non-racist sentiments within her family:

> I'm not racist at all though; I'm like my mum. My brother Gary is like my dad, but he knows if my mum hears him he'll get a mouthful. But my dad doesn't care what my mum thinks, whereas Gary does, he listens to my mum and so doesn't bad-mouth them in front of her. My sister is like me and my mum. But my dad's generation and my granddad's is really bad, you can't change them 'cause they know no better. I think my generation is better and Jade's [Vicki's two-year-old daughter] hopefully will be even better, it's just time. But my boyfriend and his mates were bad. He wants to get back with me but there is no way I'd have him back. I reckon that if Jade got to know him then she'd be racist but I won't let that happen. Jade will stay with me and I won't teach her to be like that.

Vicki understands racist attitudes to be held specifically by the White male members of her family. Vicki's brother's attitudes are shaped, conditioned and influenced by his father's racism, which in turn mirrors her grandfather's and ex-boyfriend's beliefs. In contrast, Vicki and her sister identify with their mother and so have inherited their White mother's critical attitudes on racism. Vicki explained to me that, although her father was in no way physically violent, he was authoritarian in his relationships with his wife and children. Also Vicki left her boyfriend after he physically beat her. Vicki's experience of male dominance and violence in her personal relationships undoubtedly shapes and affects her perception that those men's attitudes on race are aggressive and immoral.

Vicki also thinks that her inheritance of the sensibility necessary to cultivate anti-racist attitudes enables her to teach, socialise and inform her daughter to reject her father's, and her grandfather's, racist attitudes. There is a danger, however. Parental influences have the potential to eclipse gendered patterns of identification and affiliation. Thus Vicki thinks that if Jade's father were to bring her up, she might become taught, shaped and socialised by him to hold racist attitudes.

It is clear from Jim's and Vicki's accounts that racism is not always reproduced generationally nor internalised without deliberation. Jim's critical questioning of his own and others' racist attitudes is partly shaped by his experience of moving between the ethnically diverse townscape of Stoke-on-Trent and the predominantly White townscape of Coalville. Unlike her brother's identification with her father's conventional racist attitudes, Vicki's acceptance of BrAsians becomes manifest through her gendered identification with her White mother's more critical attitudes on racism.

Vicki's questioning of her father's racism reveals the more fragmented intergenerational lines of racialised thinking and sense-making of young White people. Vicki thinks that the reproduction of such conventional racist attitudes within her family is intertwined with male patterns of identification and affiliation. Her insights raise interesting questions for future study on the gendered nature of racist and anti-racist sentiments in White working-class areas.

Paradoxically, however, this questioning of White racism includes and incorporates the reproduction of notions of White cultural difference that resonate with colonial discourses of race and difference. It is Jim's reflections on his experience of seeing Black men as the frightening Other that enables him to challenge others' racist views. Moreover, Vicki's perception that BrAsian culture is essentially different from White culture becomes incorporated into her critical reflections on the racism of others. In this sense, neither Jim nor Vicki can escape or avoid interpreting the world 'through the rigidly binominal opposition of "ours" and "theirs"' (Said, 1978, p. 227). My analysis illuminates the totalising aspects of discourse of coloniality that demarcates the White Western self from racialised Others, but also the ways in which this worldview is questioned and challenged.

Julie

I return now to Julie, one of the young White women with whom I lived during my stay in the area. She gives a different perspective on the ways in which one's family relationships have the potential to open up a creative space that provides the conditions for racialised acceptance. It is not that Julie considers her nuclear and extended family members to be racist. Rather, her White father's Czech identity becomes the impetus and driving force behind her questioning of a White friend's racist attitudes. One Friday evening, while getting ready to go out socialising in the town, Julie explained to me her attitude towards her father's Czech identity:

> It's slightly different for me because my dad is Czechoslovakian. He's not Black but he's still a minority group. ... When my dad came they wanted cheap labour and so the foreigners came. ... I want to stress to people that my dad was invited over to this country. He worked hard labour for five years and he didn't come here with his hand out and get something for nothing. He's worked hard and now everything he's done, he's done on his own back. He hasn't fed off the state.

Julie's defence of her father's minority status and immigration to England demonstrates her knowledge of the conventional belief in the area that immigrants to Leicestershire either unfairly take local jobs, or do not work and so illegitimately feed 'off the state' and thus are unfairly supported by White labour. In this sense, Julie's emphasis on her father's 'hard work' over the years, and his 'invitation' into the country to work, makes him 'respectable' with regard to the value placed on work and entitlement to welfare. Later on in our discussion Julie revealed the ways in which her father's immigrant status becomes the prism through which she reflects on BrAsian settlers' experiences of migration and economic exploitation in England:

> It's like with my dad, Asians did the shitty jobs and paid crap wages for hard labour. ... They had nothing, they weren't given proper houses. They lived like paupers in a relatively rich society. ... It was our need and they filled it and they got the raw end of the deal basically.

Julie's identification with her father's experience of economic exploitation as part of the migration process to England is central to the formation of her anti-racist sentiments. On the one hand, Julie's identification and association of her Czech father's immigration to England with the experiences of BrAsians conflates these two different trajectories of migration. That is to say, BrAsians' migration to England was a legacy of the British Empire, in a way that migration to Britain from other parts of Europe was not. In this regard, Julie's discussion of BrAsians is entwined with amnesia of their colonial past and their historical right to residence and to claim belonging to England and other parts of Britain. But yet, on the other hand, thinking across these trajectories of immigration pushes Julie to reflect on White people's conventional attitudes to immigration, immigrants and minorities. In other words, thinking of her father's experience of immigration to England enables Julie to deconstruct the commonsense idea that BrAsians are unfair claimants of social welfare.

During another stay with Julie, about a year after I had left Coalville, she repeated her views on her father's minority status and relationship to England by using his Czech identity as a legitimisation for her right to speak with authority about BrAsians who live in Coalville. Julie, her new lodger Nick, and myself were sitting in Julie's living room. Nick was White, 24 years old and worked as a mechanic in a nearby garage. Julie explained to Nick my research, and asked him, on my behalf, what he thought about BrAsians who live in Coalville. Nick commented that he thought 'they should go back to their own fucking country', and that he never went into the 'dirty Paki shops' in the town because they 'charge extra'. Julie then asked Nick if he knew that her dad was 'Czechoslovakian'. He said he didn't. She explained to Nick that the BrAsians living in the town were like her dad. They had worked hard and come to this country with nothing. They deserved respect and not thoughtless racist abuse. Nick remained quiet.

Nick's and Julie's contrasting attitudes on BrAsians highlight, once more, the fragmented intergenerational and gendered reproduction of conventional racist and anti-racist attitudes in this area. Like Vicki's father, Nick uses anti-immigration discourse – that BrAsians should return to their own country because they are fraudsters who live dishonestly off the honest White public. Moreover, Nick's belief that BrAsian shopkeepers are dishonest resonates with views expressed by some middle-class Whites in Greenville, explored in Chapter 2. Julie is able to challenge Nick's racist comments by claiming affinity to BrAsians on the grounds of her father's shared minority status and experience of economic hardship and exploitation in England.

In contrast to Nick's conventional racist attitudes, Julie's partner, Sam, who was 30 years old, drew on his knowledge of Julie's father's immigrant status to question the racist attitudes of his work colleagues. Sam's job involved mending and maintaining the railway in Leicestershire. He told me that 'old boys' from his work thought that there are a lot of 'Pakis' in Leicester who should be 'sent back home' (from this I assume that all of Sam's work colleagues are White; at least, he did not say otherwise). He explained: 'I thought afterwards if that is what were to happen then Julie's dad should go back home, and so should Julie and then what about me? My granddad's Irish. Where do you stop?' In this instance, Sam's relationship with Julie has provided him with the know-how to reflect affectively on the conventional racist attitudes of his work colleagues. He is aware that if one's parentage and ancestry becomes a factor for the right to claim residence in England, then Julie's and even his own claims to Englishness are contested. In this way, Sam exposes and deconstructs some of the logic that underpins the immigrant imaginary, explored in detail in Chapter 2. If BrAsians' parentage and ancestry place them outside of England into another country of 'origin', so too Julie's and Sam's own claims to Englishness are open to question.

Conclusions: White working- and middle-class backlash against multiculturalism and the legacies of Empire

Before moving on to the next chapter, I want to look at some of the comparisons and dwell on some of the complexities between my work on the constitution of White classed and racialised discourses in Coalville and Greenville. I begin by thinking across these differing classed locales to consider the appropriateness of identifying White backlash discourses exclusively with the White working classes. Looking back to Chapter 3 of this book, it is clear that some White middle-class residents of Greenville felt that BrAsians that live in the city gained advantages from the local state at the expense of the White majority. For example, Madge, a retired White resident of Greenville, suggested that Black and BrAsian residents who live in Leicester receive 'a little bit of priority treatment' from the City Council. In addition, sharing parallels with expressions of conventional racism in Coalville, some White residents of Greenville suggested to me that immigration is out of control, a point also discussed in Chapter 3. Thus, as in Coalville, some of my White middle-class co-conversationalists from Greenville depicted BrAsians as immigrants and cultural outsiders to England. My argument is that central to this discourse is White amnesia of BrAsians' relationships to Englishness formed through centuries of Empire. That is, the simple construction of BrAsians as immigrants whose origins lie outside of England, and the West, rests upon the screening out of complex historical relationships forged between Empire and the cultural, political and economic constitution of Englishness and Britishness. In other words, the web of relations that connect contemporary England to the colonial past including the exploitation of land, people and commodities vital for the formation of Englishness are negated in the depiction of BrAsians as immigrants and outsiders to England. From this perspective, it is possible to conclude that White amnesia of the colonial past is intrinsic to White working- and middle-class backlash discourses against multiculturalism.

Notwithstanding these resonances within and across White working- and middle-class discourses of backlash, White middle-class and working-class research participants expressed and interpreted their perceptions of BrAsians through contrasting notions of classed respectability. I suggest that the mobilisation of these differing frameworks of respectability illustrates how ideas and experiences of place inform the ways in which White people come to think about BrAsians who live in 'their' neighbourhood. From this point of view, White research participants from Greenville did not put the same emphasis as did residents from Coalville on entitlement to state welfare and employment. Rather, as set out in detail in Chapters 2 and 3, the dominant framework of classed respectability mobilised by White residents from Greenville referred to proper and appropriate ways of behaving needed to fit into the village environment and its community. In other words, it was the rhythms and patterns of village life that BrAsian residents in Greenville were thought not to fit into. By contrast, research participants from Coalville live in a place that has been shaped and informed by the industry of coalmining and the way of life that accompanied that industry. It is from this perspective that some White residents of this area value the importance of work and working for a living, which is diametrically opposed to a culture of dependency on the welfare state. It is precisely this ethic and ethos that informs White working-class discourses of respectability and also conventional racism. From this point of view, BrAsians are believed to claim welfare payments illegitimately and/or are thought to 'take our jobs'.

It is also worth thinking through the contrasting language and idioms that White working- and middle-class residents used to express their views on BrAsians. In Coalville I sometimes heard the abusive term 'Paki' articulated either as a way to refer directly to BrAsians (for example, Nick's use of this term) or as a way to draw attention to others' use of the term (see George's, Jill's and Sam's accounts). This expression is understood to be a racist slur within White middle-class circles. It is therefore not surprising to me that this idiom was not used by any of my research participants from Greenville. However, it seems to me that it is the sometimes more direct expression of racist language by Whites from Coalville that facilitates the conditions for some to question the racist attitudes of others. Such language and the logic of racism it connotes is considered hateful by George and Jill, and misguided by Sam.

In advancing this argument I do not mean to suggest that there was no evidence of blatant and offensive racist language and actions within the White middle-class milieu of Greenville. Indeed, I was told by a few of my co-conversationalists that someone had painted, some years ago, 'Fuck Off Wogs' on the walls of the BrAsian shop in the village. This attack was considered to be an exception to the norm, and so I assume that this is why it was only mentioned to me by a few research participants. Moreover, I was also told that a committee from the Anglican Church was organised to white-wash (note the irony here) over the graffiti on the shop walls. Such action was, of course, the decent thing to do. Nonetheless, the white-washed shop was made to appear from the outside as a respectable village shop. Racist slogans, which are considered to be out of place in a village environment, were made invisible. The significance here is that blatant acts of racism, like the very presence of BrAsians themselves, offend the quiet and peaceful community spirit of Greenville.

This example serves to highlight the ways in which some Greenville residents are actively making their suburban place into a traditional English village. By contrast to residents from Greenville who have the economic and cultural capital to maintain and control the village identity of their place, the coalmining industry that was once the centrepiece of Coalville's socio-economic infrastructure has been lost forever, as part of the widespread de-industrialisation of Western economies and societies. While my White co-conversationalists from Coalville are well aware that their mining past cannot be replicated in the present, this does not mean that the area's mining past is forgotten; rather it forms a vital component in the production of a new and innovative future. In this chapter, I have drawn on the metaphors of convention (the past) and innovation (the future) to analyse the processes involved in the reproduction and transformation of conventional attitudes on race across generations. I have argued that it is precisely the loss of the area's mining past that has opened up a space for young White adults to be critically reflective on the racism of others.

These young Whites' questioning of the formulaic and conventional racist attitudes of the members of their nuclear and extended families, and friends and acquaintances, highlights the diversity of factors and conditions that push some young White adults to become reflexive actors on racism. My analysis has shown that although some Whites question racism they do not always escape the insidious nature of racial stereotypes that are a hangover from the colonial past that infuses the fabric of their everyday lives. The complexity of this process illustrates some of the difficulties that White individuals experience in escaping and avoiding the language, logic and worldview of coloniality that infiltrates the present. From this point of view, even White discourses that set out to challenge the racism of others end up reproducing the White self through the discursive production of racialised Others. Thus, the experience of seeing Black people in a crowd of White faces as the frightening Other (Jim); the automatic association of BrAsians with shops and takeaways (Julie); and the belief that all BrAsians have arranged marriages that work better that White relationships (Vicki) are experiences and beliefs that constitute critical discourses on racism. It is perhaps not surprising that the actual appropriation and experience of racial stereotypes, emotions, sentiments, feelings and attitudes can itself provide the conditions that stimulate White individuals into reflecting on their own and others' racism. It is the conditions in which working-class Whites come to confront the racist structures that shape their lives and yet at the same time retain the ability to articulate and embrace stereotypical racialised sentiments that I shall examine in further detail in the next chapter, which draws on my study of neighbourhood-based political activism in the multicultural area of Leicester that I call 'Streetville'.

For the sisters

The sisters with whom I lived in Coalville made my time in the area one of the happiest of my life. In April 1998, only three months after I left the area, one of the sisters tragically died. I dedicate this chapter to both sisters and especially to the memory of my dear friend.

5
Neighbourhood Activism and the Ambiguities of Anti-Racism in the City

This chapter continues the book's exploration of the conditions in which White discourses of coloniality may, under certain conditions, be confronted. It continues from Chapter 4's analysis of the specific contexts and situations in which White working-class discourses of backlash to multiculturalism are reproduced but yet also confronted, questioned and criticised. The chapter draws on fieldwork that was conducted from May 2002 to September 2003 within a Residents' Association (hereafter 'RA') based in the inner city area of Leicester that I call 'Streetville'.

The White working-class residents that feature in this chapter are all members of the RA. The RA formed part of a Forum that consisted of a network of Black, BrAsian and multiethnic community organisations that worked in consultation with state and private organisations to secure funding and resources for the neighbourhood. While the Forum worked with the local City Council and other service providers, its members positioned themselves as defenders of local people's rights. In this regard, the Forum members challenged local strategies of governance that they considered to be detrimental to the neighbourhood. My exploration of the structure and organisation of this neighbourhood network will cumulate in a presentation of how the members of the Forum and the RA came to challenge local structures of governance on the grounds of institutional racism. My specific focus will be on how local activists mobilised White working-class members of the RA to work with the Forum in an application for judicial review, at the Royal Courts of Justice in London, against the Electoral Commission.[1] The residents' case centred on the Electoral Commission's failure to uphold the duties placed upon public authorities to eliminate racial discrimination in accordance with the Race Relations Amendment Act, 2000. While the Electoral Commission is a body that is independent of government and responsible for managing national and local elections, in this case it was acting on the City Council's recommendations for the creation of new electoral wards in the neighbourhood.[2] From the Forum and RA members' point of view the Electoral Commission's action was attributed to the local City Council.

In this chapter I shall examine the important role that White working-class residents played in this anti-racist collective action. My argument is that crucial to the mobilisation of White working-class support for this action was the negotiation by local activists, and other residents, of their stereotypes about BrAsians who lived in the neighbourhood. Moreover, my account explores how some White working-class residents were Othering BrAsians in the very process of anti-racist action.

Sharing parallels with the 'conventional' racist attitudes and backlash to multiculturalism articulated by some Whites in Coalville, some of the White working-class residents who participated in this collective action thought that BrAsian residents in the neighbourhood, especially Muslims, were unfair beneficiaries of local state support. These residents believed that BrAsians received unfair access to neighbourhood resources such as community centres.[3] Some White working-class residents came to feel that their Whiteness was a symbol of their disadvantage in terms of their supposed exclusion from access to material, social and cultural services. In making these claims, White residents constructed a narrative grounded on what they thought they saw and observed in the course of their daily lives.

Advancing this book's emphasis on the articulation of discourses of coloniality, my argument is that White working-class perceptions of BrAsians resonate with colonial discourses of White superiority that position those colonised as 'irreducibly Other' from the standpoint of the racially unmarked White Western self (Frankenberg, 1993a, p. 17). Once more, this discourse of White cultural superiority and Otherness is driven by the screening out and forgetting of the histories of Empire that bind BrAsians to the cityscape, the nation and the West.

I focus in this chapter on the ways in which local activists negotiated and confronted these everyday constructions of BrAsians as Other to gain White working-class residents' support and inclusion in anti-racist collective action. In so doing, they drew on the language of community to address to the residents' concerns in universal terms across class, age and gender identities. White working-class residents identified with and supported the Forum's emphasis on the empowerment of residents across ethnic and class locations, including themselves, and it was on these grounds that they participated in the collective action. However, the actual inclusion of Whites in this anti-racist collective action was not a straightforward process signalling White working-class people's attempts to escape discourses of coloniality, power, privilege and dominance. Rather, some White individuals became participants and key players in this anti-racist collective action without holding and supporting anti-racist values themselves. Nonetheless, the inclusion of working-class White residents in this action was vital for its success.

My work with the RA and the Forum not only develops the book's examination of the articulation and confrontations to discourses of coloniality, it also moves the book into a different locale and moment in time. The focus shifts spatially and temporally away from semi-rural areas of Leicestershire to the city, and from fieldwork carried out in 1997–8 to fieldwork conducted in 2002–3. This movement across time and place has opened up an ethnographic avenue for me to show that the common assumption that Whites and BrAsians live racially segregated lives are overly simplistic. In particular, this chapter undermines White stereotypical images of the Streetville area of Leicester, discussed in Chapter 3, which suggest that this neighbourhood is a 'ghetto' where Whites have simply been 'taken over' by BrAsians, Blacks and immigrants.

Introducing Streetville: The site of collective action

Historically, Streetville is the area of Leicester that has been the home of settlers to the city. Over half the population of Streetville is Muslim, and Leicester's main Mosque is located there. The Office for National Statistics (2005) neighbourhood statistics states that of the 11,180 people living in the largest ward in Streetville, 3349 were 'White: British'. The largest populations in the area were BrAsian who identified as follows: 'Asian or Asian British', 5290; 'Asian: British Indian', 3807; 'Asian British Pakistani' 259; 'Asian British Bangladeshi', 559. There were 1483 'Black or Black British' people. With regard to religion, the majority of people from this ward identified as Muslim (4954), 2840 people self-identified that they were Christian, 785 identified as Hindu, and 1321 said that they had no religion.

According to the Office of National Statistics (2005) data on employment, 1969 people from the largest electoral ward in Streetville were 'unemployed' or constitute the 'lowest grade workers' and 'on state benefit' (welfare payment). In addition, 2781 people, that is, the majority of working people who lived in this ward, were categorised as 'semi-skilled and unskilled manual workers, while 854 people were identified as holding jobs that could be classified as 'higher and intermediate managerial'.

Like many ethnically diverse and relatively poor inner city areas in Britain, Streetville has a history of state intervention aimed at the socio-economic 'regeneration' of the area. In the 1970s it was labelled by the City Council as an inner city 'priority zone'. Since 1978 the Leicester City Council has implemented an Inner Area Programme (IAP) the objective of which was to 'improve the lives of those living in the inner city' (Leicester City Council, 1991b). In the 1990s, Streetville received funding from the central government's City Challenge scheme and the Single Regeneration Budget (SRB). Both grants were for the economic and social development of inner city areas. These funding initiatives and schemes have led to the encouragement and establishment of community-based organisations in the area. When I conducted fieldwork in Streetville, the area was home to a diversity of voluntary organisations aimed at supporting a variety of ethnic and religious communities that lived in the area. Each organisation had its own history of struggle in gaining governmental and other sources of funding. The City Council's policy was to be a partner in the funding of voluntary organisations, which also had to gain funds from other sources.

It was representatives from these local ethnic minority and religious organisations that made up the Forum, including representatives of the African Caribbean centre, the Bangladeshi cultural centre, an Asian women's group, an African Caribbean women's group, the Christian Churches, Muslim associations, the Antigua/Barbuda association, and multiethnic organisations such as the RA and a local youth club. Thus, the Forum was an umbrella association that represented local community organisations, including the RA.

One of the Forum's key objectives, as set out in its constitution, was to 'speak up for the needs and concerns of the citizens of the area to all relevant authorities (i.e. the various departments of the City Council and other statutory, voluntary and private organisations) [original parentheses], including calling the latter to account when appropriate'. The Forum's politics was grounded on its members' diverse senses of attachment to the neighbourhood, formed through living and/or working in the area. Forum members thus organised across ethnic, gender and class locations, using the rich language of 'community' and not the older vocabulary of 'class alienation'.[4] It seems to me that this aspect of the Forum's agenda turns upside down some White Greenville residents' assumptions that the inner city is an unfriendly and unsettled place compared to the village, its community and its ways of life, discussed in Chapter 3.

As should be clear by now, the RA was represented in the Forum. The RA was composed of White and BrAsian working- and middle-class residents concerned with the social and economic welfare of their neighbourhood, including its upkeep and inhabitants' safety.[5] While many of the ethnic minority organisations represented at the Forum were dependent on state funds for their existence, the RA was self-funded. In other words, the majority of delegates from ethnic minority organisations were community workers, reliant on local and national sources of government funding for their employment. By contrast, the RA delegates were 'ordinary' residents who lived in the locality and thus were anonymous to the City Council, and they were often not employees of the state. This meant that RA members could represent the Forum in delicate negotiations with the state without the threat of jeopardising their organisation's funding and individuals' livelihoods. The point here is that the RA's degree of independence from bureaucratic restraints was necessary for it to be able to act against the state and its representatives. It is for these reasons that a White working-class member of the RA represented the Forum at the application for judicial review. In short, the Forum and the RA were dependent on each other in achieving their mutual goal of gaining influence over the City Council and other organisations whose plans affected the neighbourhood.

In order to appreciate the symbolic and political importance of the inclusion of diverse ethnic minority organisations at the Forum, and the multiethnic membership of the RA, it is worth reflecting on how social scientists have thought about the impact of state funding on the formation of urban ethnic and religious identities. Some social science commentators on neighbourhood-based politics in Britain have maintained that the distribution of state funds and resources on cultural, religious and ethnic grounds has led to the 'fictive' division of minority communities into 'discrete ethnic groups', which implies that each group is an 'undivided unity' (Werbner, 1991, p. 33). Indeed, Kenan Malik (2005, p. 56) insists that the state's local funding strategies aimed at the defence of 'ethnic particularism' has created a platform and audience for conservative religious leaders within British Muslim Pakistani communities. It is against this background that Malik regrets the passing of an era in which ethnic minority community groups were formed around the principles of 'secular universalism' (2005, p. 56).

Putting aside Malik's one-dimensional explanation for the rise of 'militant Islam', a critique of which is outside the scope of this book, his focus on the ethnically divisive impact of local authority funding usefully helps to contextualise and explain the multicultural politics of the Forum and the RA. In parallel with Malik's analysis, the founders of the Forum and the RA felt that the allocation of City Council funds in their neighbourhood resulted in ethnic and religious segmentation, and not inter-ethnic co-operation, at the neighbourhood level. The reason for the Forum's multiethnic composition was to undermine and reverse the state's institutionalisation of ethnic segmentation. Indeed, the allocation of local funds on ethnic grounds served to compound and reinforce some White working-class residents' feeling that BrAsian, Black and other minority groups were the unfair beneficiaries of state resources to the detriment and exclusion of themselves. As this chapter progresses, it will become clear that the RA meetings provided a space for White working-class residents to articulate these concerns. In this space, White working-class stereotypes and antagonisms formed towards specific BrAsian residents were discussed, negotiated and arrested.

Ethnographic research with the RA and the Forum

Having introduced Streetville and the structure of the RA and the Forum, I shall now turn to the details of my fieldwork. As touched upon in Chapter 1, by the time I carried out fieldwork in Streetville, I had become a postdoctoral Research Associate, which meant that I could afford to rent a one-bedroom flat in the area, rather than take up lodgings, as I had done in Greenville and Coalville. Being a tenant in Streetville was crucial for my acquisition of the credentials necessary to become a member of the RA. My work with the RA and the Forum was based solely on my participant observation and active engagement in the network's meetings, which was complemented by informal conversations and interactions with members outside of meetings. Thus, unlike my fieldwork in Greenville and Coalville, my research in Streetville did not include any tape-recorded interviews.

In order to structure my thoughts on the details of my fieldwork with the RA and the Forum, I have found it helpful to situate my reflections in relation to Westwood's (1991) study of a Black youth project based in Streetville called Red Star. Westwood's study was conducted more than a decade before my own research in Streetville. Hence, some of the contrasts between my narrative and experience of neighbourhood politics and collective action in the area in the new millennium, and Westwood's analysis in the 1980s, are effects of the temporal transformation of grassroots ethnic minority collective action in Streetville and Britain more generally. In other words, an exploration of the micro-politics of Red Star illuminates some of the ways in which political action has changed over time.

The members of 'Red Star' were young BrAsian and African Caribbean men who came to identify with a shared 'Black' identity forged in the face of racism and a distrust of White authorities, including an 'attitude' towards the police in the neighbourhood (Westwood, 1991, p. 158). While these young men came from diverse religious and ethnic backgrounds, they were working-class and had grown up together in Streetville. Westwood (1991, p. 157) describes how the members of the youth project were politicised and organised by a 'charismatic leader', a man who came from the same background as the members, but who was set apart from them in his role as a university educated 'organic intellectual'.

Red Star became locked into an ongoing battle with the City Council over their right to meet in a disused school building in the centre of the neighbourhood. When the City Council officially evicted the youth club from the building, its members organised round-the-clock sit-ins. The leader of Red Star took the City Council to court to overturn the eviction notice. Westwood (1991, p. 163) argues that 'the move into a legal battle signalled not simply the defence of the project but a claim to be part of the nation and therefore to protection under the law.'

An obvious point of contrast between Red Star, on the one hand, and the Forum and the RA, on the other, is each movement's relationship with the state and statutory authorities. Red Star positioned itself in opposition to the local Council and related bodies. In contrast, the Forum and the RA worked in consultation with the City Council and other statutory agencies that provided local services, such as the police, education and health authorities. Indeed, local representatives from these authorities attended Forum and RA meetings. Furthermore, while the young, male, BrAsian and African Caribbean working-class members of Red Star mobilised around the political category 'Black', Forum and RA members drew upon the language of 'community' to articulate interests across racial, ethnic, gender, class and age locations. Moreover, the inclusion of men and women in the Forum provides a contrast to Red Star's activism, which was developed and sustained by young men.

However, in parallel with the politically committed leader of Red Star, the Chairperson of the Forum and the founder of the RA were also erudite men who had dedicated their lives to neighbourhood politics. Sanjay, the Chairperson of the Forum, was a middle-aged BrAsian man who managed a youth club in the area. Frank, the founder of the RA, was a retired White man who had been engaged in local community politics for most of his adult life. These men worked together in formulating Forum and RA policies that they proposed to the members of their respective organisations. While I learnt, over time, that each man's engagement in local politics was shaped by personal political beliefs, these ideologies did not become in any simple or direct way the guiding principles of the Forum or the RA. The heterogeneous constitution of organisations that were represented at the Forum, and the diverse membership of the RA, meant that the processes involved in achieving political consensus and mobilisation required discussion, debate and negotiation among the members. Collective action was dependent on a complex set of interactions that drew upon existing networks and resources. Thus, by contrast to Red Star, more than the anti-racist and socialist politics of a 'charismatic leader' was needed for Forum and RA members to work together to instigate an application for judicial review against public authorities.

Westwood did not set out to research the politics of 'Black' youth or to tell the story of the Red Star project. Her study grew out of her involvement with an inner city Access Course to Leicester University, which included a group of young BrAsian men involved in Red Star.[6] My study also grew out of my professional relationships. I became involved with local politics in Streetville while conducting residential fieldwork for a research project exploring everyday understandings of inheritance, identity and genealogy, which will form the focus for Chapter 6. As a way into networking for this project, I contacted the liaison officer of the RA. After attending just a couple of meetings, I was convinced that the RA provided a foothold into the ways in which residents from this locale perceived and experienced their neighbourhood. Along with other members of the RA, I attended the monthly Forum meetings. I soon became inspired by the politics of the Forum and interested in the RA members' involvement in that politics.

From a critical standpoint, my relationship with the RA, in particular, and the Forum, in general, mirrors the imbalance of power that structures the relationship between professionals employed by the state and their clients who are designated as in need of 'help' and 'empowerment'. This was highlighted in a playful way by Frank's introduction of me to RA members as a 'police spy'. The following extract from my field notes illustrates the RA members' initial response to my presence at their meetings:

> An older White man thought that I was a policewoman and asked how the police will enforce the proposed strategy of introducing residential parking permits. I explained that I did not know and told the man and the meeting that I had completed a PhD looking at rural

racism and now I am interested in studying the city. The BrAsian Muslim Chairperson said that lots of students from the University [that is, the University of Leicester] come to study Streetville. There was a sense of weariness in his voice. He wished me luck with my research.

Along with the police, welfare workers and other university students, I was perceived as an outsider who had come to Streetville in order to achieve personal and institutional goals determined outside of the neighbourhood (see Bulmer and Solomos, 2004, p. 4 for similar methodological reflections on the social scientist of race and racism). Indeed, it must be admitted that the diverse ethnic and class composition of Streetville's population makes it an interesting place for students and academic researchers to study and by so doing enhance their own careers.

However, as time passed, I felt that my relationship with the RA and the Forum changed and genuinely became reciprocal to the extent that my professional skills, such as the ability to articulate ideas in public meetings, were useful and beneficial to the network in negotiations with public authorities. Within the first few months of my membership of the RA, I took up the position of acting secretary of the Association, which meant that I had a job to fulfil and sense of purpose in my relationship with the Association. One of my responsibilities was to take the minutes at the monthly RA meetings, a task that helped with my documentation of the research. I was sometimes called upon by the lead activists of the RA and the Forum to represent these organisations at various meetings arranged by the wider voluntary sector. For example, I was put forward as a candidate to represent the Forum on a City Council committee.

During my stay in the area I also formed relationships independently of my membership of the RA with some of the ethnic minority organisations represented at the Forum. For example, I was invited because of my professional status as a university researcher to celebrations and events organised by the Bangladeshi community centre, such as prize givings and poetry readings.[7]

Given the multiethnic, working- and middle-class, male and female constitution of this network, my identity as a White, 30-year-old, middle-class, academic woman, who lived alone in the neighbourhood, correlated with the identities of some of the other residents and community workers. For example, academics working at the University of Leicester also attended the RA's meetings. I also made good friends with a single White woman who attended RA meetings and was in her early thirties like me. In this book I call this woman 'Sophie', and will draw on her words in the final ethnographic section of Chapter 6.

My roles as anthropologist, activist and resident were often blurred. Over time I became engaged and passionate about the politics of the RA and the Forum, and thus felt like a bona fide member – positioned and included on the inside. However, in the midst of this activity, I was aware that I had to negotiate my research position, making sure that residents knew why I was present at meetings and what I was doing living in the area. In this regard, Frank, the founder of the RA, sometimes made fun of me by asking, 'are we making good subjects for your anthropological microscope?' He also regularly visited my flat with updates on the day's or week's events.

One afternoon, Frank informed me that he had spent the morning networking with local residents in the hope of gaining support for a new residents' association in the neighbourhood. He exclaimed 'how about that for a bit of anthropology – that's what we call the university of life'. Frank also gave me the minutes of local community meetings and government publications, suggesting that 'this will be interesting for your research'. My relationship with Frank and the RA is captured and conveyed in the following extract from my field notes.

> Frank turned up this morning to discuss the latest developments. You can always tell when he has had a lot on because he becomes kind of jumpy. ... When I told him that I had fixed it with Pete and Jeanette [my managers and mentors at the University of Manchester] so that I could extend my fieldwork in Streetville to include the summer months, he said 'good, you are ours for the summer', and 'we can continue being insects under your microscope'. ... I am very pleased to be staying here longer. I have the sense that I belong somewhere, if only for a short period of time, and that I am in some way useful.

Westwood (1991, p. 146) tells us that her account is not 'neutral' but drawn from the narratives of the young men involved in Red Star. My ethnographic description and analysis of the Forum's and the RA's politics is unavoidably situated and partial. My recording of the events leading to the application for judicial review, and my theorisation of its implications for understanding the mobilisation of White working-class residents, are rooted in my membership of the RA and participation in the activities of the Forum. However, I was not privy to the other Forum organisations' internal discussions on the legal action, nor did I have access to the City Council's discussions on this matter. Thus as I write I am mindful of the fact that other members of the Forum, particularly those who were not members of the RA, as well as representatives of the City Council, might produce a different interpretation of the legal action, inter-ethnic relationships and governance in this neighbourhood.

I agree with Westwood's (1991, p. 146) suggestion that the process of researching and writing about political struggle can have the effect of 'domesticating and de-politicising that struggle'. In writing about neighbourhood politics in Streetville, I hope to capture something of the excitement, conviction and drama that I shared with those involved, but without romanticising the coalition politics of this network. Moreover, as I have sought to achieve throughout this book, I want to avoid stereotyping research participants' class, ethnic and racial identities, although I fear that, given the deeply grounded difficulties in doing so, it would be surprising if I have wholly succeeded in fully realising this ambition. Thinking of my work in Streetville, I am conscious of Michael Keith's (2005, p. 41) assertion that 'the ethnographically real can ... be notably naïve about the politics of the city. For all its notion of sympathy it can lead to a humanistic celebration of the subjects of difference.'

Love thy neighbour? (But who is thy neighbour?) Negotiating White working-class backlash against multiculturalism

My research question was: how did the Forum and RA work together to instigate an application for judicial review? In this chapter I am particularly interested in the mobilisation and inclusion of White working-class RA members in this legal action because of the significance of their role in the actual application for judicial review. A close examination of the debates that were co-produced at RA meetings provides the context for accounting and explaining the White working-class residents' support of this collective action, a support that was crucial for its success. Another way of putting this is to suggest that an exploration of the micro-politics of RA meetings reveals how the White working-class residents of this locality came to perceive themselves to be part of a multiethnic 'community' united in their opposition to the local Council and its representatives. This scale of analysis provides insight into how RA meetings were the site for the negotiation of White working-class backlash discourses against multiculturalism, and further develops this book's exploration of the complexities involved in confronting White attitudes towards BrAsians that are entwined within discourses of coloniality.

Approximately two-thirds of the members of the RA were White, the majority of whom were working-class, and a third was BrAsian, most of whom, including the chairperson, were Muslim. The residents' class and gender identities did not correspond in any simple way with ethnicity. The members included, for example, elderly White working-class men and women, married couples, single White professionals who lived alone, such as myself, members of interracial families, White and BrAsian mothers of young children, White single mothers, unemployed and self-employed White and BrAsian men, local businessmen including a BrAsian shopkeeper and a BrAsian Muslim undertaker, the White members of a commune and White male and female university lecturers. While some of the residents had lived all or most of their lives in the area, others had settled to Streetville from other parts of the city, Britain and outside of Britain. Moreover, some residents owned their properties, while others rented from private or public landlords.

Social familiarity through working together as a political network and organisation did not in any simple way produce inter-ethnic co-operation between the members of the RA and the other organisations, including the ethnic minority organisations, represented at the Forum. Rather, RA meetings became heated discussions and debates across ethnic and class lines, whereby stereotypical perceptions about the ethnic identity of residents who lived in the neighbourhood were constructed, discussed and broken down. This was a recursive process in which stereotypes of ethnic difference could be deconstructed in one meeting, only to reappear in the same or similar form in another meeting. Generally speaking, it was the White working-class men and women that disseminated ethnic, racial and religious stereotypes on BrAsian Muslim residents. However, while some White working-class residents held derogatory racialised views, other White working-class residents together with working-class BrAsian residents, were involved in the process of challenging them.

One of the functions of the RA meetings was to provide a space for White backlash discourses against multiculturalism to be taken seriously. In so doing, the meetings enabled White working-class residents to express their concerns about what they perceived to be the unfair advantages and priority given to BrAsians by the local state at their expense. Thus the meetings became a place where these concerns were listened to, engaged with by some, and confronted by the other residents, including White middle-class and working-class residents, as well as middle- and working-class BrAsian residents. In this sense, the meetings enabled residents and activists to drive a wedge between the White working-class residents' legitimate worries and racialised modes of articulations of those fears.

The positive effect of these discussions was that they made possible the production of 'intercultural dialogues' across ethnic, racial, religious and class boundaries. Back and Keith (2004, p. 69) argue that such 'dialogues' are premised on 'transcending' and 'escaping', however momentarily, 'particular kinds of disciplined selves' and so 'sharing' and 'communicating something with a stranger'. One consequence of this process is that the White working-class members gained a sense that they were involved and at the heart of neighbourhood life rather than ignored and consigned to the periphery. I shall now turn to some examples of this process that provide insight into how some White working-class residents' racialised views were confronted; and how the White working classes were mobilised in support of the wider anti-racist agenda of the Forum by activists and other White and BrAsian residents who were also members of the RA. These ethnographic examples are reconstructed from my participation in RA meetings, my notes taken at the meetings and the official minutes of the meetings.

Frank told me that 'you will find no racism in Streetville, but you will find low level resentment from some of the older White people'. While I would dispute Frank's distinction between 'resentment' and 'racism', I did observe many examples of such resentment expressed by middle-aged and retired White working-class residents against BrAsians who lived in the area, particularly Muslims. My contention is that an analysis of the production of White working-class stereotypes about BrAsians provides a further lens through which to view the articulation of discourses of coloniality in the present. In this regard, underlying White working-class residents' attitudes towards BrAsians was the construction of absolute cultural differences separating Whites from BrAsians.[8]

For example, consider how White working-class members of the RA complained when during the holy month of Ramadan, the RA's meeting could not be held in its usual place of a Muslim community centre.[9] Nora, a White woman, who played a vital role in the judicial review (details of which follow shortly), felt this was unfair given that the White Christian members of the RA were not given time off from meetings at Christmas and at Easter. Furthermore, Nora expressed her dissatisfaction that the BrAsian Muslims who ran the community centre, in which the meetings were held, did not attend the meetings even though they were specifically invited. In addition, a retired White working-class woman, who ran the neighbourhood watch scheme in her street, blamed BrAsian youths from the local Mosque for the vandalism to cars in the street in which she lived.[10]

I am struck by the resonances between these White discourses on BrAsian Muslims and the ways in which White middle-class residents from Greenville portrayed BrAsians. Echoing Greenville residents' belief that wealthy BrAsians isolate themselves from the village community, Nora thinks that those BrAsian Muslims who had been specifically invited to attend RA meetings should have accepted the invitation because she and other members were fighting for them. In parallel with some White middle-class Greenville residents' perceptions of BrAsians as excessively religious, Nora implies that Muslims are excessively religious, compared to Whites, for taking time off from meetings during Ramadan. In addition, the idea that BrAsian youth are vandals resonates with the views of my Greenville co-conversationalists who felt that BrAsian shopkeepers were dishonest in their business practices. My supposition is that these White representations of BrAsians produced in different classed milieus and contexts are in part the legacy of colonial discourses that supported 'the culturally sanctioned habit of deploying large generalizations' to separate and demarcate 'ours' from 'theirs' (Said, 1978, p. 227). Thus while Whites are differently located in terms of class location and geographical belonging, they share a common heritage in the categories and ways of thinking given to them as subjects of postcolonial Britain.

However, in stark contrast to the village setting of Greenville, where these views were uncontested and unchallenged, the racialised views aired in the public arena of RA meetings were confronted, debated and discussed by other working- and middle-class White and BrAsian residents. In this regard, Frank, the organiser of the RA, and Helena, a White middle-class academic, explained the significance of Ramadan to Nora and other residents. Moreover, a young White working-class mother defended the BrAsian Muslim community workers' non-attendance at meetings. She suggested that it was not always easy to find the time in the evenings to attend meetings particularly given the pressures of work and family life. Furthermore, the Chairperson of the RA, a BrAsian Muslim man who was the local undertaker, expressed his surprise at the suggestion that youths from the Mosque were responsible for the vandalism of cars. However, he agreed that he would investigate the matter further with members of the Mosque.

Consider also the following exchange among residents concerning the BrAsian Bangladeshi organisation's new premises in the neighbourhood. Sharon was a White single mother in her fifties. She believed that her racially tolerant attitudes were exemplified by her role as a temporary foster parent for African Caribbean children in social care. One evening, Sharon conveyed her anger and frustration to the meeting regarding the plans for a new community centre for Bangladeshi people from Streetville. At this meeting, she suggested that the residents organise a petition against the new Bangladeshi premises on the grounds that she said she was 'sick' of ethnic groups having their own centre where others could not go. Sharon pointed out that the residents of the RA did not have a centre of their own in which to meet. By contrast, she argued that the Bangladeshis in Streetville already had a community centre, which she thought was closed to non-Bangladeshi people from the area.

Fred was a retired White man who had lived with his White wife in a rented terraced house in the area for many years. He remarked that when he walked past the Bangladeshi centre he wondered, 'What is it all about? It looks foreign, alien and strange to us [that is, White non-Bangladeshi residents]. It looks like a place that we cannot go in and that we know nothing about what is going on inside.' Fred, like Sharon, believes that Whites were excluded and not welcome in the Bangladeshi centre.

It is worth exploring how this point of view resonates once more with some of the ideas expressed by my White middle-class co-conversationalists from Greenville, discussed in Chapters 2 and 3. For Fred and Sharon, supposed Bangladeshi cultural differences from Whites alienates and excludes Whites from entering their centre, whereas, for some of my White co-conversationalists from Greenville, BrAsians are thought to isolate and thus cut themselves off from the local village community. Either way, it is the perception that BrAsians are culturally Other to the White majority that is thought to be the reason for the supposed lack of interaction between 'us' and 'them'.

Tahir, a BrAsian resident of Streetville and a community worker at the Bangladeshi centre, explained that the current Bangladeshi centre was for use by anyone who lived in the area, regardless of ethnic identity. Tahir pointed out that the 'Bangladeshi' community group did not own the new premises but planned to rent them. Tahir was accompanied at the meeting by a member of the Bangladeshi community group who I did not know.

Frank, the founder of the RA, suggested that the Bangladeshi residents were the wrong target to blame for the RA's lack of premises, and that the City Council was the proper and appropriate target. The Council was at fault because it did not fund community groups like the RA. In this vein, the minutes of the meeting read: '[Frank] raised the ongoing need for a City Council funded meeting place that supported the wider and diverse Communities of Streetville.'

The meeting finally concluded, and I quote again from the minutes: 'those Streetville residents who proposed a petition objecting to the initiative [of the new Bangladeshi centre] ... in principle did not object to the centre although they wished to address to the owners questions regarding planning'. In this way, the residents' concerns were directed not at the BrAsian Bangladeshi community group but the owners of the new centre. With the residents' objections to the new Bangladeshi centre settled in this pragmatic way, the members agreed that if the RA had its own premises a space would be provided for people of different ethnic and religious locations from Streetville to meet. Such a place, it was suggested, would, potentially at least, facilitate the dissolution of inter-ethnic fears and misunderstandings. The minutes of the meeting read: 'as residents of the area we need to meet together as individuals to look to ways in which Multicultural groups can co-exist and share ideas under one roof'. Tahir offered his practical help and knowledge to prepare a funding application for such a centre. Time was ticking on. The caretaker of the building in which the meeting took place came in to see if we were getting ready to leave. Sharon commented: 'This is why we need our own premises – we cannot thrash out all these important issues in a couple of hours once a month in the evening.' Sharon then turned to Tahir and asked him if the RA could have a room in the new Bangladeshi centre. Tahir suggested that this could be arranged.

Sharon's and Fred's resentment towards the new Bangladeshi centre illustrates the ways in which the distribution of social provision, funding and support had the potential to create racialised antagonisms, cultural stereotypes and resentments towards BrAsian residents. From the standpoint of the White working-class residents, BrAsian Bangladeshis and other minority groups received funding from the state to pay for 'culturally' specific 'community' centres and the resources that were thought to equip these centres, such as kitchen equipment and computers. The White working-class residents came to feel that they were excluded from access to local government funding on the grounds that they were White. Hence the production of seemingly exclusive ethnic zones within the neighbourhood became one impetus for White residents' hostility and resentment towards BrAsians and other minority groups. My supposition is that these feelings of resentment were framed by discourses of coloniality to the extent that BrAsians were depicted as fundamentally Other to the racially unmarked White self. It is exactly in the face of these discourses of White backlash against multiculturalism that the RA meetings provided a space for the discussion and debate of these negative views about racialised Others. In the meeting described above, the repositioning and restoration of White working-class people's sense of belonging to the neighbourhood and its community was facilitated by Tahir and Frank.

Tahir was in his early thirties, a working-class BrAsian resident of Streetville, a member of the RA, an employee at the Bangladeshi centre and a part-time university student. At the meetings he represented the Bangladeshi centre's interests, but he was careful to identify himself with the RA by introducing himself as an RA member and a resident of Streetville. Tahir's offer of practical help to the residents, as well as use of the Bangladeshi centre's new premises, positioned the Bangladeshi organisation in a reciprocal relationship with the RA. In this way, Tahir manoeuvred a space for an alliance between the Bangladeshi residents and the other residents by breaking down the stereotype that the Bangladeshis were 'taking over' Streetville to the detriment of others.

Frank was concerned with the maintenance of good relationships between the RA and the other organisations represented at the Forum, including the Bangladeshi organisation. He knew that if the RA hindered the Bangladeshi centre's expansion into new premises the RA's relationship with the Forum would be damaged. Frank argued that the City Council's failure to fund multiethnic community groups like the RA made them the appropriate target for Sharon's and Fred's frustration and anger, and not the Bangladeshi centre. In this way, Frank's argument negotiated Sharon's and Fred's concerns that the Council funding policies unfairly benefited ethnic minorities by suggesting that the Council failed to fund organisations that were multicultural and multiethnic. Thus the RA's lack of funds became indicative of the failure of the Council's funding policies rather than the fault of those people, especially BrAsians, who appeared to benefit most from the Council's policies.

The effect of Frank's and Tahir's arguments was to confront and challenge Sharon's and Fred's representations of BrAsians as irreducibly Other and 'alien' to Whites. In so doing, the City Council was positioned as a mutual antagonist that had the potential to unite the residents not only with each other across ethnic, gender and class identities but also with the other organisations represented at the Forum. In other words, Tahir and Frank drew upon their understanding of what constituted good 'community' relationships in Streetville in their attempts to negotiate Sharon's and Fred's sense of the racial disadvantages experienced by Whites in the neighbourhood.

Importantly, Tahir's and Frank's arguments had effect and made sense to the White working-class residents because they drew upon and fed into their already existing frameworks for positioning the Council as an outsider and an adversary. For example, the minutes that I took at the RA meetings provided a record of the myriad ways in which the residents across ethnic and classed identities regularly complained about and ridiculed the City Council's management of their neighbourhood, including: holding the Council responsible for refuse discarded on the streets and back alleyways, disdain for the Council's closed-circuit television camera positioned in the centre of the neighbourhood, and complaints about the Council's slowness in replacing a public post (mail) box situated on the pavement (sidewalk) that local youths had blown up with fireworks. On a more intimate level, the state and its various agencies shaped the personal lives of some of the poorer working-class White residents. For example, some residents were dependent financially upon welfare payments and a few RA members had dealings with social workers and the police.

It is against this background of experiencing the City Council as an outsider that the members of the RA, including the working-class White residents, lent their support to the Forum's legal action against the Council, and they did so through perceiving themselves to be the members of a multiethnic community. In other words, the residents' involvement in the Forum's legal action was not determined by their support for 'abstract ideological criteria' (Fantasia, 1988, p. 230) but was in part motivated by their dissatisfaction in their everyday dealings with the Council. However, sharing some parallels with my analysis of White working-class critical reflections on racism discussed in Chapter 4, the White working-class residents did not suddenly become anti-racist angels through their involvement in the Forum and its politics. Rather in spite of their inclusion in anti-racist collective action, some of the people that I came to know continued to express and embrace racialised stereotypes and opinions rooted in their belief in the fundamental cultural differences separating Whites and BrAsians. The ways in which Whites continued to hold on to and express racialised attitudes in this way illuminates the encompassing aspects of discourses of coloniality. In the following section, I turn my attention to an examination of the events that led up to the application for judicial review, the actual details of the White working-class residents' involvement in this legal action and an account of the eventual court hearing.

The application for judicial review: 'Battle of the boundaries'

At the time of the application, the Forum members' concern was to ensure that Streetville was not overlooked in the City Council's plans for urban development. The area's two electoral wards were the first and third most economically and socially deprived in the city. One strategy proposed by the Council to address this urban poverty was to develop 'Area Forums', which would consist of local people from the economically deprived electoral wards of the city. One suggested aim of these Forums was to provide residents with the tools to 'empower' themselves to take control of the management of their communities. The Streetville Forum was particularly apprehensive that the proposed new 'Area Forums' would lead the City Council to ignore their demands. Moreover, at the time of the legal action, Forum members were campaigning to ensure that they would be given fair representation on the newly formed City Council-led Strategic Partnership. The latter committee was a partnership between the statutory, voluntary and business sectors. The Partnership was responsible for the distribution of urban renewal funds.

While these plans for development were taking shape, proposals were announced for the reconfiguration of the electoral boundaries in the city. The Forum was stirred to instigate an application for judicial review on this issue for the following reasons. It was felt that the new electoral wards proposed for Streetville would have the effect of disguising the real socio-economic poverty and deprivation in the neighbourhood by amalgamating part of the area with an affluent neighbouring suburb. The members of the Forum were particularly worried that the amalgamation would impair the neighbourhood's access to urban renewal funds that were vital for the area's economic regeneration. Moreover, members were concerned that the changes would hinder the Forum's participation in the proposed new structures for local democracy. In this regard, the Forum was alarmed about the potential repercussions of these boundary changes for the representation of Streetville on the Strategic Partnership and the proposed new 'Area Forums'. Furthermore, the suggested boundary changes would require the de-selection of two local government, elected Councillors, which the Forum members considered to be undemocratic. If this de-selection were to occur there would be no elected representative on the Council accountable solely to the people of Streetville. In short, the Forum felt that the changes to the electoral boundaries constituted gerrymandering on the part of the Electoral Commission.

At the time of the court hearing, the Forum's press release explained the racial inequalities inherent within the proposed boundary changes as follows: 'Our challenge to the Commission's view ("the racial or cultural make up of the population in any ward is not a relevant consideration; no-one is being disenfranchised by reason of race or cultural background" [original parenthesis]) is likely to set a precedent for all public bodies in relation to their duty under the Race Relations Act.' From this point of view, some Forum members denounced the failure of the Electoral Commission to fulfil its statutory duty to protect the interests of ethnic minorities as a moral outrage, a feeling that fuelled the belief that their legal action was righteous and just.

Not all RA members supported or even appreciated the anti-racist motivations for the legal action. Some members, including some of the White working-class residents that were directly involved in the application for judicial review, did not support this action because of its explicitly anti-racist aims. These RA members instead focused upon the impact of the suggested boundary changes on the quality of their own lives. For example, a White working-class mother expressed her concern at an RA meeting that school trips would no longer be subsidised by the Council if the boundary changes took place. This was because she feared that as a new, less impoverished ward, the people of the area would no longer qualify for subsidies. Moreover, White and BrAsian, working- and middle-class members suggested that the amalgamation would lead to the break-up and transformation of the identity of their neighbourhood, a theme that we have seen articulated in differing ways by my White co-conversationalists from both Greenville and Coalville. This sentiment was encapsulated in Streetville by the slogan printed on a poster that some residents displayed in the windows of their houses: 'STREETVILLE FOREVER'.

The organisations that made up the Forum raised the money needed to employ a London-based lawyer, a barrister (a lawyer that is an advocate in a court of law) and a QC (which stands for 'Queen's Counsel' and is the highest rank of barrister in Britain), to initiate the legal challenge to the new electoral boundaries. The RA made a considerable donation towards these legal costs from their funds. Importantly for my focus on the role of the White working-class members in this legal action, an RA member, Nora, who we met above complaining about the BrAsian Muslims' failure to attend meetings, represented the Forum at the court hearing. This was in spite of the Electoral Commission's attempt to obstruct her right to legal aid (financial assistance provided by the state available to those unable to meet the full cost of legal proceedings) on the grounds she was a City Council employee in her job as a 'lollypop lady' (one who escorts young children across busy roads by stopping the traffic with a large sign – 'Stop' – that looks like a lollypop). Nora was persuaded to represent the Forum at the application for judicial review by Frank and Sanjay, the Chairperson of the Forum. In being asked to play such a significant role in this collective action, Nora was given the feeling that she was a valued, trusted and respected member of the neighbourhood and community.

I shall now turn to an account of the day's events from the residents' perspective. This aspect of my analysis will illustrate the ways in which Nora and other Whites continued to hold on to derogatory racialised sentiments in spite of their participation in the multiethnic network. My contention is that this observation highlights some of the potential ambiguities inherent within Whites' participation in anti-racist action, as well as illuminating the reach, depth and hold of discourses of coloniality in the present.

The day's events from the residents' point of view

On the day of the court hearing, Nora travelled to London in a minibus, loaned by a local youth club, with members of the RA. Her supporters consisted mainly of White working- and middle-class people who were not in full-time employment, such as Frank (the White founder of the RA who had retired from paid work), Sharon (who we met above) and her youngest daughter (who was White and about seven years old), Nora's partner (who was an unemployed White man), Archie (a retired White university lecturer), Fiona (a White mother with her baby), Sanjay (the BrAsian Chairperson of the Forum), Edward (a Black youth worker) and myself (the White female secretary of the RA and anthropological researcher).

We met at 7.00 a.m. outside a local primary school. Frank, Sanjay and a community worker had been to London the day before to meet with the Forum's legal representatives. Frank told me on the telephone that they had spent much of the day in London colouring maps to show where the current and proposed ward boundaries lie. Apologies for absence were received from the RA's BrAsian Chairperson, who was also the local undertaker, because he was unexpectedly busy owing to the death of an important local BrAsian Muslim doctor. Complaints were made about his absence by Nora and Sharon. In this regard, they each expressed their dissatisfaction with BrAsians and Muslims for not being reliable.

The class divisions between the residents came sharply into focus on the journey to London. For example, Sharon asked if anyone had a newspaper that she could read on the journey. Frank passed her his copy of *The Independent*, a quality British newspaper. Sharon laughed and said 'that is not a [news]paper'.

Once we had arrived at the Royal Courts of Justice we spent about 45 minutes waiting outside the courtroom for proceedings to commence. This allowed time for us to be introduced to our legal team. Sharon turned to me and said, 'I can see why he is representing Streetville, he looks very Streetville'. Our senior barrister (QC) was a BrAsian Sikh man who wore a turban, and our lawyer a BrAsian man. I was immediately struck by the disjunction, on the one hand, between Sharon's comments that emphasised and connected the racial identity of the Forum's legal team with the BrAsian population that lived in Streetville, and, on the other hand, the multiethnic politics of the RA and Forum and the anti-racist aspects of this collective action aimed at challenging institutional racism. Sharon's remark, combined with her and Nora's complaints that BrAsians are not reliable, exemplify the ways in which they both continued to interpret and classify individual BrAsians' identities and actions through a rigidly dualistic worldview of 'us' and 'them', 'ours' and 'theirs' (Said, 1978). This had the consequence of repeatedly positioning BrAsians as 'Other' when juxtaposed to the racially unmarked White self.

We waited in the same corridor as the Electoral Commission and City Council and their legal team. Each group kept a polite distance from the other. But we noted that they had four barristers. The strength of the Council's representation combined with the seniority of their leading barrister was interpreted by Frank as already a victory for the residents. That is to say, this legal action was clearly taken very seriously by the City Council.

After the hearing we had our photograph taken outside the High Court. We held our banners that said 'STREETVILLE FOREVER' and 'SAVE STREETVILLE – DON'T LET THEM CRUSH DEMOCRACY'. I was very proud to be part of this.

The case was adjourned for the weekend. This made Nora anxious because she would need a further day off from work and required someone to write a letter on her behalf to her employers at the City Council. Frank agreed to write the letter. Sanjay played Bob Marley's song 'Chant down Babylon' on the way home. He laughed and told Frank to write in the letter that Nora has to 'chant down Babylon one more time'.

The case for the prosecution

This account of the court hearing is constructed from notes that I took sitting in the public gallery combined with my research on the Race Relations Amendment Act (2000).

The Forum's case was that while the Electoral Commission had taken cognisance of Section 19b of the Race Relations Amendment Act (2000), it had failed to comply with Section 71, which imposed a more stringent duty. The Race Relations Amendment Act (2000) is a direct result of the MacPherson report (1999), which examined the racist assumptions guiding the Metropolitan (London) police investigation of the racially motivated murder of the Black teenager Stephen Lawrence. In deciding on the new electoral boundaries, the Electoral Commission, it was contended, had focused on Section 19b of the Act, which makes 'it unlawful for a public authority ... to do any act that constitutes discrimination'. The Forum's Counsel advocated that Section 71 prescribes that it is the duty of public authorities, which would include the Electoral Commission, 'to eliminate unlawful racial discrimination and to promote equality of opportunity and good relations between persons of different racial groups'; and it was this directive that the Electoral Commission had failed to fulfil.

The prosecution's Counsel argued that the creation of a new electoral ward in a multiethnic area that would be 24 per cent larger than the average electoral ward in the UK, and this entailed the de-selection of Councillors, should have rung alarm bells in relation to the access of 'minority ethnic' people to their Councillors. In short, it was suggested that these proposed changes distorted the relationship of the electorate to the elected that would be detrimental to the rights of 'minority ethnic' people.

The judge questioned this proposition, stating that he could not see how the new electoral wards interfered with the equality of opportunity for the residents because they still had the right to vote.

The Forum's Counsel argued that this missed the point. Section 71 places a duty on public authorities to ensure and promote equality of opportunity for 'minority ethnic' people, which includes the elimination of prejudice within the electoral system. It was on these grounds that the Forum's Counsel asked for a declaration that the new wards were unlawful.

The case for the defence

In response, the Electoral Commission's Counsel reasoned that the Electoral Commission had consulted with the Commission for Racial Equality (CRE) on the equality implications of the new wards. (The CRE was the agency that monitored race relations and racial equality in British society at the time of the application for judicial review.) The Electoral Commission's Counsel argued that neither the Electoral Commission nor the CRE knew about the separate duty of Section 71. Thus the case for the Electoral Commission was that they could not be expected to implement a duty that they knew nothing about. The judge conceded that he also did not know about the specific duty of Section 71.

Furthermore, the Electoral Commission's Counsel maintained that unless the old electoral wards were reinstated immediately it would be impossible to proceed with the imminent local elections. It was argued that the effect of this would be to cause chaos to democracy and the electoral system in the city. A letter from the Deputy Prime Minister's office that endorsed these sentiments was presented to the court.

Crucially for the Electoral Commission's case, their Counsel focused on the Forum's failure to take legal action within the three months time span allowed for objection. Counsel explained that the Forum was consulted in all discussions about the electoral boundary changes. Thus when the decision to change the electoral wards came into effect, the Forum had all the information necessary to bring legal proceedings within the permitted time.

The verdict

The Forum's delay in bringing legal action led to the residents' defeat; this was in spite of the residents' plea that allowances should be made for the delay because the Forum had limited funds and no experience of litigation. The members of the RA and the Forum were disappointed by this verdict. However, Frank and Sanjay diminished the verdict's significance by arguing in their feedback on the legal hearing to the members of the Forum and the RA that the Electoral Commission's victory was dependent on a 'legal technicality'. Furthermore, Frank and Sanjay suggested that the Electoral Commission's triumph was diminished by the judge's decision to take the weekend to deliberate on the case owing to its considerable importance. Frank and Sanjay also perceived the judge's use of the word 'regretfully' three times in his judgement to be significant. In short, members of the Forum and RA were convinced that they had achieved a moral victory.

This reaction to the verdict illustrates how for contemporary social movements the idea of 'success' is overshadowed by the 'symbolic' import of the protest directed at 'challenging and upsetting dominant codes upon which social relationships are founded' (Melucci, 1988, p. 248). Clearly, this action illuminates in stark terms the ways in which some public authorities are ignoring the Race Relations Amendment Act's directives on institutional racism. Thus the court hearing pushed elites to 'admit what was previously excluded from the decision-making arena' (Melucci, 1988, p. 254). The government, from the upper echelons of the Deputy Prime Minister's office to the local state, had to listen to the Forum's and the RA's arguments, take them seriously, and include them in their deliberations. It is in this sense that the residents entered the public culture of the nation and claimed a place on the political agenda. Yet the outcome of the legal action demonstrates that when local people work together as a community across ethnic, class and gender locations to challenge strategies of governance that are institutionally racist and undemocratic, public and local authorities have the legal machinery, financial clout and power to silence and dissipate dissent and rebellion, as well as to reinforce policies that reproduce unequal power relations and racial discrimination.

Conclusion: The ambiguous process of confronting discourses of coloniality

While my analysis of young White adults' critical reflections on racism in Coalville focused upon the conditions in which individuals came to confront racism within their own families, my focus in this chapter has been on the mobilisation of White working-class individuals within multiethnic community politics and anti-racist collective action. Residents and community workers came together in opposition to the local Council to make demands that they considered to be of interest to the residents of their neighbourhood across ethnic, racial, gender and class lines. Central to this process was the inclusion and mobilisation of White working-class residents in this collective action, which involved the complex negotiation of White backlash to multiculturalism. In order to unpack further how this was achieved, it is worth reflecting in more detail on Hewitt's (2005) analysis of the ways in which the local state in Britain has both fuelled and managed White backlash.

The area to which Hewitt's ethnography refers is Eltham in London, the scene of the aforementioned racist murder of Stephen Lawrence. In the wake of Lawrence's murder and other racially motivated attacks in Eltham, the local Council felt it necessary to establish Black and ethnic minority-only residents' associations to combat racism. Hewitt (2005, p. 95) argues that this proposal provoked 'a backlash' from White members of the established residents' associations. The White residents felt that the recognition of Black issues undermined elderly White residents' victimisation by Black and White youths in the neighbourhood. Hewitt (2005, p. 101) concludes that this conflict demonstrates 'a clash between universalistic liberal principles of justice on the one hand and a communitarian claim being made on the other'. In other words, the White residents drew upon 'universal liberal principles of justice' and equality that took meaning in opposition to the Council's 'communitarian' privileging of minority rights.

By contrast to the singularly communitarian politics of Eltham Council, the Forum's legal action appealed both to universal principles of democratic justice, and communitarian issues focused on the defence of ethnic and racial equality. In other words, the legal action, like the broader politics of the Forum and the RA, drew upon the language of community to speak in universal terms to the members' concerns and interests across ethnic, class, age and gender identities. It was not the anti-racist politics of the legal action that the White working-class residents supported as such. Rather, they participated in this political action because they believed that the neighbourhood's access to local funding and resources for urban renewal was at stake. From this standpoint, it is possible to understand how some White working-class individuals came to play a central and leading role in this anti-racist action without holding anti-racist views themselves, and even more than this, continued to express what they perceived to be the fundamental distinctions that mark Whites off from BrAsian Others. This observation serves to illuminate the encompassing and entrenched constitution of discourses of coloniality in the present and the complexities involved in any attempt to escape its hegemony. In this regard, my work in Streetville supports my conclusions drawn from the Coalville study, namely, that White confrontations of racism is not a straightforward process. That is to say, some of the young White adults with whom I came to know from Coalville drew upon the internalisation of their own racialised attitudes, feelings and emotions to question what they considered to be the racist views of others. In a similar vein, the White working-class residents whose support was crucial to the success of this anti-racist action were not anti-racists themselves and continued to reproduce stereotypical assumptions about BrAsians, even while standing outside the courtroom.

It is in the next chapter, which examines the identities of the members of interracial families from Streetville, where we will see discourses of coloniality unambiguously and unequivocally questioned, challenged and broken down.

Part III
Postcolonial Genealogies

6
Slave Ancestries and the Inheritance of Interracial Identities

In this chapter my focus of attention shifts away from analysis of how White working- and middle-class people represent and imagine the lives of BrAsians, to an examination of the Black, White and interracial identities of members of interracial families. This aspect of my work provides insight into the ways in which slave histories and ancestries inform the identities of members of interracial families. To do this, I shall draw upon in-depth interviews that I conducted with Black, White and interracial members of interracial families from Streetville. I am interested here in the ways in which members of interracial families think about ideas of ancestry, descent, inheritance and belonging when they reflect on their ethnicities and relationships across the colour-lines. I shall pay detailed critical attention to how aspects of the slave past become meaningful to members of interracial families within the broader context of their ideas about the inheritance of identity.

Crucially, this chapter's focus on members of interracial families' evocations of the slave past provides a stark contrast to this book's examination of White amnesia with regard to colonial histories in White people's constructions of BrAsians, examined in detail in Chapters 1, 2 and 3 and traced throughout the discourses of coloniality scrutinised in Chapters 4 and 5. Thus far I have explored how White people screen out the significance of the colonial past for interpreting the meaning of BrAsians' relationships to the village, the countryside, the city, the nation and ultimately the West. In this chapter I shift gear, so to speak, to scrutinise how some Black, White and interracial members of interracial families positively identify with an aspect of the colonial past when they think about the formation of their own ethnicities and those of other family members.

It has been suggested by some ethnographers working in Britain that interracial families provide a microcosm of the broader racial politics and inequalities that structure and shape society (Parker and Song, 2001). So, the experiences of members of interracial families bring into sharp relief dominant folk concepts of racial difference that associate phenotype (skin colour, hair type, body shape) with 'just' White or 'just' Black parentage and ancestry and a particular set of cultural practices and beliefs (Ifekwunigwe, 2001; Parker and Song, 2001). Central to the diverse experiences of members of interracial families, including the White, Black and 'Asian' parents of interracial children and interracial people themselves, is the ways in which others judge, label and classify their racial identities, cultural locations, biological parentage and ancestries on the basis of their physical appearance. Interracial people are frequently confronted with the 'what are you?' question from outsiders to interracial families who seek to fix and pin down their identities. Thus, it is quite often assumed that members of interracial families must be purely White, purely Black or purely 'Asian' parentage and descent. Moreover, outsiders and onlookers often think that members of interracial families are not logically related to each other. For example, it is sometimes thought that White mothers of interracial children are not the child's biological parent, and that the child's biological mother must be the adoptive parent (Ali, 2008). Putting this in terms of the concepts that I have deployed in this book, members of interracial families' ethnicities and experiences confront, challenge and dismantle discourses of coloniality in the present. In this chapter, I trace how some members of British interracial families that I came to know and interview drew upon slave histories and ancestries to explain and understand their experiences of racism and rejection, and to make sense of the complexities of their ethnic identities.

My focus on the formation of interracial identities also provides a further avenue through which to explore the dynamics, structure and content of Whiteness that has been a central theme of this book. From this point of view, members of interracial families that I interviewed are differently located in relation to Whiteness. They are either the White parents of children who self-identify as 'Black', self-identify as 'Black' themselves, or they are of interracial descent and have a White parent.[1] This chapter explores how members of interracial families who grew up in White racist milieus came to break connections with their own White family members because those members were racist, and thereby deepens this book's analysis of the conditions in which individuals can become reflexive actors on racism, a theme discussed in Chapter 4.

I will also trace and analyse the ways in which class distinctions and notions of respectability become intermeshed with White and interracial people's experiences of relationships across the colour-lines. In addition, in this chapter, I will elaborate upon how a sense of belonging to Streetville as a place and a neighbourhood mediates the formation of ethnicities, a theme discussed in the previous chapter. I will trace how my interracial, Black and White co-conversationalists' experiences of belonging to Streetville informs their emerging identities and how this can have both positive and negative effects. Some of my co-conversationalists' claims to belong to Streetville became associated with the positive aspects of community associated with solidarity, belonging and kinship. In this regard, Streetville is a site for the formation of positive kinship ties of love and genealogical affiliation and relatedness across the colour-lines. Yet Streetville can also be a place where interracial relationships and subjectivities are contested and rejected by family, neighbours and acquaintances from the locality. The perception that members of interracial families transgress racial boundaries generates social stigma and gossip. So claims of belonging to Streetville can potentially link residents into their neighbourhood, but yet competing claims to belonging can also alienate them.

At this juncture I must justify my use of the term 'interracial'. I prefer 'interracial' to the more popular term of 'mixed-race' in English vernacular and academic accounts. The term 'mixed-race' implies 'pure' biological races have been 'mixed' to produce a 'third' race (Parker and Song, 2001, p. 11). I think that the term 'interracial' suggests an ambiguity that might begin to trouble the reproduction of racial binaries associated with this image of 'mixing' discrete biological and cultural types. With similar sentiments in mind, some of my co-conversationalists used the terms 'dual heritage' and 'mixed-heritage' to describe their identities or those of their children. In reporting my co-conversationalists' voices, words and ideas, I will stay faithful to their own self-descriptions, as has been my approach throughout this book.

Before proceeding to the ethnography I want to consider how my work on the genealogical constitution of interracial families' identities is situated within, and contributes to, sociological studies that explore how histories of slavery became configured in the formation of contemporary racial identities in Britain. I will also set out how my approach to genealogy and identity has been influenced and shaped by a body of literature known as the 'new' kinship studies in social anthropology.

Interracial identities, genealogy and ancestral slave pasts

Frances Winddance Twine's work on the formation of interracial identities in Britain is particularly relevant to my project because her work is also based in Leicester and focused upon the formation of White and interracial identities. Twine's research draws on in-depth interviews mostly with White mothers of interracial children from Leicester, as well as interviews with other White and Black family members (2000, 2004, 2006, 2010, 2011).[2] Central to Twine's study is her examination of the myriad ways in which White mothers of children fathered by men of African Caribbean descent develop what she calls 'racial literacy'. She defines the latter as 'proactive anti-racist' strategies to prepare their children to negotiate their inevitable experiences of racism (2000, pp. 96–101).

Significantly for my examination of how everyday understandings of slave histories mediate the formation of interracial identities, Twine (2004) explores how some White mothers, and White fathers, with whom she worked wanted their interracial children to learn about Black history. This included Black people's contribution to world history, knowledge of the Caribbean and Africa as well as the histories of slavery and colonialism (2004, pp. 886–7). These White parents believed that the appropriation of this knowledge was necessary for their interracial children's identification with the African Caribbean community in Leicester. Moreover, a feeling of relatedness to the Black community was considered by some White parents to be important because they thought that their children would at some point in their lives experience racism and rejection from other White people. One site for learning Black history was Saturday school and weekday after-school clubs run exclusively by Black people for African Caribbean children (2004, pp. 888–9). These schools and clubs were particularly important for White parents who lived with their children in predominantly White suburban neighbourhoods. For these parents, Saturday schools enabled their children to socialise in a Black environment, to be with teachers who understood racism and what it means to be Black in contemporary Britain. Significantly for the focus of this chapter, these clubs were thought to provide a crucial place where children could learn about Black history including the histories of slavery.

Building on Twine's ethnographic insights, I am interested in how members of interracial families have a sense of belonging to the slave past, which becomes incorporated within a broader narrative of racial literacy that includes ideas of inheritance, relatedness, ancestry and belonging across the colour-lines. The questions that I explore in this chapter include: How do members of interracial families come to learn about the slave past and its significance for interpreting the present? In what ways does knowledge of slavery inform people's ideas of relatedness to other members of their families? To what extent does a sense of ancestral connection to the slave past mediate feelings of connectedness to the Black community in Leicester and to members of the Black community in other diasporic times and places? How does a feeling of ancestral relatedness to slavery enable members of interracial families to confront racism, including experiences of rejection from both Black and White relatives and neighbours?

The 'new' kinship studies help with these questions (see Franklin and McKinnon, 2001). This literature examines how kinship ideologies become reconfigured in the context of the new reproductive technologies, for example, ova and sperm donation. These recent clinical practices have opened a space for anthropologists to examine how ideas about biogenetic relatedness within families and across generations become intersected with ideas about the inheritance of cultural attributes of identity passed on through upbringing, example and experience (Edwards, 1999, 2000; Edwards and Strathern, 2000; Thompson, 2001). Drawing on the insights of these studies, I examine what constitutes interracial people's ideas of biological and cultural relatedness within their families and across racial categories.

In this vein, I follow Peter Wade's (2002, pp. 83–7) suggestion that these anthropologists' reflections on the biological and social 'origins' of persons can be deployed to unpack 'everyday' understandings of the relationship between ideas of 'race', 'nature' and 'culture'. In his review of anthropological approaches to the study of race, Wade (2002, p. 15) contends that, 'People ... move between the biological and the social, the given and the developing, the permanent and the changeable, in ways that blur the boundary between them.' I will be examining the ways in which members of interracial families imagine the fixity, malleability and intersection of biological and cultural attributes of identity when they think about the inheritance of their own identities from colonial times.

Alongside the new kinship studies, I have also found Stuart Hall's work on 'new ethnicities' useful to the task of analysing genealogical narratives. In his famous essay, Hall provides insight into ways in which Black Britons might draw upon genealogy, ancestry and descent – including affiliation to slave pasts and histories – to self-fashion an identity that is neither eternally fixed nor endlessly fluid (Nash, 2002). One of Hall's (1992, p. 257) aims is to promulgate awareness of the 'Black experience as a diaspora experience'. This means that Black Britons must embed feelings of relatedness to places within and outside the UK in a sense of the 'rediscovery' of hidden and forgotten slave histories. For some members of the Black diaspora, dispersed through slavery, Africa has become an iconic symbol that serves to create a sense of coherence (Hall, 2003, p. 235). For example, in reflecting on his upbringing in the Caribbean, Hall (2003, p. 240) describes how Africa remained the 'unspeakable presence' in Caribbean culture. He tells how 'Africa is "hiding" behind every verbal inflection, every narrative twist of Caribbean cultural life' (2003, p. 240). In this way, Africa features as an imaginary geographical and historical homeland for the descendants of slaves scattered across the globe. For Hall (1992, p. 258), remembrance of this shared slave ancestry does not involve a 'simple return' to 'ancestral pasts' and 'cultural roots', nor does it entail disposing of 'shared points of departure' and 'forms of experience' (Nash, 2002, p. 33). Rather, Hall (1992, p. 258) insists that mutual feelings of 'deep inheritance' must be 're-experienced and re-interpreted' through the 'categories of the present'. Thus he argues that new ethnicities need to be 'constructed historically, culturally, politically' (1992, p. 257).

Hall illuminatingly illustrates how concepts of genealogy, ancestry and descent provide a useful vehicle for thinking about the significance and meaning of the slave past in the formation of Black ethnicities in the present. But yet, as Suki Ali (2003) argues, Hall's focus is exclusively on the formation of 'just' Black subjectivities. So what Hall has to say is of clear significance for Black people, but he does not address interracial or White people in interracial families. This should not be surprising if we take on board Hesse's (2002) argument that White European narratives of slavery more often than not construct slavery as a 'one off event' and thus something that happened in the past. That is to say, in tune with my analysis of White amnesia in the earlier chapters of this book, White European and American hegemonic histories of slavery become detached from 'contemporary social relationships, governance and cultural representations' (2002, p. 157). Thus, what is screened out, displaced and 'ritually forgotten' within White hegemonic narratives of slavery is the 'numerous interdependencies that obtained between Christianity and slavery, liberalism and imperialism, democracy and racism' (Hesse, 2002, p. 160). One important consequence of this narrative is for the people who were enslaved to be 'airbrushed out' of Western history. However, as I alluded to in this book's Introduction, historians of slavery, and more recently population geneticists, have shown that the legacy of the forced dispersal of African descent people across the globe is that to be of Black descent is constitutive of the genealogies of most White British and American families too. Thus, if they were taught how to White British and American people might also recognise their identities in Hall's 'new ethnicities' and also be concerned to trace and follow their ancestries to slave and colonial pasts. Some of the White, Black and interracial members of interracial families that I interviewed, and who feature in this chapter, did not need to trace their family tree in order to articulate their feelings of relatedness to the slave past. Rather, this knowledge was always already entwined within their genealogical imaginations, which had been learnt in diverse ways from their parents, husbands, grandparents, and at after school clubs.

Ethnographic inquiry with members of interracial families from Streetville

My fieldwork with members of interracial families from Streetville was conducted between May 2002 and June 2003, and formed an important and central component of my study on everyday understandings of race, genealogy and genetics (see also Tyler, 2005, 2007, 2008, 2009). The oral testimonies presented in this chapter are drawn from 36 in-depth interviews conducted with a cross-section of past and present residents of Streetville in terms of racial, ethnic, age, religious, class and gendered locations. The aim of the interviews was to explore how people reflect upon the constellation of genealogical aspects that make up their racial identities, which are inherited in diverse ways from their parents and extended family. Some of the people who participated in this project included members of the Residents' Association and the neighbourhood Forum discussed in Chapter 5. My participation in this neighbourhood network provided one valuable pathway for me to get to know residents of the neighbourhood. Meeting people in this social context enabled me to invite and encourage individuals to participate in my project on genealogy and racial identity.

Seventeen members of interracial families, comprising 14 women and three men, participated in this research on genealogy and identity, and seven members of interracial families agreed to be interviewed more than once. As I have already highlighted, the majority of my co-conversationalists from interracial families were members of White British and Black British African Caribbean descent families, which reflected the largest ethnic composition of interracial families in the area. All of the interviews were tape-recorded and were conducted either in people's homes, their workplaces or my flat in Streetville.

I came to know and network with some of my co-conversationalists from interracial families through contacts that I had formed with local organisations in the area, including, for example, centres for African Caribbean people. In addition, in networking with members of interracial families in the area, I drew upon relationships formed outside the fieldwork context. For example, an old school friend introduced me to an interracial couple who lived in Streetville. Moreover, some members of the Residents' Association, discussed in Chapter 5, put me in contact with people who they thought would want to help my research. Notwithstanding the significance of these networks, the most plentiful source for meeting research participants was through my co-conversationalists themselves, who introduced me to their family members and friends.

The predominance of female members of interracial families in my study is partly dependent upon my racial and gendered location as a White woman, which, echoing my fieldworks in Greenville and Coalville, inexorably shaped the research. At times I became painfully aware that some of my research participants, across racial, class and gendered locations, felt that my White identity might intrude to prejudice the research process. For example, a Black woman that I interviewed only told me after our discussion that her daughter's father was White. She felt that I needed to be 'educated' in the history of the African Caribbean community from Streetville before sharing personal information about her family with me.

On another occasion a female co-conversationalist who self-identified as 'mixed-heritage' gave me the telephone number of Robin, a male friend who she thought would be keen to participate in the project. I spoke with Robin a couple of times on the telephone and he seemed pleased to meet up with me. But when we did actually meet, it was instantly clear that he was disappointed by my White physical appearance. My Whiteness was immediately visible to him and was taken to be an indicator that I was not interracial. Robin had assumed that I would be interracial, or the member of an interracial family, and I had not told him otherwise. We were both disappointed. I felt bad that I had not made my ethnic identity and family relationships explicit to him on the telephone, which would have avoided putting him in an awkward situation. I regretted wasting Robin's time; he said he felt bad for turning me away without an interview.

With hindsight, this incident reminds me of my conversation with Simon, a White, middle-aged man from Greenville. The reader may recall that Simon was wary and suspicious of me and my project when I introduced myself to him on the telephone. Simon had thought that I might be an 'Asian girl' trying to trick him. By contrast to Robin, Simon was relieved that I was White. These examples provide insight into some of the ways in which my Whiteness intervened in contrasting ways to shape, facilitate and also at times hinder fieldwork.

Moreover, also during the course of my time networking with members of interracial families, I understood that some women with whom I came to interact believed it appropriate for me to talk with other women, from different racial locations, about what they took to be personal and intimate family matters. As the fieldwork progressed, I became interested in the inter-resonances between my co-conversationalists' narratives in terms of their experiences as wives, mothers and daughters and the ways in which their narratives were complicated by varied life stages, age, racial and ethnic locations. I also became interested in how feelings of ancestral connection to slave histories mediated my co-conversationalists' accounts.

In what follows, I draw extensively on the personal testimonies of three female members and one male member of African Caribbean Black and White descent interracial families: Emily identified herself as a 'White' mother of five children of African Caribbean descent. Her husband John described himself as 'Black'. Sandra self-identified as a 'mixed-heritage' woman who grew up with White adoptive parents. Clare was brought up by her Black Antiguan grandmother and White Irish mother, and despite her White physical appearance had come to define herself as 'Black'.

There are a number of reasons why I have chosen to focus in this chapter on these four people's personal testimonies. Firstly, the contrasting ways in which these individuals are located in relation to Whiteness illuminates in interesting ways how Whiteness mediates the formation of interracial identities. Secondly, I was drawn to these individuals' accounts because they each evoke and incorporate images and relationships from the slave past to interpret and make sense of the present, a process of meaning-construction that not all members of interracial families that I interviewed engaged in. Finally, my editorial decision to focus on just three women's and one man's testimonies is partly inspired by Jayne Ifekwunigwe's (1999) 'retelling' of the lives of six interracial women of Black and White parentage out of a total of 25 research participants in her book *Scattered Belongings*. She explains that by focusing in depth on the 'oral testimonies' of just six women she hoped to produce a narrative that neither 'fragmented nor trivialized' their 'lived experiences' (2001, p. 50). Likewise, I hope that by focusing in detail on just four people's narratives that I avoid undermining the complexity of research participants' particular understandings and experiences.

In this chapter, my ethnographic writing also shares parallels with a 'representational strategy' adopted by Sherry B. Ortner (2002, p. 10), which she calls 'critical documentary ethnography'. Like my work with members of interracial families, Ortner's account of her high school peers' memories of growing up in the post-war US is primarily based upon interviews. To achieve the 'maximum effect' from her interviews and to convey the passion with which her co-conversationalists talked with her, Ortner draws on 'the extensive use of people's own words, voices, styles, and emphases to communication not only the substance of the point, but its affect' (2002, p. 28). Ortner's (2002, pp. 10, 28) representational style is inspired by documentary films and ethnographic texts that are suffused with 'social criticism', which emerges through the 'voices and interactions of the people in the film or text' with relatively little authorial interruption. The effect of this approach in her ethnographic writing is to produce 'a kind of piling up of [interview] texts' so that the inter-resonance between individuals' testimonies is made visible. Inspired by Ortner's ethnographic writing, I have come to believe that drawing extensively on my co-conversationalists' 'choice of words, the emphases, the pace' (2002, p. 28) is the best way to communicate the emotion, feeling and passion with which my co-conversationalists talked to me about the intimate details of their lives. By 'piling up' each co-conversationalists' words, I also wish to render explicit the inter-resonances between their accounts, with the aim of producing a text that is 'more than the sum of its parts' (Ortner, 2002, p. 28).

Emily: A White mother of 'Black' children

Let us begin by considering the way in which Emily thinks about the inheritance of her children's racial identities. Emily's husband, John, introduced me to Emily. I knew John from his work as a youth worker at a local college in Streetville. Emily is a White woman who is the mother of five children who self-identified as 'Black'. When we met, her children spanned the ages of nine to 17. Emily was 42 years of age and had been married to John for nearly 20 years. John's parents migrated from Antigua to Streetville before he was born. While Emily and John did not live in Streetville, John worked as a youth worker in a local college and the family returned regularly to visit John's mother who had lived in the area for over 40 years. Emily was brought up in a predominantly White suburb of Leicester where her parents prohibited her from forming interracial relationships. During the course of my fieldwork, I met and interviewed John twice at his workplace and once at the family home. In addition, I interviewed Emily once at the family home, and John joined in my discussion with Emily towards the end of our conversation. My relationship with Emily and John was based on listening and learning about their experiences of becoming and being the parents of interracial 'Black' children. In the following account I have chosen to draw on lengthy extracts from my interview with Emily that highlight the racial and classed stereotypes that contributed to the breakdown in her relationships with her family of White origin. In the following section of this chapter, I will complement Emily's account with John's thoughts and reflections. But first, let us consider how Emily described her White parents' reaction to her interracial family:

> My dad believed that Whites should be with Whites and Blacks should be with Blacks. ... I became the black sheep of the family by marrying a Black man. I met this friend at school and she lived in Streetville ... and that's where I met John. ... I started to learn about other people and other ways of doing things. ... And like I said I met this friend at school and she lived in the Streetville area and that is where I began to find my way out of where I didn't want to be. ... She started introducing me to different people, different colours and different races ... [When her mother met John] She said, 'What the f-ing hell have you brought in here?', from then ... I used to stay a lot at the weekends at John's mum's in Streetville. ... The more children I had the less interest they [her parents] showed.

For Emily, Streetville is the site where relationships are made across the colour-lines, which is pitched in opposition to her experience of the weakening of genealogical ties to her family of origin. Her friendships formed in Streetville pushed her to reflect on her family's racism. From her parents' perspective, Emily's relationship with a Black man diluted her White racial identity, thereby rendering her the 'black sheep' of the family and so weakening their biogenetic relationship with their grandchildren. In her White parents' eyes, Emily has joined the wrong racial group. In this regard, an essentialist view of race shapes the perceived inappropriateness of intimacy across the colour-lines.

This view resonates with widely held colonial sensibilities on interracial sex. Respectable White bourgeois European colonial culture forbade White women from having any sexual intercourse with Black men. Interracial sexual relationships were thought not only to pollute and defile the purity of White bourgeois women's bodies, but also to threaten the health and strength of the nation and ultimately the European White race

(Stoler, 1995). Emily also described how her White parents believed that her relationship with a Black man indicated a loss of her social standing in terms of her class status:

> I mean when I had the twins that was a big thing from my side of the family because my granddad was a twin. And they [her parents] came up to the hospital to see them and after that they didn't bother. They didn't take them out as babies, and the more children I had the less and less interest. And what hurts me the most is that when I see them with my brothers' and sisters' children and they take them out to the seaside. And that is when I hurt the most, because I hurt for my children. And I did hurt for myself before but now I am hurting more for my kids. I mean it was my decision to marry John. I think that they [that is, her White parents] had the impression that if you marry a Black man then you are going to get beaten. And they [Black men] will put you out on the street – you know it is all this bad side. In my life with John I have had nothing. I mean it is my brothers and sisters that have had the bad things [that is, personal problems]. And my mum and dad have had more problems with them. I mean, I have had nothing with John.
>
> KATHARINE: And they can't see that?
>
> EMILY: I mean they can see it now. And all they can see now is Emily is alright [Emily refers to herself here]. I mean to their mind we shouldn't have had a house like this. And we shouldn't have had five kids. But again that perception and thinking you have married a Black and you shouldn't have that. And they come down [her parents visit infrequently, but do not offer the kind of relationship that she would like] and [they think] 'wow you've got your house', and my kids are brilliant [this is Emily's view and not her parents' perception of their grandchildren].

Emily's narrative draws on a discourse of White working-class respectability that is simultaneously raced, classed and gendered. By contrast to the ways in which my White working- and middle-class co-conversationalists' perceptions of class distinction became transparent in their views on racialised Others, Emily's sense of her family's classed respectability and status becomes apparent in her negotiation of how others judge her through the lens of respectability. Her parents feared that their White daughter's marriage to a Black man would result in her being mistreated by her husband. In this regard, Emily's marriage across the colour-lines signifies for them a loss of gendered and classed respectability associated with a decent home and a husband who cares for and provides for his family. The reality is that Emily and John have five 'brilliant kids', a happy marriage and a comfortable family home. Emily's parents' surprise at their daughter's happiness highlights how the economic (having a nice home) and cultural (being a good mother, husband and so on) capital associated with the reproduction of a respectable family is thought by some to be unavailable and lost to White women who marry across the colour-lines.

There is a parallel to be drawn between Emily's parents' assumptions and the ways in which the material capital of Wealthy BrAsians in Greenville is not legitimated by White middle-class people there (see Chapter 2). In both cases, racial difference is thought to devalue, eclipse and render worthless the acquisition of norms and capital that are valued and esteemed by most Whites, such as economic stability and material and emotional comfort. Emily and her children's experiences of snobbery, racism and rejection from her White parents have contributed to the conditions in which her children self-identify as 'Black'. Once more, Emily explained it to me like this:

> We had this discussion about the [British Census] forms. My children put themselves down as Black and not dual heritage [her term, not an official Census classification] and that for me was a big thing. At first I did mind and I thought well they are my kids as well. I am their mother. ... But then, I could see where they [her children] were coming from because they have had such a strong bond with John's family. ... I didn't mind because they couldn't have had that with my family, what with their views. ... They [her children] have always been brought up in the Streetville way. ... Like with their hair, I wouldn't have known to put grease on their hair if John's mum hadn't told me. ... For nine months they are growing inside of you and it would be hard to say that they are not mine because they are.

In her narration of her children's inheritance of their 'Black' identities, Emily intersects ideas about her biological connection to them formed through gestation with ideas about her cultural affiliation. Initially she was concerned that her children's self-identification as 'Black' on the British Census forms rather than 'dual heritage' negated their maternal connection to her. As she says 'I am their mother' – a relationship that is made self-evident by her children's gestation in her womb – yet which seems to be screened out in their self-identification as 'Black'.

However, Emily realises that the weakening of her relationship with her White family of origin has been instrumental in the formation of her children's 'strong bond' with their Black kin and so has facilitated the inheritance of their 'Black' identities. In fact, Emily goes further, to suggest that her children's identification with her husband's Black family becomes interwoven and synonymous with their sense of belonging to Streetville as a place. As she says of her children, 'They have always been brought up in the Streetville way'. In this regard, Emily describes how her appropriation of Black cultural knowledge from her mother-in-law, such as her ability to care for her children's hair, has played an important part in fixing their 'Black' identities. Suki Ali (2003, p. 81) argues that the ability of White mothers to care for their interracial children's Afro-style hair is not just about 'appearance; it is values, caring, kinship and culture'. Thus while in some contexts Emily's cultural and biological relationship to her 'Black' children might not be clearly visible, it is certainly not negated. That is, Emily's genealogical affiliation to her children disrupts the bounded and discrete folk categories of 'Black' and 'White' that associate skin colour with a particular racial location and ancestry. In short, Emily's account renders explicit the role that some White women play in the reproduction of the 'Black' English population.

Emily repeatedly draws on the ideas of 'teaching' and 'learning' from her husband and his family to describe her cultivation of Black 'racial literacy' and 'maternal competence' (Twine, 2000). In this way, Emily stressed that John and his family 'taught her everything'. For example, she explained how she had learnt from her mother-in-law: 'West Indian nursery rhymes', the necessity to 'cream' her children's skin because 'it gets dry', and knowledge of life in Antigua. Central to this process is Emily's learning of Black history. On this she said:

> And I am learning more than I did at school. ... They didn't teach you things about slavery, whereas John will sit here and tell me things. ... We went to the Maritime Museum in Liverpool and they talked about girls getting raped [that is, Black girls and women being raped by White men]. And I was like, 'oh gosh' – that was a real shellshock. I wouldn't say that I was ignorant because I just didn't know. And we came home and he [John] talked me through the situation ... because they [teachers at school, her family, adults generally when growing up] don't teach you things about that. And I wouldn't say that I was being ignorant it is just that they don't teach you otherwise. ... I am

still learning now. ... I have to learn that or otherwise I end up ... thinking that the White way is the right way and you can't be like that. ... And if I had stayed at home [her White parents' home] I would have been stuck with their way of thinking. ... And that goes for my grandparents as well. They used to look down on Black people like a piece of dirt.

It is significant that Emily considers herself not to be 'ignorant' of the histories of slavery because she was not taught it when growing up in a White family in a predominantly White working-class suburb in Leicester in the 1960s. Emily's comments are profoundly significant because they provide insight into the ways in which White amnesia of the slave past is reproduced within English society. From this point of view, institutionalised White amnesia of the slave past within English schools, combined with White people's general lack of knowledge about that past, ensures that White individuals are unaware of the ways in which slavery has shaped the formation of Black interracial and White English ethnicities in the present. Interestingly, Emily's visit to the Maritime Museum is part of her process of learning about slavery. This exhibition formed part of a surge in the late twentieth and early twenty-first century in exhibitions that 'sought to reclaim the histories of oppressed minorities and their struggles against imperialism' (Thompson, 2005, p. 234). It is thus the process of learning about slavery from her husband, together with her cultivation of Black cultural practices learnt from her extended family, that has transformed Emily's way of thinking about the histories that connect Black, interracial and White people in the present. Hence she fears that if she had not met and fallen in love with John she might never have come to question and challenge her White parents' and grandparents' racist values and attitudes.

John: 'politicising' a White mother

Following on from Emily's narrative it is useful to explore her husband's views on the meaning and significance of his wife's acquisition of racial literacy, including her knowledge of slavery. One afternoon, I met and interviewed John in his office at the college in which he works. During our conversation he explained the following:

> With my wife there has been a lot of learning for her. ... And the whole thing about her understanding the effects of racism and what she would say to the kids if they come home [with issues and

problems regarding racism]. ... And all those things about slavery ... liberation and Black history. ... So the thing about politicising is very important. Because again the mother instinct takes over as well – it is one thing when you have to go up and fight on behalf of the child but it is quite another thing when it is a White mother challenging racism.

John suggests that knowledge 'about slavery ... liberation and Black history' is crucial to Emily's development and appropriation of racial literacy. He believes that it is the intersection of the 'mother instinct' with her appropriation of knowledge about Black history that makes her challenge to racism as a White mother a powerful political expression of anti-racist sentiment. Like Emily's beliefs and experience, John's thoughts disrupt the hierarchical racialised tensions in English society that classifies and defines individuals as either 'Black', 'White' or 'Asian'.

John eloquently and poetically elaborated upon the ways in which histories of slavery are integral to the contemporary formation of his family's relationships with each other and with the wider Black community. In the following extracts from my interviews with John, he described the connections between the slave past, Emily's ability to cook Caribbean food and his family's appreciation of music and dance:

> From my point of view there was a whole lot to teach her [Emily]. ... The whole thing about the way African Caribbean people cook our food, how we dance. ... So you know my wife, even at a point without promoting from me, she took on a Caribbean cookery course. ... From my point of view that shows her willingness ... to engage in not just our relationship but that I [he is speaking her from Emily's point of view] also need to engage in the culture and its values.
>
> KATHARINE: Why is food particularly important?
> JOHN: Historically ... food as a community has had a major significance. ... If you go back to the slave days that is why ... Caribbeans are so good at using spices, because as slaves we got the leftovers from the main upper class people. So when we were getting it last, we thought hang on a minute this tastes bland, and so we had to make it to our tastes. And so there is a whole historical link particularly with food, you know, how it was developed and how stuff was prepared ...
> KATHARINE: You just mentioned dance: can you expand on that?
> JOHN: For me dance and music, in order to understand your culture and your history, you have to understand how all these things came about. ... Things have been passed

from generations about how we are. ... It [music] was one of the spiritual ways in which slaves had their free time. It was one of the ways in which slaves had of relieving their tensions, was through song and dance. ... So in one sense it is inherited because that spiritual and historical presence has moved along with Black communities throughout. ... It has always been spiritual – church and stuff like that gospel. Gospel music has played, you know, and gospel was part of that era, through the fifties and sixties the church was inspiration in terms of us having hope that things will get better. ... When the wife was pregnant a lot of the gospel music and soul music we played all of that. Even to the point with one of my daughters, we swear blind that one of my daughters was dancing in the wife's stomach. Funnily enough, since all our children have been born – I've got three daughters who sing and a son who performs in a rap group. So because music plays such a central role that follows up. And again understanding that historical context where it has come. ...

In a different discussion with John, he drew upon this theme as follows:

In Africa the drum is the heartbeat, the melody and the tunes is the blood flowing through you. And because you have to remember the slaves couldn't communicate. There was one way of communicating through the drum, da dum, da dum [John flattens his hand and makes a boom, boom sound on his chest like a heart beat]. The sound hits your heart and resonates. It was the life beat of the community, and if you look at it now one of the most popular things that have come out of Black music now is the drum and base. Even with my son who is into ragga music [a genre of reggae] and you go back to the historical context you know where that has come from.

John constructs an intricate and complex chain of biological and cultural metaphors to describe how the 'spirit', 'blood', 'heart' and 'soul' of the slave past is passed on across generations in the everyday routines and rhythms of Black and interracial families and communities, including his own family. John understands music to have offered pleasure and hope to Black families and individuals across time and space including his White wife and children. Thus John describes how the African drum – the 'heartbeat' of slave communities – and its tunes – the 'blood flowing through you' – intimately relates his children's musical talents and Emily's enjoyment of soul music to the slave past, and to past and present generations of Black people. Emily's White body and her cultivation of racial literacy are central to John's account. This is made evident by the way that Emily's preparation of Caribbean food binds Emily and John's family to the histories of slavery. It is noteworthy that in this context food is not just a fixed and static marker of cultural distinction, as curry too often is within White notions of cultural difference (as discussed in Chapter 3). Rather, in John's narrative, Caribbean food becomes integral to the formation of his family's identity and ancestry. John also evokes a connection between the heartbeat and blood of African slave music and one of his daughters dancing to soul music in her White mother's womb. Reading across Emily's and John's accounts, it becomes clear that their returns to the slave past highlight some of the ways in which a feeling of ancestral relatedness to that past can come to shape the everyday formation of contemporary Black, White and interracial ethnicities and relationships in the present.

Sandra: Growing up White

Like Emily, racism intervened to truncate Sandra's sense of relatedness to the White family that brought her up. Sandra was brought up by a White adoptive family, and when she reached adulthood she cut all ties with them. Sandra described herself as 'mixed-heritage'. Her birth mother was a White woman from Leicester, and her birth father was born in Antigua and came to Leicester as a child. A White family fostered Sandra when she was 10 days old and this family subsequently adopted her. When I met Sandra she was 33 years of age. I came to know Sandra through her work as co-ordinator of a project based in Streetville that provides support for the parents and children of interracial families living in Leicester. One of the members of the Streetville Residents' Association put me into contact with Sandra. I first met Sandra at her office. At this meeting I talked with Sandra and her colleagues about their work with interracial families from Leicester. One morning Sandra visited my flat in Streetville. It was at this meeting that we spoke at length about her experiences of growing up, her search for her birth parents and the impact that coming to know her birth parents had upon her sense of identity. Sandra began her story by describing her feeling of alienation and loneliness growing up in a White family that was racist:

> I would do things like scrubbing my skin ... to stop the racial abuse. ... It wasn't because I hated it – my skin being brown – it was just that

I wanted to fit in. ... I always felt not part of that family because it was something that I always knew that I was very distanced. I don't know but maybe because of the name-calling that made me step back and as a child there was no affection. ... I found it very hard to call them 'mum' and 'dad' ... it was kind of like why am I calling them that? I was very intrigued by anyone who was Black or of colour on the television that used to fascinate me, because I felt that was part of me that I did not know. ... It took me years to pluck up the courage to say, 'Pack it in'. ... When I did I used to get comments back so I just thought forget it.

While growing up, Sandra experienced her 'brown' skin as a visible, fixed and naturalised marker of her racial identity that distinguished and separated her from her White adoptive family. In this way, she expresses her experience of racism as a child in naturalised terms centred on the physicality of race. This experience pushed her to form a sense of connection and 'fascination' with 'Black' or 'of colour' people on the television.

When she was 18 years old Sandra moved to Streetville and began the task of tracing her birth parents in the hope of finding people to whom she would belong. Her desire to search for her birth parents illustrates how the idea of genetic and racial ancestry can be alluring. By contrast, the weakening of Emily's kinship ties with her White birth family highlights how relations based upon the idea of genetic kinship and racial ancestry can be seen as impermanent and unstable.

Sandra's search led to her discovery of unexpected connections between people, places and cultural knowledge. Her genealogical journey 'widened the possibilities of what counts as kinship out from under the long shadow of genealogy and biology', that set her search in motion (Franklin, 2001, p. 317). Once Sandra had traced her White birth mother to London, her friends in Streetville drew upon their memories of their past relationships in the area to identify her father and other members of her birth family. She explained her reaction to finding out that her neighbours in Streetville were her sisters as follows: 'It was like No! I had known these girls for a couple of years ... and they are my sisters!' Sandra's journey not only affiliates her to neighbours in Streetville in surprising ways but also makes her reinterpret her relationship to the cityscape. In her own words:

It is interesting in this area this is where my dad was living with his auntie and that is where I was conceived basically. She [Sandra's birth mother] used to meet my dad at the health centre [when this building was a community centre, before it became a health centre]. And it is interesting because when I was 18, I moved into this area and I used to live in the tower block at the back of the health centre. And like now, I work and live here, which is kind of weird that the area I have been in is where I began.

For Emily and Sandra, Streetville is the place where interracial relationships and identities are formed and negotiated. Moreover for Sandra, Streetville is the locale where she discovered that she was 'made'. Sandra and her twin daughters visit her father regularly. She talks with her White mother on the telephone but has only met her once. Sandra explained further her relationship with her birth parents and the effect of these new relationships on her life thus:

My mum is like my friend who I've known all my life, and my dad ... I'm learning a lot about my identity and my culture from him. He tells stories to the kids [her twin daughters] ... and I'm like, oh I've got to hear this because no one has ever, do you know what I mean? So it is like, I am 10 and 11 and I'm listening to stories. And it is like I love it. I just soak it all in. He says, 'In Antigua this', and I say, 'tell me some more'. So I think that is what I'm craving, I need that, and I'm reborn kind of thing. ... I don't need much on the White side because I've had that [all my life], like I know who my mum is, and if I have the contact great and if I don't no big deal. But my dad is like a big part of me that I have never had. ... I have not been brought up around that and things like cooking and stuff like that. He says, 'I am going to get you a Caribbean cookery book', and it is like I wish you would because I've not been shown. And like my daughter has got really thick long black hair, a bit like mine, and nobody showed me how to do that. It was things like, I had to pick it up. And going into the Black hairdressers [located opposite my flat in Streetville] ... I didn't dare go into that ... but now my confidence has grown and it is like – yeah I'm going to go into that. ... When I was growing up people were very much like, 'You are Black', and I think ... I had a very limited Black experience as a child. It was only as an adult that I got more. ... And as a young child I used to say I was 'White'. ... But it was once I got that balance I was quite happy to say, 'I'm mixed-heritage'. I am not going to deny either side of my family because ... why should I deny my mum or my dad? It was both of them that made me.

In Sandra's narrative 'the social' and 'the biological' are 'foregrounded at a different moment and for a different purpose, but each requires the other for its purchase' (Edwards, 1999, p. 318). As a child, Sandra used to say that she was 'White' because she was not brought up by a Black family, while others identified her as 'Black', an assumption that rests on the folk belief that physical appearance signifies 'just' Black or 'just' White biological parentage. It is only when Sandra's knowledge of her interracial ancestry becomes melded with her inheritance of Black cultural knowledge from her birth father, friends and neighbours from Streetville that she feels 'reborn' as an interracial woman.

As with Emily, White culture and identity is the backdrop against which Sandra's acquisition of racial literacy becomes transparent. Growing up in a White family and society has ensured Sandra's knowledge of White cultural practices. So, she does not 'crave' and 'desire' the same close relationship with her White mother as she does her Black father. Moreover, once more in parallel with Emily and John, Sandra identifies her learning and knowledge of how to care for her daughter's hair and her ability to cook Caribbean food as central to the acquisition of racial literacy. This reinforces the point that the cultivation of these practices symbolises the embodiment of African Caribbean identity, kinship and a sense of relatedness to the wider Black community. In this way, for Sandra, parenthood not only represents the biological making of persons but also the passing on of identity, values and culture. Sandra's knowledge of her genetic 'origins' thus becomes a 'coding for ethnicity' (Thompson, 2001, p. 81) when it is intersected with her inheritance of racial literacy, cultural knowledge and social relationships across the colour-lines, without which her interracial parentage and 'origins' would not make much sense to her.

Sandra's relationship with her father not only mediates and is mediated by her relationships with friends, neighbours and new kin from Streetville but also affiliates her to the African Caribbean diasporic home of Antigua and to her White birth mother. Thus, Sandra's sense of her identity is chosen, self-constructed and made through a 'changing constellation' and 'constant weighting' (Stoler, 1997, p. 104) of ideas about her interracial genetic parentage, her affiliation to local and diasporic homes and the inheritance of Black and White cultural practices that disrupt the binary folk racial categories of 'Black' and 'White'. It is in the context of this narrative of relatedness that Sandra draws upon the slave past to articulate her ethnicity. She said:

> I have always been into – I have loved listening to music – and that I've never played an instrument or anything like that, but I've been very much into it. Where it links in – I mean carnival is about

a celebration of the end of slavery and getting together. Music is a big thing – a big part of Black culture. But again it depends on the individual families and what kind of music they are into. Like some families are big churchgoers and they have a different kind of music there. So it comes in different forms, and it is not just a religious thing. It is a very strong influence in the culture. ... It is passed on from way, way back and the songs, as well in some of the books I've read about slavery and freedom and it is the life experiences that make the good music.

Sandra's emphasis on always liking music allows her to relate her experience of growing up in the absence of Black parents to the wider Black community and histories of 'slavery and freedom'. Moreover, as with Emily's experience, Sandra did not learn about slave histories from the White people who brought her up. However, her emphasis upon reading about slavery and freedom forms a contrast to Emily's learning about the histories of slavery from her husband. From this standpoint, a sense of connection to the slave past does not feature as prominently within Sandra's account as it does for my other co-conversationalists who appear in this chapter. Nonetheless, it is significant that to make sense of her liking of music while growing up, Sandra draws upon her reading of Black history and the importance of music to that history. In this way, as with Emily's and John's accounts, aspects of Sandra's everyday life and biography become woven into histories of slavery and freedom.

Clare: Looking White, being Black

By contrast to Emily and Sandra, Clare was brought up in what she describes as a 'Black' milieu. Clare was a 26-year-old youth worker at an African Caribbean women's centre in Streetville, where she grew up. The manager of the women's centre introduced Clare to me. I interviewed Clare at her workplace. She explained what she calls her 'heritage' thus: 'My father is African Caribbean Antiguan heritage and my mum is White Irish heritage.' She described herself physically as: 'Very fair – people think that I am Irish because I have got bits of red hair and freckles. I would work quite well over in Ireland.' Clare had never visited Ireland, nor had she met her White Irish grandparents. She told me: 'They weren't too pleased that we were Black. They weren't accepting of us.'

Clare's parents divorced when she was four years old and her Antiguan grandmother and White Irish mother brought her up. She told me how her mother, the eldest of 11 children, did not go to school because her emotional and physical labour was needed at home. Clare said of her mother's childhood and adolescence: 'she was more of a fetcher, a carrier, a runner', who as an adult 'scrubbed toilets' so that Clare and her sister received 'the things she never had', such as extra math lessons and ballet classes. In this way, Clare's mother worked hard to ensure that her children acquired the cultural and social capital necessary to become respectable.

Throughout our conservation Clare drew on idioms and metaphors of 'culture', 'environment' and 'upbringing' to narrate what she perceived to be the sensual, cultural, psychological and physical characteristics that constituted her inheritance of a Black identity. In her words:

> I have been lucky enough to have been brought up as a Black person, in a Black environment, growing up with a Black grandma. Although my mum is White, I have always been pushed to the forefront of being Black. ... Although I'm very fair ... that is my heritage ... part of who I am. ... And to be able to talk about food and the characteristics, like the way I speak. I was told by a couple of women in the centre [the African Caribbean women's centre where she works] that they don't see my colour. ... They just see Clare as being Black. And they say, 'That's because of your whole make-up'. ... In some ways I'm more Black than some Black people. I am very aware of my roots.

The food, the way that she speaks, thinks and sees blend together to 'make up' her 'Black' 'heritage', 'roots' and identity. It makes no sense for Clare to distinguish between, or see any contradiction in her upbringing in a Black cultural milieu, her White ancestry marked by her skin colour, and her embodiment and internalisation of a Black identity. In fact, Clare insists that her cultural upbringing is as important in creating and fixing her Blackness as any physical inheritance. In this way, she contests and destabilises a naturalised definition of Blackness grounded on inherited biological and phenotypical characteristics. This does not mean that Clare simply naturalises culture. Rather, she intersects and blurs the metaphoric domains of nature and culture, thereby disrupting the boundaries between folk racial categories of Black and White.

Clare's narration of her inheritance of a Black identity is interwoven and entwined with her reflection on her Black friends' and neighbours' reactions to her White physical appearance. Clare's claim to membership of the Black community from Streetville is contested by others. To counter this, she has to negotiate the folk conception of race that defines an individual's racial identity, parentage and ancestry by their physical appearance:

> If I was darker then I would have been more accepted by Black friends. ... When I spoke Patwa [a language spoken in the Caribbean] ... or when I talk about back home – that is how I was always taught, Antigua was always back home – and I think people would think, 'who is she?' Or they think I was being disrespectful.

Like Sandra's sense of affiliation to Antigua, Clare's feeling of relatedness to the wider Black diaspora spreads beyond the family and Streetville to Antigua, a place that she calls 'home'. However, in contrast to Sandra, who describes herself as having 'brown skin', Clare's White physical appearance means that her claim to belong to Antigua is questioned and truncated by others.

In relation to this contestation over her identity, Clare spoke about an emotional and defining episode in her life, when her Black neighbours from Streetville objected to her becoming the Carnival Queen at Leicester's annual African Caribbean Carnival. In reflecting on this event, she mobilises knowledge about her Black 'roots', images of the slave past and White ancestry to reinterpret and transform her experience of rejection by some Black people in Streetville. Central to this narrative of belonging was Clare's description of the class distinctions that she felt separated her from others. She told me:

> I have eventually got to achieve the status of being Carnival Queen – the atmosphere after that was horrible because I just wasn't accepted. ... That experience was very hard for me – living in Streetville all my life – being very active in the Black community. ... Wherever I have experienced racism from Black people ... it was ignorance and jealousy. ... It is something that has gone on for generations and generations. You know it goes back to the slave trade. And a lot of people perceive that with me ... being fair and having really long hair and those kinds of things, and being accepted as well [by White people]. ... It wasn't nice, I mean to be called the 'White witch', 'the White queen' on the actual evening ... blew me away. It was like the natural progression of the lively person that I am ... because I have always made the costumes. I have always been part of it. But to be brought back down to earth like that with a big bump – I do think that is ignorance. It is something that has gone on for generations. ... You know it goes back to the fair-skinned one being

able to work in the house in the slave trade [that is, the plantations], and the darker you were you were out in the fields. ... The negative that is pushed out there, within the Black community via Black people in Leicester is really saddening. It just seems really sad to me. I don't know if it is just Leicester, but for every one step that someone makes to better themselves everyone just wants to pull them down ... to a negative. And it is a difficult situation because, on the one hand, you are proud of who you are, and what you are, and then you constantly get knocked by your own.

By contrast to Emily and Sandra, who experienced Streetville as a positive site for the formation of interracial relationships, Clare experienced Streetville as a place where her Black identity is rejected by some Black people. In their eyes, Clare's White skin and body demarcates her as purely White. These onlookers assume that the body provides a straightforward signifier of ethnic identity and location. From this point of view, Clare's self-identification as Black and her detailing of social and cultural capital (such as growing up in a Black milieu, working for the 'community') to support her claim is not recognised and legitimated by others. To reformulate and subvert this misunderstanding of her ethnicity, Clare articulates an inclusive sense of her Black identity. In so doing, she traces her Black ancestry to slave times. In this way, Clare evokes and recalls a time when Black men and women had no ownership over their bodies and thus no claims to identity – a state of being that the historian Orlando Patterson (1982) famously calls 'social death'. As in Hall's concept of 'new ethnicities', Clare's return to, and remembrance of, the past does not signal a simple return to ideas of origins associated with the fixity of cultural and ancestral purity. However, whereas Hall concentrates on the formation of Black subjectivities, her sense of relatedness to 'fair-skinned' interracial slave ancestors neither negates nor celebrates her White physical appearance and mixed ancestry. Clare thus carries the suffering of her White, interracial and Black slave ancestors both physically and experientially within herself.

Notwithstanding Clare's profound feelings of relatedness to other Black people, this image of shared ancestry is interwoven with a sharp sense of class distinction entwined with ideals of working-class respectability and rooted in her desire for self-improvement. By contrast, to those members of the Black 'community' who Clare thinks constantly 'pull' her and others 'down ... to a negative', she is determined to 'better' herself. In this sense, Clare has ambitions to gain social status associated with class mobility and the value of recognition. Moreover, she thinks that her desire for self-betterment echoes distinctions that existed between her enslaved ancestors, separating those with 'dark skins' who worked in 'the fields' from those with 'fair skins' who worked in 'the house'. Clare knows that some slaves were more trusted with domestic work than others. And because of this, she believes domestic work in the house was more 'respectable' than work in the fields. It is precisely this historically embedded concept of respectability that Clare feels explains some Black people's negative reaction towards her physical appearance, and 'jealousy' towards her social ambition in the present.

It is noteworthy that the figure of the White slave owner is the absent ancestor in her narrative. From this standpoint, Clare does not identify with White middle- and upper-class people. This should not be surprising given that Clare relates to White people, like her mother, who has not benefited in any clear-cut way from the power and privilege associated with Whiteness (see also Gatson, 2003, on this point, discussed in Chapter 7).

Later on in our conversation Clare described how she had come to learn about the history of slavery and develop a sense of the historical injustices inflicted upon Black people:

KATHARINE: And where has this sense of historical injustice come from?
CLARE: For me myself it comes from being a child. I read an old school report last week and I was 12 years old. I had just gone up to my second year and it was a history report. ... I wrote: 'I do enjoy history, but why can't we do any work on Black history? Or at least try'. ... I just got this feeling that there was a lot more to learn. And I was lucky because I went to Saturday school. ... But I was shocked reading this report and seeing how passionate I was all those years ago. So it can only come from being a child – listening to my grandma and hearing and ... This is something that my mum pushed. And I'd learn all about Black history and I'd learn all about the slave trade. ... And I must have been about 8 or 9 [years old]. ... I was coming here to the Centre [that is, attending Saturday classes at the Black women's centre where she now works] and mixing with a lot of Black girls and learning a lot more. Just that sense of thinking that people suffered just for us to be here.

Like Emily, Clare highlights how she was not taught Black history at school and so points towards the institutionalisation of White amnesia of the slave past in England. However, in stark contrast to Sandra and Emily, who each grew up in White environments where they were taught nothing about slavery by the adults around them, Clare learnt about slavery from her grandmother, her White mother and at Saturday school. This difference in each woman's experiences brings to the fore the contrasting ways in which Whites, Blacks and interracial people are socialised differently, or not at all, within their families into thinking about Black history, including the histories of slavery and its significance for the formation of the present. Clearly, for some Black and interracial children growing up in England, like Clare, and Emily's and John's children, the learning of slave histories is not left to chance. Rather, their retelling of slave histories in the home and between family members, and the interweaving of the significance of that history into the daily rituals and pleasures of family life, such as cooking and listening to music, ensure that these histories become 'imprinted on the bodies of children and carried with them into adulthood' (Hall, 1998, p. 456).

Before moving on to the final section of this chapter it is worth pausing for a moment to draw out some of the contrasts and complexities in my co-conversationalists' accounts, and the ways in which their narratives connect to some of the wider themes explored in this book. Central to my co-conversationalists' narratives is the ways in which Whiteness mediates the inheritance of interracial identities. Emily and Sandra both experienced racism from the White people who brought them up. In this way, their White relatives' racist attitudes destroyed the intimacy of their family relationships. Form her White parents' point of view, Emily's marriage to a Black man negatively diluted the purity of her White racial identity and signified a loss of respectability in terms of class status and gender identity. Sandra's experience of racial abuse growing up in her White adoptive family motivated her to search for her biological parents. For both Emily and Sandra, Streetville is the site where positive relationships of intimacy and love are formed across the colour-lines. For Clare, by contrast, Streetville is the place where her claim to be Black is rejected by those who can only see her White skin colour.

Crucial to Clare's Black ethnicity and Emily's experience of mothering children who self-identify as Black is each woman's emphasis on learning about Black history and its significance for the formation of their identities and, in Emily's case, her children's identities in the present. In this way, knowledge of the slave past becomes entwined with each woman's sense of identity, understanding of racism, becoming and being a member of the Black community in Leicester and the wider diaspora.

In short, knowledge of Black history and the slave past provides a lens through which my co-conversationalists in their unique ways come to interpret and make sense of patterns and rhythms of the everyday. In so doing, their narratives illuminate how knowledge of the slave past and its significance for the present holds the potential to disrupt the White, colonially inherited, worldview that classifies and interprets individuals through a racialised binominal lens of 'us' and 'them'. Thus it is here, in the narratives of members of interracial families, that a discourse through which to challenge the contemporary articulation of colonial discourses of race, culture and difference arrives and emerges. A feature crucial to this counter-narrative is the remembering of aspects of the colonial past and its significance for the present.

A White woman's view on slavery and genealogical identities

I shall end and conclude this chapter by moving away from its focus on members of interracial families to explore how ideas of genealogy, interracial identity and images of the slave past are put to work by Sophie, a woman who self-identifies as 'White' and does not belong to an interracial family. My introduction of Sophie's views illuminates some of the processes involved in the displacing, forgetting and screening out of the significance of the slave past for interpreting and understanding the formation of interracial relationships in the present. In one sense, by bringing in Sophie's views at this juncture I turn the book full-circle by returning to some of the processes and consequences of White amnesia of the colonial past explored in detail in Part I of this book.

I met Sophie, who owned a small terraced house in Streetville, through her participation in the Residents' Association. Sophie was 32 years of age and moved to the city when she was 18 years old to study languages.

Sophie and I had much in common. We were both female, White, middle class, university graduates, settling into our thirties and we lived in close proximity to each other. During my fieldwork we became friends. We often shared wine and neighbourhood gossip after Residents' Association meetings. At times my work became the stimulus for serious discussion.

In the following, I draw upon Sophie's reaction to a film we watched together as part of my fieldwork on ethnicity and genealogy. The film is entitled *Motherland: A Genetic Journey*, and I showed it to Sophie because it raises some of the themes that I wanted to discuss with residents of

Streetville for my work on ethnicity and genealogy. In this respect, the documentary raised issues concerning the ways in which ideas of ancestry and descent mediate the inheritance of ethnic and racial identities. Our discussion of this programme provides insight into how a White woman (who, as I have said, is not a member of an interracial family) negotiates the possibility that one of the legacies of slavery is that she might have a Black ancestor. I draw here on an extract from my conversation with Sophie after watching *Motherland*, but first, a little more about the documentary.

The programme was inspired by an experiment carried out by geneticists at the Universities of Cambridge and Leicester. This experiment deployed advances in population genetics to trace the ancestral identities of Black Britons. The programme forms part of a recent surge in the number of television documentaries, books, websites and commercial companies that have popularised and marketed genetic techniques to trace family genealogies (Cross, 2001; Brodwin, 2004; Nash, 2004; Tutton, 2004). The programme analysed the DNA of 228 Black African Caribbean descent men and women living in Britain. The research participants were selected on the criteria that they had two generations of paternal and maternal grandparents that were of Black African Caribbean descent. Over a quarter (26 per cent) of the Black male participants were told that their Y chromosome, inherited through the male line, traced them back to a European ancestor. The tests also showed that the mitochondria DNA that is inherited through the maternal line affiliated many of the research participants with ancestors from African tribal groups. The DNA results of the project participants thus confirmed the historical evidence that White European men had frequently reproduced children with Black slave women, invariably through force and coercion.

The programme followed the journeys of three research participants who used their newly acquired 'genetic kinship' (Nash, 2004) to interrogate either their Black/African or their White/European ancestry, depending on which aspect of their identity was important to them. At this point in the documentary, the viewer is left with the impression that an individual's DNA can be objectively coded, separated and divided into its racially distinct component parts. Moreover, each individual's 'quest for self-hood' (Strathern, 1998, p. 3, cited in Franklin, 2001, p. 306) appears to reflect the way in which 'objective' scientific knowledge can have 'intimate and personal effects' (Franklin, 2001, pp. 306, 307). However, when the research participants embarked on their journeys to forgotten African and Caribbean ancestral home places, they unexpectedly discovered the entanglement of White and Black people's colonial and slave histories, ancestries and origins. In this way, when knowledge of genetic ancestry is combined with social relationships, colonial and slave histories can be put to work to undermine the idea of racially pure lines of descent within families.

In the knowledge that Sophie was tracing her paternal Irish family's history, I asked if she would find the technologies deployed in the *Motherland* experiment useful to her quest. She spontaneously replied as follows:

> I know that out of curiosity I would do it. ... But I don't know how I would feel about the results. ... You would never ever find an end or a beginning to your heritage. ... When I started doing my family tree, I wanted to know a bit about my heritage. And now, I want to know a bit more. ... And my God, if I discovered that I had cousins in Zambia! My God – it would be unbearable – just never ending, thinking and worrying. ... Because you would want to know it all and you wouldn't be able to. ... It would be a logistical nightmare. ... How do you go that far back? ... How many records and places to go to? How many hundreds of pounds would that cost you? Oh, I would be mental. But it would be quite nice.
>
> KATHARINE: So why nice?
> SOPHIE: Well, because everyone likes a bit of an exotic background, don't they? ... I am convinced that there is no such thing as true English, which is proved by my family. But I would be interested in –
> KATHARINE: How diverse?
> SOPHIE: Exactly.
> KATHARINE: I would take delight in seeing myself as being more connected.
> SOPHIE: Connected to what, though? I wouldn't pin anything on it. I would take it with a pinch of salt.

Sophie acknowledges the possibility that Black and White ancestries are merged and interconnected. However, by contrast to the members of interracial families that feature in this chapter, who draw upon the slave past to interpret and make sense of their identities and daily lives in the present, Sophie describes potential African ancestors through the objectifying idiom of 'exotic'. Thus, in this extract from our conversation, Sophie constructs and maintains a sense of distance and racialised distinction separating her racially unmarked and bland White identity from that of exotic ancestors. While Sophie's fragmented sense of Englishness relates her to people outside of England (mainly to White people in Ireland), she does not consider these relationships to be 'diverse' enough to constitute an 'exotic' background. One might say that they are too close to home, too White and thus perhaps too 'normal' to constitute the 'exotic'. Rather, it is people who are unfamiliar, identified by their faraway origins, and who also happen to be racially marked, that would be considered by Sophie to be suitably 'exotic'.

Having focused upon what Sophie actually says in this particular extract, it is worth taking a moment to examine what is absent in her account. While Sophie says that she 'would want to know it all', her thoughts here on the formation of her potentially interracial ancestry displace and screen out any direct reference to or engagement with the histories of slavery and the atrocities that constitute that history. This absence is particularly surprising given the centrestage that colonial and slave histories play in the documentary programme that formed the stimulus for our discussions. Sophie's side-stepping of the power dynamics that underpin the realities of the slave past illuminates further how White, Black and interracial people are socialised in different ways to think about the importance of slavery for the formation of postcolonial identities. But more than this, my contention is that it is precisely Sophie's screening out of White domination that lies at the heart of the slave relation, and thus the significance of this for interpreting the present, which underlies her sense of distinction between the White self and the exotic Other. In this way, Sophie's account illustrates that it is not simply a case of knowing about the inheritance of ancestors across the colour-lines that counts, rather it is the ways in which such knowledge is put to work to interpret and inform the present that matters. I return to this point in the next and final chapter of this book.

7
The Co-Existence of Whiteness, Social Class and Coloniality in Britain and the USA

In this concluding chapter, I take a step back from the ethnographic material presented earlier to reflect upon the ways in which the theme of coloniality and social class running throughout this book might contribute to the theoretical framework that informs Whiteness studies. I aim to juxtapose some of the key findings of my study on race, class, place and coloniality in Leicester/shire with similar phenomena in the USA. In so doing, I seek to deploy ethnographic and theoretical insights from the USA to think analytically about how to draw together some of the themes and conclusions of my work in Leicester/shire. In placing some of my arguments and conclusions in a broader comparative framework, I do not want to eclipse or screen out the differing histories of Empire, racial segregation, slavery and immigration that have formed and continue to shape the identities of the British and American nations and the people that live there. Nor is it my intention to provide a general review of the contrasts and complexities that inform British and American approaches to White ethnicity (see Garner, 2006). Rather, my motivation for doing this is to engage in conversation with the US-biased field of Whiteness studies in order to widen at least a bit this area of inquiry. My comparative approach will thus seek to place the issues that I have examined in this book in another Western English-speaking context that is culturally, economically and politically on the surface similar to Britain. A further interesting aspect of this comparative approach is that the USA is itself, of course, a former British colonially.

Race, class and place through a comparative framework

Central to the study of Whiteness in Britain and the USA is an exploration of how racial and classed identities are entwined with and co-constituting of each other. In Chapter 1, I examined how sociologists analyse the articulation of Whiteness, class and place in the context of Britain. At this juncture, I would like to return to some of these ideas in order to think through the contrasts and complexities in the articulation of Whiteness, class and place in the USA and England. In so doing I will situate some of the findings of my work with middle- and working-class Whites in Leicester/shire (discussed in Parts I and II of this book) in relation to the work of anthropologists and sociologists who examine the embedding of race, class and place in the formation of White ethnicities in the USA.

What is ethnographically interesting about my approach to the formation of White classed identities is the finding that my White co-conversationalists rarely defined themselves and Others explicitly in classed terms. In this sense, social class is hidden within my White co-conversationalists' accounts in that classed ideas of respectability and acceptability were rendered explicit in racialised attitudes towards BrAsians. From this standpoint, my contention is that the icons, myths and metaphors mobilised by my White middle- and working-class co-conversationalists to depict and define BrAsians reveal the constellation of elements that constitute the White classed self. By contrast, there is some evidence from my work with the members of interracial families to suggest that classed notions of respectability became apparent in the ways in which others perceived and judged them in racialised and classed terms. However, in each case, the point remains firm that race and class, as modalities of being and relating to the world are embedded in, entwined with and co-constitutive of each other. But more than this, I would like to make an argument for the embedding of race, class and place in the formation of White ethnicities in Britain. In order to reflect on the mobilisation of race, class and place in my study of White working- and middle-class ethnicities, I now turn my attention to ethnographic studies that have been conducted in the field of Whiteness studies in the USA, beginning with John Hartigan's work.

Race, class and place in the USA

Hartigan (1999, 2003, 2005) is one of the most influential and well-known theorists on the formation of Whiteness and social class in the USA. I have been struck by the parallels between Hartigan's (1999) ethnography on Whiteness and social class in the city of Detroit and my ethnographic study of Whiteness in Leicester/shire, and so it is his book on race and class in Detroit that I shall discuss here. Like my study, Hartigan's work is based on residential fieldwork and interviews with White people across class locations in three differing neighbourhoods that varied in terms of racial and class composition. Also in parallel with my study of Leicester/shire, Hartigan's (1999) account explores the formation of White ethnicities and classed identities of both middle- and working-class White people.

Hartigan's (1999) study of Whiteness in Detroit relates to the cultural phenomenon known as 'White flight'. Resonating with some aspects of the post-war movement of White middle-class English people out of the inner cities to the suburbs and the countryside, 'White flight' in the USA refers to a general post-war trend of Whites moving en masse from urban areas to the developing 'leafy' suburbs to be with members of their own race and class (Sibley 1995; see also Johnson and Sharpiro, 2003, for contemporary instances of this phenomenon, in the case of White Americans moving to areas with 'good', that is, White schools for their children). Hartigan reports that between 1950 and 1990 Detroit lost 1.4 million of its White residents to the suburbs through White flight (1999, p. 10). Thus Whites in Detroit had become in the minority. Hartigan explores the ethnic identities of those remaining White residents in Detroit. He does not attempt to define what Whiteness is, but rather sets out to examine the articulation of Whiteness in specific social interactions and places. Hartigan argues that Whiteness becomes visible in relation to its own internal divisions defined by class distinction. For Hartigan, internal class distinctions between White people are so deeply ingrained and inscribed in American cultural formation that he labels such distinctions 'intraracial'. By deploying this term to highlight class distinctions among Whites, Hartigan is pointing to the ways in which class categories share many of the properties usually associated with racial categories. In this sense, White people can be identified as belonging to a specific classed category of person by the way that they look, how they speak, where they live and their family history. For Hartigan (1999, p. 16) '*intraracial* distinctions are a primary medium through which Whites think about race' (original emphasis). That is to say, the identification of Whites with a specific intraracial classed category reveals something about their attitudes towards those considered to be racialised Others. It is from this standpoint that Hartigan argues that when White people in Detroit spoke about race they invoked classed distinctions between themselves and their White neighbours. They considered a situation racial, not on the basis of Blacks being involved, but rather by reflecting upon which kind and class of Whites were involved (1999, p. 17).

At the heart of Hartigan's work is his analysis of the role of place in informing local articulations of intraracial identities among Whites. He writes: 'The fundamental assertion made here is that racial identities are produced and experienced distinctly in different locations' (1999, p. 14). For example, in an area of Detroit called 'Briggs', certain Whites were labelled and self-identified as 'hillbilly', a term that operates at both national and local levels as 'a stigmatised intraracial distinction, articulating a sense of refinement and sophistication that these "rude", out-of-place Whites could not attain' (1999, p. 18). In another area of the city, called Corktown, White professionals debated who among them constituted a 'gentrifier', that is, an upwardly mobile individual intent on 'improving' the area through, for example, the physical improvement and gentrification of their houses. And in 'Warrendale', Whites were labelled 'racist' by the local media for opposing the opening of the Afrocentric Malcolm X Academy, known locally as a 'Black school'. In reaction to this media designation, White residents debated among themselves who were the 'real racists'. Central to this neighbourhood debate was the articulation of wider national classed notions of respectability and decorum. As Hartigan argued, 'the basis for their designation of "racist" involves subtle distinctions of class – those who ruptured middle-class decorum were typically assumed to be more racist'. The everyday policing, appropriation and rejection of these labels of 'hillbilly', 'gentrifier' and 'racist' by White people within specific locales illustrates for Hartigan (1999, p. 14) how place becomes a means of identifying individuals and situating them in a locally and nationally sanctioned racialised and classed order.

The interplay between race, class and place in the formation of White ethnicities is also explored by Ruth Frankenberg (1993a, 1993b), whose approach to the postcolonial constitution of Whiteness I have drawn on throughout this book. Frankenberg scrutinises how memories of racial segregation in terms of neighbourhood and friendship networks informed White women's accounts of their childhoods. By contrast to Hartigan's ethnographic work, which is rooted in specific neighbourhoods of Detroit, Frankenberg's empirical material is not situated in a particular locale. Rather, she develops the notion of 'social geography' to analyse White women's memories of the racial and classed constitution of the neighbourhoods, streets, friendship groups and schools in which they grew up. Frankenberg found that White middle-class women's experiences of racial segregation were marked by the absence of 'people of colour', whereas White working-class women's accounts were defined by the presence of 'people of colour'.

White middle-class women discussed how they grew up in all-White neighbourhoods where 'Black people were the "significant others"' (1993a, p. 48). White middle-class women's experiences of racial segregation were in part dependent upon their families' economic ability to live in exclusive all-White areas. Frankenberg is intrigued by how two White middle-class women mentioned as an afterthought that their families had employed 'Women of colour' as maids. What surprised Frankenberg is that the presence of non-White maids did not disrupt these White women's perceptions of their childhood networks and environment as totally racially White and thus segregated from Blacks and other 'people of colour'. Frankenberg (1993a, pp. 50–1) writes:

> It may be the status of domestic workers from the standpoint of White middle-class women, or the status of people of colour from the purview of a White and middle-class childhood, that made these women invisible and stripped them of subjectivity in the landscapes of childhood.

By contrast, White working-class women grew up in 'quasi integrated' environments in which interethnic relationships were formed across the colour-lines. However, Frankenberg (1993a) argues that even close interethnic friendships at school and with neighbours were mediated by racial tensions. She writes: 'growing up in a racially mixed context did not mean that racism was absent, nor that the environment was not racially structured' (1993a, p. 65). Thus, Frankenberg concludes that the White women in her study, across class locations, experienced at best only a 'partial or qualified integration' when growing up. Frankenberg (1993a, p. 69) argues that this is inevitable in a racist society, 'if racial integration is taken to mean the absence of race hierarchy and racist ideas'.

The desire on the part of some modern-day White middle-class Americans to segregate and thus cut themselves off totally from racial and class Others is brought sharply into focus in Setha M. Low's (2003) study of gated residential communities. Low reports how 'gated communities' are a phenomenon in the USA that began in the 1990s.[1] They consist of houses of a similar design and type that are enclosed by walls and accessed by a central gate that is patrolled by guards. These communities are home to White middle-class families. Low draws on interviews with White middle-class residents of two gated communities situated on the boundary of the cities of San Antonio and New York. She argues that one reason White interviewees gave for moving away from the city was a fear of violence and crime, an image that was reinforced daily in local and national media. Low suggests that individuals' fear of urban crime 'encodes' other social concerns, including fear of racial and class Others. Critical discourse analysis of interviewees' narratives revealed that this anti-urban discourse included a fear of the poor, workers, 'Mexicans', 'newcomers' and so-called ethnics. In short, Low's White middle-class interviewees felt that they were safer living in a 'community' behind walls rather than an ethnically diverse neighbourhood. Low's work is interesting because it highlights how White middle-class people's search for cultural homogeneity can result in total isolation from those considered to be different in terms of racial and class locations. From this standpoint, Low reveals a world in which White middle-class people's search for cultural uniformity examined in my study of Greenville can be extended to such an extreme that there is literally no space for those considered to be racial and class Others.

Reflections on race, class and place in Leicester/shire

Reading across my discussion of Hartigan's (1999), Frankenberg's (1993a) and Low's (2003) studies, and my work in Leicester/shire, prominent themes come to the fore. These are the co-constitution of racial and class identities; and the importance of place to understanding articulations of Whiteness and class identities, whereby belonging to a particular locale becomes interwoven with the formation of classed and racialised identities. I shall now explore some of the ways in which the discourses of race, class and place are expressed, articulated and constructed within White racialised discourses in Leicester/shire.

Following Hartigan's analysis, I would like to make an argument for the entwining of race, class and place in the formation of White ethnicities in Leicester/shire and Britain more generally. My contention is that an ethnographic approach to place is crucial to an analysis of the ways in which White classed identities are lived and experienced. That is to say, the socio-economic constitution of place, combined with White people's ideas on the *proper* constitution of their place – be it village, post-industrial mining town or inner city – is interwoven and bound up with classed identities that become transparent in relation to talk on racialised Others. From this perspective, it becomes possible to identify the contrasts and complexities in White working- and middle-class attitudes towards BrAsians within and across specific locales.

There is evidence from my fieldwork in Coalville and Streetville to suggest that some White working-class people from these places are concerned with BrAsians' and recent immigrants' seemingly unfair access to public resources. This discourse of White backlash and resentment to multiculturalism is articulated in different ways in each specific place. Thus, for example, in Coalville this sense of resentment was expressed in general terms aimed at all immigrants and BrAsians who were thought not to work, pay no taxes and thus unfairly claim welfare payments. While in Streetville, some of the White working-class people that I came to know believed that particular groups of BrAsians, and especially Muslims who lived in their neighbourhood, received unfair access to local government resources to the detriment of themselves and other Whites who lived in the area. My argument is that these discourses tell us more about White working-class notions of respectability, fairness and the proper constitution of place than they do the actual distribution of public resources. In Greenville, my White middle-class co-conversationalists were less concerned with BrAsians' access to public money and resources, although this did bother some (see Chapter 3). Rather, residents from Greenville were more focused on the perceived inability of BrAsian neighbours to display the aesthetic tastes, neighbourly attitudes and social practices that were valued in the village.

In light of my comparative approach to the formation of White classed ethnicities across differing locales, I resist and reject ideas and arguments advocated by some academics and politicians that it is the White working classes in Britain, and not the White middle classes, that produce a backlash to multiculturalism. I cannot argue strongly enough that my work in Leicestershire suggests that White middle-class people commonly harbour ambivalence and reticence towards racialised Others. Thus it seems to me that while the racialised form of White working- and middle-class people's ideas remain the same, the distinction between their racialised discourses is to be found in the differing content of ideas of appropriate and proper ways of behaving in one's social environment. This distinction within White working- and middle-class worldviews affects and shapes the ways in which White people perceive the presence of racialised Others in 'their' place.

The main emphasis of Chapters 4 and 5 was on the conditions in which some White working-class people become potentially reflexive actors on racism, and not the White middle classes. But it is not my intention to suggest that the White English middle classes cannot also be critical of racism. Clearly such a claim would go against the grain of much ethnographic evidence to the contrary. However, I have suggested that some White working-class people are placed in conditions and circumstances whereby they come to confront racism, in a way not noticeable in the White middle classes. I want to resist making any formulaic and general argument for the distinctions between White working- and middle-class people's attempts at confronting racism. Rather, my detailed ethnographic analysis of the formation of White ethnicities within and between specific locales reveals the circumstances and conditions that can prompt Whites to confront the racism of others including pernicious, unfounded stereotypes, racist structures and policies, admittedly to varying degrees of success. I shall return to this point later.

Notwithstanding the distinctions between White working- and middle-class discourses within specific places, my argument is that intrinsic to White racialised discourses across class and geographical locations is the reproduction of White discourses of coloniality in the present. This aspect of my analysis has been inspired and influenced by Ruth Frankenberg's (1993a) work in the USA. As discussed in the Introduction to this book, Frankenberg (1993a) contends that White dominance in the USA is supported by essentialist notions of culture and difference that are the aftermath of the colonial period. This discourse reproduces and maintains a racially dichotomous worldview in the present that underpins the co-construction of a racially unmarked White American self (and British self, as my work exemplifies) in relation to racially marked Others.

Following Frankenberg's analysis I have traced the manifestation of this hierarchical worldview of cultural superiority in everyday White middle- and working-class representations of BrAsians in Leicester/shire. In addition I have also examined the impact of White amnesia – the not knowing, the forgetting, silencing and screening out – on the implications of colonial histories within everyday White constructions for the presence and national membership of BrAsians. The effect of this is to depict and position BrAsians as eternal immigrants and outsiders to the nation and ultimately to the West.

Central to my analysis of coloniality is the idea that its hegemony remains to be seen even in those moments in which Whites question the racism of others. In making this critical point, I do not want to denigrate and disregard the significance of the ways in which the young White working-class adults that I met in Coalville challenged the racism of their family members. Nor do I want to belittle the significance of the participation of White working class-residents in anti-racist collective action in Streetville. Nonetheless, my study of young White adults' moments of questioning the racism of others in Coalville is a reminder of just how difficult it is for Whites to step outside the discourses of coloniality even when they are intentionally confronting racism. From this standpoint, the internalisation of beliefs and emotions founded upon a sense of White Western cultural superiority is part of the base from which individuals engage in critical reflections on the racism of others. Moreover, my work with the Residents' Association in Streetville illuminates how even White people who become involved in anti-racist collective action may still interpret and view the world through a racialised lens that is inherited from the colonial past. This aspect of my study illustrates how difficult it is for White individuals to step outside of a worldview that partly constitutes their way of being, inhabiting and engaging with the social world. However, my work with the members of interracial families who unequivocally confront and challenge White privilege and power illuminates one pathway through which individuals' transcend these frameworks, a point to which I shall return to in the final sections of this chapter.

White amnesia of the colonial in everyday constructions of British and American imaginings of nation

I now want to explore further the ways in which the colonial past informs American and British concepts of racial difference and nation. To do this I shall focus on how amnesia of the colonial past informs everyday and public discourses on nation within the USA. Once more, I shall use my discussion of the American context as a platform from which to reflect on some of the findings of my fieldwork in Leicester/shire. In relation to what interests me here, Britain's and American's very different imperial and racial histories are not as significant as the similarities within everyday articulations of nation. That is, my argument is that central to everyday imaginings of each nation is the collective remembering of a sanitised version of the colonial past. One consequence of this process is for contemporary American and British nations to be imagined as White in terms of ethnicity and history.

White amnesia and the British colonisation of the USA

I begin this section by discussing how the actual existence and origins of modern-day America are interwoven with its colonial relationship with Britain. This history was recently marked in 2007 in public commemoration of what was officially termed 'America's 400th anniversary', which remembered the establishment of the first permanent British colony in America in 1607. Georgie Wemyss (2008) explores the screening out and silencing of slave histories in public events and speeches organised in both London and Virginia (the site of the first British colony) to mark this anniversary. To do this, she traces the mobilisation of the tropes of 'commemoration' and 'celebration' by politicians and exhibition organisers involved in marking this anniversary. Wemyss highlights how the significance and meaning attached to these terms provides a pathway through which to examine and expose White hegemonic discourses on nation and colonial history.

Native American and African American groups in the USA rejected the term 'celebration' to describe this anniversary because they were keen to show that this event was seen to be a 'celebration' of the formation of the British colonisation of the USA. Following this lead, the official 400th anniversary publicity in both London and Virginia took care to mobilise the term 'commemoration' and eschew 'celebration'. Nonetheless, despite this response to criticism on the part of the organisers, there were times when the language of 'celebration' was deployed. For example, the US Embassy reported: '19 December 2006 Ambassador Tuttle *celebrates* the origins of Jamestown [the site of the first British colony in the state of Virginia]' (Wemyss' emphasis, 2008, 3.3). Moreover, the screening out of the atrocities of the colonial past shaped an exhibition held at a museum in the London Docklands entitled 'Journey to the New World: London 1606 to Virginia 1607' (23 November 2006 to 13 May 2007). The London Docklands was the place from which three British ships set sail to Jamestown. While the exhibition did include some reference to 'the genocide of Native Americans', the history of African American slaves was mostly absent. Wemyss (2008, 3.8) writes:

> The museum exhibition highlighted the labour shortages of the early years of the colony, the English indentured labourers and the triumph of Virginia tobacco. However, apart from three short references to African slaves in the 17th century chronology (on the back of a leaflet), the final solution to the labour shortage – African slaves – were absent.

In stark contrast to the screening out of the histories of African slavery in London and by some officials in the USA, the Virginia General Assembly became the first State Assembly to apologise for its role in slavery. The Assembly also expressed regret for the exploitation of Native Americans and linked these apologies directly to the 400th anniversary events (2008, 3.9).[2] But yet, in a speech made by President Bush addressed to the British Queen on a state visit to the USA to mark the 400th anniversary, the language of 'celebration' once more took centrestage. President Bush linked the shared colonial histories of the two nations to contemporary American and British global hegemony. He said:

> Based on our common values, our two nations are working together for the common good. Together we are supporting young

democracies in Iraq and Afghanistan. Together we're confronting global challenges such as poverty and disease and terrorism. And together we're working to build a world in which more people can enjoy prosperity and security and peace. Friendships remain strong when they are continually renewed, and the American people appreciate Your Majesty's commitment to our friendship. We thank you for helping US *celebrate* the 400th anniversary of the Jamestown settlement. We're confident that Anglo-American friendship will endure for centuries to come.

(www.Whitehouse.gov/news/releases/2007, cited in Wemyss 2008: 3.10, original emphasis)

This extract highlights how a celebratory version of shared British and American colonial histories can creep into political discourse to support contemporary American and British hegemony, which some social commentators argue is the most recent manifestation of contemporary forms of Western imperialism. In the shadows of Bush's speech is the historical reality that contemporary 'Anglo-American' political alliances rest upon the historical genocide of Native Americans and the enslavement of African peoples that perpetuated trade routes between the USA and Britain and Africa in which cotton, sugar, tobacco and slaves circulated. The ways in which Native American colonial histories are screened out by ordinary White American people in the course of their daily lives is examined by Jane H. Hill, a linguistic anthropologist, in her book *The Everyday Language of White Racism* (2008). It is to the details of her work that I shall now turn.

White amnesia of Native American histories within in the USA

In Chapter 3 of her book, Hill (2008) examines the controversy in the Phoenix area of Arizona surrounding the renaming of a mountain that was known as 'Squaw peak' to 'Piestewa Peak'. The new name was that of a Hopi woman, Lori Piestewa, who died in March 2003 while serving as a soldier in the US Army in Iraq at the time of the American invasion of Iraq. Hill traces the controversy surrounding the name change of the mountain in a web-based message board set up by a local newspaper for public debate on the name change. While Hill does not describe Whites' desire and determination to retain the name 'Squaw Peak' as an example of White amnesia of the colonial past, it is clear from her analysis of this debate that those Whites who wanted to keep the name had indeed screened out and displaced the racist connotations and colonial histories associated with the term 'squaw'. I suggest that this episode highlights some of the processes and consequences of amnesia of the colonial past in everyday White American people's imaginings of nationhood.

Hill categorically states that 'squaw', like the notorious 'N-word', is a racist 'slur' in American culture. The word first became meaningful in English in the seventeenth century, when scientific racism was in its early stages. For example, in a 'Plea for the Indians' written in 1859 by John Beeson (who was an English settler to the US and advocate for the rights of Native Americans), Beeson declared:

> [I]t was customary to speak of the Indian man as a buck; of the woman as a squaw; until, at length, in the general acceptance of the terms, they ceased to recognize the rights of humanity in those to whom they were so applied.
> (McWilliams, 1943, p. 52, cited in Hill, 2008, p. 59)

In spite of the dehumanising and racist connotations associated with this word, many Whites still falsely believe it to be a 'technically correct' way to refer to Native American Indian women (Hill, 2008, p. 62). Indeed, the naming of the mountain in the Phoenix area of Arizona as 'Squaw Peak' means that almost 'every non-Indian in Arizona had for many years uttered without a second thought the name "Squaw Peak"' (Hill, 2008, p. 62). Hill (2008, p. 63) highlights how according to the American folk theory of racism if a word is a racist slur then those people who use that word are racists. Hence, the public debate about the meaning of 'squaw' was highly charged. Many Whites in the area had used the term 'squaw' all their lives and they firmly rejected the idea that they were racists for doing so. In stark contrast, Native Americans expressed their pain at having to encounter this word in their daily lives. In this way, Native American contributors to the debate argued that this word is equivalent to 'bitch'.

Nonetheless, the majority of White people who participated in this debate genuinely believed that 'squaw' was not an abusive term and thus was not a racist slur. In so doing, White Americans showed how they have the ability to screen out and displace the histories of genocide and segregation of Native Americans and are 'actively oblivious' to their daily concerns (Hill, 2008, p. 86). The extent of White amnesia of the colonial past became apparent in the widespread belief that contemporary 'Indians "take and take" while Whites "give and give"' (2008, p. 84). Hill (2008, p. 84) argues that this assertion takes meaning in the context of 'a well-known history where Whites used every device of power including genocide to strip resources from Indians'.

Some Whites countered that the name 'Squaw Peak' emphasised Native American tradition and their contribution to the building of Arizona. Yet, as Hill eloquently writes: 'early White American settlers relabelled the entire landscape using their own conventions. ... Thus when "tradition" is invoked in favour of "Squaw Peak", it is White tradition, not Native American "tradition", that is being honoured' (2008, p. 85). In this sense, the histories of White dominance and genocide of Native Americans are literally inscribed on the contemporary landscape. However, the power, inequality and genocide intrinsic to these histories is denied and ultimately forgotten by Whites. The consequence of this process is for White people to reassure themselves that they are not racist by wanting to keep the name 'Squaw Peak'. Rather, from the point of view of the majority of Whites who participated in this debate, it is a minority of Native American activists and the local state who are 'the problem' by taking a misinformed and 'politically correct' stance. Native Americans thus become portrayed as overly sensitive, unpatriotic and unfairly benefiting from local government support at the expense of the White majority. This ethnographic vignette illustrates one of the ways in which amnesia of the atrocities of the colonial past infiltrates everyday and contemporary White discourses in the USA on the construction of place and nation.

White amnesia in Leicester/shire

Reading across my account of White representations of BrAsians in Leicester/shire, and Hill's analysis of White depictions of Native Americans in Arizona, it becomes apparent that the silencing of the histories of the imperial past within everyday and ordinary local English and American contexts has the effect of positioning postcolonial minorities outside of hegemonic imaginings of nationhood that become intimately associated with Whiteness. In Chapters 1, 2 and 3 of this book, I have shown how everyday constructions of the English village and the English countryside in Leicester/shire are reproduced and maintained as White spaces through the erasure of colonial histories and their legacies. The city thereby is depicted as the site of a BrAsian settlement, which remains a disconnected place set apart from the true site of Englishness, history and tradition, which lies elsewhere in the countryside.

At key moments in my study colonial histories embedded within the social fabric of the Leicester/shire landscape have threatened to break the silence of this White amnesia. Thus, I have discussed how Wood's archaeological work in the Leicestershire village of Kibworth unearthed a brooch from the East Indian Company. Moreover, two elderly residents of Kibworth were employees of that company. William, one of my White co-conversationalists from Greenville, was born in Calcutta during the colonial period. His father worked in the imperial jute industry. In addition, Mark, also from Greenville, served in the British Army in the former British colonies of India, Sri Lanka and Singapore. My argument is that even in these moments when colonial histories come to the surface the full implications of the legacies of Empire for interpreting the meaning of the present are side-lined, which serves once more to render BrAsian outsiders to the Leicestershire countryside and ultimately the nation. It is not simply a case of *remembering* the colonial past that matters, but rather the *ways* in which people think about the legacies and implications of the colonial upon the formation of the present that counts.

Genealogical imaginations: The mobilisation of slave ancestries in the USA and Britain

My research with members of interracial families from Leicester provides ethnographic insight into how one aspect of the colonial past – that is, the slave past – is remembered, reflected upon and incorporated into ideas of ancestry across the colour-lines. My work with members of interracial families illustrates how it is through relations of kinship that ancestries and histories of the slave past inform contemporary interracial relationships and identities. This aspect of my study in Leicester highlights how slave histories and ancestries can come to form part of White, Black and interracial people's senses of who they are. But more than this, the way in which such histories are remembered and put to work has potential to dismantle and fragment White privilege and power. In short, my work with members of interracial families turns my analysis of the processes of White amnesia of the colonial past in England upside down and inside out.

Turning back to the American context, the myriad ways in which slave ancestries inform interracial, Black and White Americans' ethnicities are explored in studies that examine the narratives and accounts of individuals who are engaged in the genealogical project of tracing their family trees. The members of interracial families whom I interviewed from Leicester were not as such tracing their family trees in any formal way. However, my contention is that their emphasis on relatedness across the colour-lines within their nuclear and extended families resonates with how slave histories mediate Black and interracial American people's genealogical searches for their ancestral identities. The American literature on the formation of genealogical identities also explores how discourses of race and class become entwined in the search for forgotten slave ancestors, which provides a further lens through which to think about the embedding of discourses of race, class and coloniality in the USA.

The sociological study of genealogy in America highlights how Black, interracial and White people are socialised differently into remembering and forgetting the significance and meaning of their nation's slave history. Thus White, interracial and Black African Americans often draw upon different aspects of the slave past to make sense of the present. In a similar vein, I have examined in Chapter 6 how the members of interracial families who grew up in White families did not learn about slavery from their White family members. By contrast, some people who grew up in Black and interracial milieus came to learn about the significance of the slave past in the routines and rituals of everyday life. The contrasting ways in which African Americans, interracial and White Americans interpret their ancestral relationships to slavery is explored by Sarah Gatson (2003) in her 'autoethnographic account' of her search for knowledge of her racial ancestry.

Gatson describes herself as a sociologist who is a 'biracial African American' (2003, p. 21) and as such she places emphasis on the formation of an 'amorphous multiracial position that allows her to emphasize one identity at one time and another under different circumstances' (Parham, 2008, p. 17). Gatson's study charts the complexities of forming a sense of ethnicity that acknowledges and incorporates 'Black', 'White' and 'multiracial' ancestries. Throughout her genealogical journey, Gatson found that White genealogists more often than not interpreted their relationship to America's history of slavery differently from herself. For example, she explains how she corresponded online with a White woman who shared her surname. Gatson's (2003, p. 30) contact wrote: 'Our ancestors were also slave owners and there are many African American Gatsons now too. I am White ... I am very excited to hear from you because you mention names that I have never heard.' When Gatson revealed to this White woman that her family were African American, her White correspondent's sense of their genealogical connection 'diminished'. Gatson concludes that this White woman had constructed an interpretation of her surname that had two distinct and separate Black and White genealogical lineages. However, Gatson remarks that for her knowledge of her Black identity had 'always allowed for Whiteness to be part of it' (2003, p. 31).

Moreover, Gatson describes how her ancestral connections to Whites did not mean that she automatically identified with the White 'romance of the Old South' (2003, p. 38). She felt no sense of relatedness to the plantation owner's wives, who she described as 'the ladies in the big house'. She writes that 'I was used to identifying with oppressed Whites, thanks to my Irish-identified grandmother, and with radical Whites more generally – people who at least questioned racial privilege, not those who instituted and celebrated benefiting from it' (2003, pp. 38–9). It seems to me that Gatson's work illustrates how it is not simply a case of *remembering* the colonial past that matters but rather *how* that past is remembered and *how* one interprets its legacies for the present that are crucial.

In a similar vein to Gatson's embracing of both Black, interracial and White genealogies, the members of interracial families that I interviewed mobilised diverse racial connections to the slave past that were put to work to illuminate the complexities of their families' and their own ethnicities and ancestries in the present. Moreover, sharing some parallels to Gatson's account, the members of interracial families who feature in this book acknowledged the power and violence intrinsic to the slave past. Their knowledge and understanding of this violence facilitated the pathway for the formation of politicised White, Black and interracial ethnicities in the present.

The diverse ways in which Americans across ethnic locations come to think about their relationships to slave pasts is also examined by Angel Purham (2008) in her study of the genealogical identities of White European-American and Creole members of genealogical societies based in post-Katrina New Orleans. While the members of both genealogical societies traced their ancestries from Louisiana to the migration of slaves, 'free people of colour' and Whites from Haiti in the eighteenth and nineteenth centuries, Parham (2008) argues that the general mood and the approach to thinking about how the past relates to the present was quite different for each genealogical society. Members of the White European-American genealogical society focused on the classed status and origins of ancestors rather than their ethnicity or their role in slavery. On this point, Parham (2008, p. 27) writes: 'There was an air of old respectability about the ... research centre that evoked old books, old families, and old money.' For members of the Creole genealogical society, on the other hand, the slave past took on a spiritual quality and significance in becoming constitutive of members' understanding of their present experiences of racism. Purham (2008, p. 27) writes on this contrast as follows:

> [For members of the Creole society] The practice of slavery becomes something with which the genealogist interacts and enters into.

There is a sense of 'rescuing' ancestors from being forgotten, of validating their past struggles by recognising them today. Within this approach, history is seen as being more than simply a context for doing genealogy, instead it is seen as constitutive of who one is today. This difference is in line with what some historians have found – that people of colour tend to link their family history to larger national narratives of oppression and progress more often than do European Americans.

Like 'people of colour' in the USA, the members of interracial families who feature in this book also draw on diverse senses of ethnic and class connections to slave pasts, which become part of who they are and enables them to interpret and make sense of their own and their families' experiences of racism. In stark contrast, I have discussed in Parts I and II of this book how colonial discourses of White Western cultural superiority are articulated in the present by White middle- and working-class English people to support their place in the world in relation to BrAsian Others. My supposition is that underlying the reproduction of this colonial mentality is the screening out and not knowing of the histories of Empire that bind BrAsians to Englishness and Britishness. From this standpoint, one of the legacies of Empire in the present is White people's unwitting inheritance and internalisation of a colonial worldview that ensures the co-construction of a racially unmarked and culturally superior White Western self in relation to racially unmarked Others. Perhaps one way to break out of this impasse is for those of us whose ancestries can be traced to the histories of European colonialism to gain an understanding of our shared colonial and slave ancestries across the lines of race, nation, class and place when we think about who we are, where we come from and who we might become. Any such project must be reflexive about how the colonial past is remembered and its consequences for the present. I have come to realise this through the process of writing this book, and thus its epitaph is that *how* we think about and interpret the legacies of Empire in the present matters to us all.

Notes

1 Frameworks, Fieldworks and Inspirations

1. 'English' refers in everyday usage to the people of England, which is one of the nations, along with Scotland, Wales and Northern Ireland, that makes up the United Kingdom (UK), which is also called Britain and even referred to sometimes as 'Great Britain' (GB). 'British' is used in the everyday to refer to the peoples of England, Scotland, Wales and Northern Ireland collectively. England, Scotland, Wales and Northern Ireland are distinct national identities, and are for some purposes, such as sporting participation, considered distinct nations. England, Scotland and Wales have varying degrees of political autonomy and devolution, but the nation state Britain/UK encompasses all of them. Recently, there has been a certain aggressiveness to assertions of Englishness as a distinct nation and cultural identity, which is at times associated exclusively with White ethnicity. By contrast, the term 'British' has become associated with a more multiracial and ethnically inclusive image of nation and national belonging. In this book I shall use the terms 'England', 'English'; 'Britain', 'British' and 'UK'. I shall invoke the most appropriate term to capture and convey what is meant by my research participants and myself. I have come to conclude through the process of writing this book that from the standpoint of my White research participants not much hangs on the distinction between these terms.
2. When I refer in this book to 'Empire' and 'the colonial', I mean the histories of the British Empire, the Atlantic and West Indian/Caribbean slave trade. In this sense, it is a generalised imperial vision rather than any historically situated concept of Empire and the colonial that is deployed in this book.
3. I deploy the term 'racialised' to describe the social beliefs and practices that my White research participants mobilised to define those they consider to be racially other to themselves. Whilst most of my co-conversationalists did not refer explicitly to physical markers of difference associated with the idea of race, many of them did define Others by a set of cultural markers of distinction, for example language, family structure, religion, food and so on. The articulation of cultural markers of distinction associated with the idea of race is crucial to the formation of racist beliefs and practices.
4. The 1991 and 2001 official national Census data has consistently shown that Leicester is the city with the largest British Asian Indian population in England. However, White people remain in the majority in the city. According to a Leicester City Council (1991a) report on the findings of the 1991 Census, 71.5 per cent of the total population of Leicester were 'Whites', 2.4 per cent 'Black'; 22.3 per cent 'Indian'; 1.0 per cent 'Pakistani', 0.4 per cent 'Bangladeshi'; 2.4 per cent 'Chinese and Others'. The 2001 Census showed that while the White population decreased, it remained the dominant ethnic category. According to a Leicestershire County Council report (2001a) on the 2001 Census results, 63.9 per cent of the total

population were 'White'; 2.3 per cent 'Mixed'; 29.9 per cent 'Asian'; 3.1 per cent 'Black' and 0.8 per cent 'Chinese Other'.

The following statistics highlight the contrast between the multiethnic composition of the population of the city of Leicester and the predominantly White constitution of the population of county of Leicestershire. According to a Leicestershire County Council (2001a) report on the 2001 Census, 94.7 per cent of the total population of the countryside of Leicestershire was 'White' compared to 63.9 per cent of the city. In 2001 the total 'Asian' populations of Leicestershire constituted 3.7 per cent whereas the total 'Asian' populations of the city constituted 29.9 per cent. The number of 'Black' people in the countryside was put at 0.3 per cent of the total population and 3.1 per cent in the city.

It is also noteworthy that the idiom of 'county' in England refers to a region of England. For example, Leicestershire is the county in which the city of Leicester is situated. In this book, I shall at times indicate that my fieldwork was conducted in both the county of Leicestershire and the city of Leicester by using the shorthand term of 'Leicester/shire'.

5. Throughout this book, I shall refer to the people that participated in this study as 'research participants' and/or 'co-conversationalists'. The term 'research participant' refers to those people that I came to know during the course of my fieldwork, but did not necessarily interview. I use the term 'co-conversationalists' to refer to those research participants that I interviewed.
6. In this book, I shall use the real name of the town Coalville. The name of the town is an important fact that is necessary to retain in order to convey and fully understand the meaning and significance of the town's coalmining history to research participants. However, unlike Coalville, the place names of 'Greenville' and 'Streetville' are pseudonyms. I use pseudonyms for these places because their real names play no inherent role in the significance attached to place by the people that live there. All research participants' names are pseudonyms to protect their personal identities.
7. My thanks to Steve Fenton for telling me about this series. I focus here upon the BBC television series and not Wood's (2010) book that accompanied the series.
8. My emphasis upon the forgetting of Empire within the White English imagination is informed by the findings of my ethnographic fieldwork in Leicestershire and my interpretation of Wood's documentary. Indeed, Wood's series reinforced what the fieldwork had already primed me to think. In making this argument it is not my intention to deny the recent popular interest in Britain's imperial past within the media more generally. There has also been a surge in museum exhibits that focus on the legacies of Empire. However, an analysis of these various representations of Empire and public reactions to them is beyond the scope of this book. Suffice to say that Thompson (2005, p. 236) argues 'there is a perennial tendency to think of Empire in terms of a "moral balance" sheet – imperial costs or benefits are weighed as either good or bad'.
9. The predominance of White villagers in this project reflects the ethnic composition of Kibworth. According to Leicestershire County Council (2001b) 'area profiles' based on the 2001 Census, the ethnic composition of the District within which the village of Kibworth is located was as follows: 94.7 per cent of this

District was 'White'; 0.75 per cent 'Mixed'; 3.70 per cent 'Asian or British Asian'; 0.32 per cent 'Black or Black British'; and 0.36 per cent 'Chinese Other'.
10. I am inferring about the middle-class identities of the villagers from the size of their gardens and houses that were featured in the programmes, as well as their comportment and accents.
11. Guildford is a suburban market town situated within commuting distance from London. The majority of the residents of Guildford are very affluent, White and middle to upper middle class. The audience that attended Wood's lecture reflected this population profile.
12. This body of literature is contentious to the extent that it risks recentring and reaffirming White ethnicities as the norm through its investigation of Whiteness (Ahmed, 2004).
13. Throughout this book the sexual identities of my research participants remain invisible, unmarked and unexamined. One consequence of this is that the normative constitution of heterosexual identities is reaffirmed, which raises a host of interesting questions about the invisible articulation of Whiteness and heteronormativity that I do not address here.
14. This research was funded by an Economic and Social Science Research Council Doctoral Studentship (1996–1999).
15. This research formed part of a larger project entitled 'Public Understandings of Genetics: A Cross-Cultural and Ethnographic Study of the "New Genetics" and Social Identity', funded by the European Commission Fifth Framework Programme: Quality of Life and Management of Living Resources. Contract number: QLG7-CT-2001-01668.

2 BrAsian 'Invasion' of White Suburban English Village Life

1. I shall write about Greenville in the main in the present tense, especially when I am revisiting the conversations that I held with the White residents. While I shall mostly introduce research participants and our discussions in the past tense, I will keep my analysis of our conversations in the present tense. In settling upon this mode of representation I want to acknowledge the debates within social anthropology concerning the use of the ethnographic present (see, for example, Clifford and Marcus, 1986). One line of argumentation is that writing in the present tense traps research participants in a timeless space that lies outside of real time. In writing about Greenville in the present tense, I hope to avoid these negative implications. Rather I find writing in this way is the most natural and least forced way to describe and express my interactions with residents, especially when engaging with conversations and interviews that we shared.
2. During a cricket match it is usual for the players of both teams to break for tea. This is a light meal, which includes sandwiches, cake and a cup of tea to drink.
3. This cricket team included BrAsian players. However, while preparing and serving the tea for the team, I learnt that this team were not members of the 'official' Greenville cricket club, but was a team from a club based in a neighbouring ethnically diverse suburb. This club rented the village club house from the official Greenville cricket club, whose members were all White.

226 *Notes*

4. My judgement of my landlady's age, like that of most research participants from Greenville, Coalville and Streetville, is based on my estimates. On the whole, I did not ask interviewees and other adults who were (or seemed) considerably older than me their age for reasons of politeness.
5. I draw upon Census data that refers to the time that I conducted the fieldwork.
6. All names that I give to places, streets, roads and buildings in Greenville are pseudonyms.
7. According to the Collins English Dictionary, 'wog' is: 'Brit. Slang, derogatory. A foreigner, esp. one who is not White [probably from Golliwog]'. On Golliwog the following is written: 'a soft doll with a black face, usually made of cloth or rags [C. 19: from the name of a doll character in children's books by the American Bertha Upton (died 1912), writer, and Florence Upton (died 1922), illustrator]'.
8. William Blake's poem 'Jerusalem' has become a non-official national anthem in England. While it has national overtones, it is also thought to be an anthem that critiques the negative aspects of the Industrial Revolution and calls for criticism of England's present circumstances.

3 The Racialisation of the Country, the City and the Forgetting of Empire

1. Belgrave is an area of Leicester that has historically been the home to some of Leicester's BrAsian populations. Belgrave is the real name of this area of Leicester, which is identified on the websites.
2. Melton Mowbray is a market town approximately 14 miles north east of Leicester.
3. Thanks to Cathrine Degnen for this insight drawn from her fieldwork in Dodworth, a former mining village that formed part of the Barnsley coalfield; see Degnen, 2012.
4. The Melton Road is not a pseudonym. It is the central road in Belgrave and is mentioned on the public website, and so I have not attempted to disguise its identity.

4 The Questioning of Racism in a Former Coalmining Town

1. As I noted in this book's introduction, Coalville is the real name of this town. I have decided not to use a pseudonym in order to be able to discuss the meaning that residents attach to their town's name. I have also not used pseudonyms for the towns and cities surrounding Coalville. However, I have chosen not to reveal the name of the village near to Coalville where I lived during my stay in the area. This is to protect the identities of the people with whom I lived.
2. Unemployment rates have remained relatively stable in the region. According to the 2001 Census, 2.42 per cent of North West Leicestershire's population were unemployed.

3. Morrisons is a famous chain of supermarkets to be found across the UK, associated with low prices.
4. It is unusual for a woman to hold the post of secretary in an otherwise male dominated union in terms of membership.
5. The fact that Jill and George had lived in Coalville all of their lives raises an important biographical contrast between the identities of the residents' of Greenville and Coalville. That is to say, some of my older and younger White co-conversationalists from Coalville, but not all, had lived in the area their entire lives. This was not the case for my White middle-aged co-conversationalists from Greenville.
6. GCSE stands for General Certificate of Secondary Education, which are public examinations that pupils at school in England routinely take at 16 years of age.

5 Neighbourhood Activism and the Ambiguities of Anti-Racism in the City

1. It is important to note that this collective action centred upon an application for a judicial review and not an actual judicial review.
2. An 'electoral ward' is the district into which British cities are divided for administration and the election of local and national government representatives. An 'electoral boundary' is the boundary that demarcates the electoral ward.
3. I do not think, as might be thought, that Whites' objectification of Muslims is specifically associated with a hegemonic Euro-American post-9/11 worldview that identifies Muslims as the Other. Rather BrAsian Muslims are the largest ethnic and religious minority in this neighbourhood and thus are thought by some White residents to be unfair beneficiaries of local state support.
4. See also Gilroy's (1987) analysis of urban social movements in Britain that mobilise ideas of community and neighbourhood belonging to unite members, rather than a sense of shared class alienation.
5. While the RA's lack of Black African Caribbean members was striking, I do not have an explanation for this absence.
6. An Access Course provides the foundational knowledge and skills necessary for entry to an undergraduate degree programme at British universities. This course is designed for mature students who wish to attend university but have not acquired standard qualifications.
7. I deploy the term 'Bangladeshi' here because this is the term that was used by the 'Bangladeshi' organisation themselves, and was also deployed by the members of the RA, as we shall see later in this chapter.
8. My observations on White working-class racialised discourses in Streetville are based on fieldwork with members of the RA. See Joanna Herbert's (2008, Chapter 2) study of White residents' oral histories from this area of Leicester for a wider discussion of the dynamics of White attitudes.
9. Ramadan is a holy month in Islam when devout Muslims fast from daybreak to sunset.
10. The neighbourhood watch scheme is a national scheme where residents work with the police to monitor crime in their neighbourhood.

6 Slave Ancestries and the Inheritance of Interracial Identities

1. Like most ethnographic studies of interracial subjectivities in Britain (see, for example, Ifekwunigwe, 1999; Twine, 2000, 2004; Ali, 2003), the majority of my research participants were members of Black British African Caribbean and White British descent families. This represents the majority of interracial families that live in Leicester. In the 2001 national Census classifications, the ethnic composition of interracial people in Leicester was as follows: 'Mixed: White and Black Caribbean' 1.01 per cent; 'Mixed: White and Black African' 0.19 per cent; 'Mixed: White and Asian' 0.68 per cent; 'Mixed: Mixed Other' 0.44 per cent.
2. Twine's (2011) book on the 'racial literacy' of the White mothers of interracial families from Leicester was published while I was in the final stages of writing this manuscript, and so I am unable to draw substantially on it.

7 The Co-Existence of Whiteness, Social Class and Coloniality in Britain and the USA

1. The rise of gated communities in Britain has been discussed in the British media, but has received much less attention from academics.
2. See Thompson, 2005 for a discussion of apologies for the atrocities of Empire made by members of the British government.

Bibliography

Agyeman, J. (1989) 'Black-People, White Landscape'. *Town and Country Planning*, 58(12): 336–8.
Agyeman, J. and Spooner, R. (1997) 'Ethnicity and the Rural Environment', in P. Cloke and J. Little (eds), *Contested Countryside Cultures: Otherness, Marginalisation and Rurality* (London: Routledge).
Ahmed, S. (2004) 'Declarations of Whiteness: The Non-Performativity of Anti-Racism'. *Borderlands* (ejournal) 3(2), http://www.borderlands.net.au/vol3no2_2004/ahmed_declarations.htm.
Ali, N., Kalra, V. S. and Sayyid, S. (eds) (2006) *A Postcolonial People: South Asians in Britain* (London: Hurst and Company).
Ali, S. (2008) 'Mixed "Race", Families and Belonging'. Paper presented to the Centre for Research on Nationalism Ethnicity and Multiculturalism, University of Surrey, 18 February.
Ali, S. (2003) *Mixed-Race, Post-Race, Gender New Ethnicities and Cultural Practices* (Oxford: Berg).
Back, L. (2002) 'Guess Who's Coming to Dinner? The Political Morality of Investigating Whiteness in the Gray Zone', in V. Ware and L. Back (eds), *Out of Whiteness: Color, Politics, and Culture* (Chicago: The University of Chicago Press).
Back, L. (1996) *New Ethnicities and Urban Culture: Racism and Multi Culture in Young Lives* (London: UCL Press).
Back, L. and Keith, M. (2004) 'Impurity and the Emancipatory City: Young People, Community Safety and Racial Danger', in L. Lees (ed.), *The Emancipatory City? Paradoxes and Possibilities* (London: Sage).
Baunman, Z. (1997) 'The Making and Unmaking of Strangers', in P. Werbner and T. Modood (eds), *Debating Cultural Hybridity: Multi-Cultural Identities and the Politics of Anti-Racism* (London: Zed Books).
Blokland, T. (2001) 'Bricks, Mortar, Memories: Neighbourhood and Networks in Collective Acts of Remembering'. *International Journal of Urban and Regional Research*, 25(2): 268–83.
Blommaert, J. and Verschueren, J. (1998) *Debating Diversity: Analysing the Discourse of Tolerance* (London: Routledge).
Bonnett, A. (2000) *White Identities: Historical and International Perspectives* (Essex: Pearson Education Limited).
Bourdieu, P. (1984) *Distinction* (London: Routledge).
Brodwin, P. (2004) 'Genetics, Identity and the Anthropology of Essentialism', in J. O. Ifekwunigwe (ed.), *Mixed Race Studies: A Reader* (Routledge, London).
Bryne, B. (2006) *White Lives: The Interplay of 'Race', Class and Gender in Everyday Life* (London: Routledge).
Bulmer, M. and Solomos, J. (2004) 'Introduction: Researching Race and Racism', in M. Bulmer and J. Solomos (eds), *Researching Race and Racism* (London: Routledge).

Butler, T. and Robson, G. (2003) 'Negotiating Their Way In: The Middle-Classes, Gentrification and the Deployment of Capital in a Globalising Metropolis'. *Urban Studies*, 40(9): 1791–809.
Butler, T. and Savage, M. (eds) (1995) *Social Change and the Middle Classes* (London: UCL Press).
Cashmore, E. (1987) *The Logic of Racism* (London: Allen and Unwin).
Chakroborti, N. and Garland, J. (2004) *Rural Racism* (Devon: Willan).
Charlesworth, S. J. (2000) *A Phenomenology of Working Class Experience* (Cambridge: Cambridge University Press).
Clifford, J. and Marcus, G. E. (eds) (1986) *Writing Culture: The Poetics and Politics of Ethnography* (Berkeley: University of California Press).
Cloke, P., Phillips, M. and Thrift, N. (1995) 'The New Middle-Classes and the Social Constructs of Rural Living', in T. Butler and M. Savage (eds), *Social Change and the Middle-Classes* (London: UCL Press).
Cohen, A. P. (2000) 'Peripheral Vision: Nationalism, National Identity and the Objective Correlative in Scotland', in A. P. Cohen (ed.), *Signifying Identities: Anthropological Perspectives on Boundaries and Contested Values* (London: Routledge).
Cohen, P. (1997) 'Labouring Under Whiteness', in R. Frankenberg (ed.), *Displacing Whiteness: Essays in Social and Cultural Criticism* (Durham, NC: Duke University Press).
Colls, R. (2002) *Identity of England* (Oxford: Oxford University Press).
Cross, K. (2001) 'Framing Whiteness: The Human Genome Diversity Project (as seen on TV)'. *Science as Culture*, 10: 411–37.
Degnen, C. (2012) *Years in the Making: Ageing Selves and Everyday Life in the North of England* (Manchester: Manchester University Press).
Diacon, D. (1990) *Regeneration of a Mining Town, Coalville into the 1990's – A Future Without Coal?* (Memorial Square, Coalville: The Building and Social Housing Foundation in Association with Loughborough University).
Doane, A. W. (2003) 'Rethinking Whiteness Studies', in A. W. Doane and E. Bonilla-Silva (eds), *White Out: The Continuing Significance of Racism* (London: Routledge).
Dyer, R. (1997) *White* (London: Routledge).
Edwards, J. (2000) *Born and Bred: Idioms of Kinship and the New Reproductive Technologies in England* (Oxford: Oxford University Press).
Edwards, J. (1999) 'Why Dolly Matters: Kinship, Culture and Cloning'. *Ethnos*, 64(3): 301–24.
Edwards, J. and Strathern, M. (2000) 'Including Our Own', in J. Carsten (ed.), *Cultures of Relatedness: New Approaches to the Study of Kinship* (Cambridge: Cambridge University Press).
Eley, G. (2002) 'Beneath the Skin. Or: How to Forget about the Empire Without Really Trying'. *Journal of Colonialism and Colonial History*, 3(1). http://muse.jhu.edu/journals/journal_of_colonialism_and_colonial_history/v003/3.1eley.html.
Essed, P. (1991) *Understanding Everyday Racism* (London: Sage).
Evans, G. (2007) *Educational Failure and Working Class White Children in Britain* (Basingstoke: Palgrave Macmillan).
Fantasia, R. (1988) *Cultures of Solidarity: Consciousness, Action, and Contemporary American Workers* (Berkeley: University of California Press).

Ferber, A. L. (2007) 'Whiteness Studies and the Erasure of Gender'. *Sociology Compass*, 1: 265–82.
Frankenberg, R. (1993b) 'Growing Up White: Feminism, Racism and the Social Geography of Childhood'. *Feminist Review*, 45: 51–84.
Frankenberg, R. (1993a) *White Women, Race Matters* (London: Routledge).
Franklin, S. (2001) 'Biologization Revisited: Kinship Theory in the Context of the New Biologies', in S. Franklin and S. Mckinnon (eds), *Relative Values: Reconfiguring Kinship Studies* (Durham, NC: Duke University Press).
Franklin, S. and Mckinnon, S. (2001) *Relative Values: Reconfiguring Kinship Studies* (Durham, NC: Duke University Press).
Gabriel, J. (1998) *Whitewash: Racialized Politics and the Media* (London: Routledge).
Garner, S. (2009) 'Home Truths: The White Working Class and the Racialization of Social Housing', in K. P. Sveinsson (ed.), *Who Cares About the White Working Class?* (London: The Runnymede Trust).
Garner, S. (2006) 'The Uses of Whiteness: What Sociologists Working on Europe Can Draw from US work on Whiteness'. *Sociology*, 40(2): 257–75.
Gatson, S. N. (2003) 'On Being Amorphous: Autoethnography, Genealogy, and a Multiracial Identity'. *Qualitative Inquiry* 9(1): 20–48.
Giddens, A. (1994) 'Living in a Post-Traditional Society', in U. Beck, A. Giddens and S. Lash (eds), *Reflexive Modernization: Politics, Tradition and Aesthetics in the Modern Social Order* (Cambridge: Polity Press).
Gilroy, P. (2005b) 'Why Harry's Disoriented About Empire, The Chronic Pain And Loss Feeds Our Melancholic Attachment', 18 January, *The Guardian*, http://www.guardian.co.uk/uk/2005/jan/18/britishidentity.monarchy.
Gilroy, P. (2005a) *Postcolonial Melancholia* (Columbia: Columbia University Press).
Gilroy, P. (1987) *There Ain't No Black in the Union Jack: Cultural Politics of Race and Nation* (London: Hutchinson).
Hall, C. (2000b) 'Introduction: Thinking the Postcolonial, Thinking the Empire', in C. Hall (ed.), *Cultures of Empire: Colonizers in Britain and the Empire in the Nineteenth and Twentieth Centuries* (Manchester: Manchester University Press).
Hall, C. (ed.) (2000a) *Cultures of Empire: Colonizers in Britain and the Empire in the Nineteenth and Twentieth Centuries* (Manchester: Manchester University Press).
Hall, C. and Rose, S. (2006b) 'Introduction: Being at Home with the Empire', in C. Hall and S. Rose (eds), *At Home with the Empire: Metropolitan Culture and the Imperial World* (Cambridge: Cambridge University Press).
Hall, C. and Rose, S. (eds) (2006a) *At Home with the Empire: Metropolitan Culture and the Imperial World* (Cambridge: Cambridge University Press).
Hall, J. D. (1998) '"You Must Remember This": Autobiography as Social Critique'. *The Journal of American History*, 85(2): 439–65.
Hall, S. (2003) 'Cultural Identity and Diaspora', in J. E. Braziel and A. Mannur (eds), *Theorising Diaspora* (Oxford: Blackwell).
Hall, S. (2000) 'Conclusion: The Multi-Cultural Question', in B. Hesse (ed.), *Unsettled Multiculturalisms: Diasporas, Entanglements, Transruptions* (London: Zed Books).
Hall, S. (1992) 'New Ethnicities', in J. Donald and A. Rattansi (eds), *Race, Culture and Difference* (London: Routledge).
Hartigan, J. (2005) *Odd Tribes: Towards a Cultural Analysis of White People* (Durham, NC: Duke University Press).

Hartigan, J. (2003) 'Who are These White People?: "Rednecks," "Hillbillies", And "White Trash" as Marked Racial Subjects', in A. W. Doane and E. Bonilla-Silva (eds), *White Out: The Continuing Significance of Racism* (London: Routledge).

Haritgan, J. (1999) *Racial Situations: Class Predicaments of Whiteness in Detroit* (Princeton: Princeton University Press).

Herbert, J. (2008) *Negotiating Boundaries in the City Migration, Ethnicity, and Gender in Britain* (Farnham, Surrey: Ashgate).

Herzfeld, M. (1993) *The Social Production of Indifference: Exploring the Symbolic Roots of the West* (Chicago: University of Chicago Press).

Hesse, B. (2002) 'Forgotten Like a Bad Dream: Atlantic Slavery and the Ethics of Postcolonial Memory', in D. T. Goldberg and A. Quayson (eds), *Relocating Postcolonialism* (Oxford: Blackwell).

Hesse, B. (1997) 'White Governmentality: Urbanism, Nationalism, Racism', in S. Westwood and J. Williams (eds), *Imagining Cities: Scripts, Signs, Memory* (London: Routledge).

Hesse, B. (1993) 'Black to Front and Black Again: Racialisation through Contested Times and Spaces', in M. Keith and S. Pile (eds), *Place and the Politics of Identity* (London: Routledge).

Hesse, B. and Sayyid, S. (2006) 'Narrating the Postcolonial Political and Immigrant Imaginary', in N. Ali, V. S. Kalra and S. Sayyid (eds), *A Postcolonial People: South Asians in Britain* (London: Hurst and Company).

Hewitt, R. (2005) *White Backlash and the Politics of Multiculturalism* (Cambridge: Cambridge University Press).

Hill, J. (2008) *The Everyday Language of White Racism* (Oxford: Wiley-Blackwell).

Home Office (2000) *Race Relations (Amendment) Act*, http://www.homeoffice.gov.uk/comrace/race/raceact/amendact.html.

Hutnyk, J. (1999) 'Magical Mystical Tourism', in R. Kaur and J. Hutnyk (eds), *Travel Worlds: Journeys in Contemporary Cultural Politics* (London: Zed Books).

Ifekwunigwe, J. (2001) 'Re-Membering "Race": On Gender, "Mixed Race" and Family in the English-African Diaspora', in D. Parker and M. Song (eds), *Rethinking 'Mixed Race'* (London: Pluto Press).

Ifekwunigwe, J. (1999) *Scattered Belongings: Cultural Paradoxes of 'Race', Nation and Gender* (London: Routledge).

Johnson, H. B. and Sharpiro, T. M. (2003) 'Good Neighbourhoods, Good Schools: Race and the "Good Choices" of White Families', in A. W. Doane and E. Bonilla-Silva (eds), *White Out: The Continuing Significance of Racism* (London: Routledge).

Keith, M. (2005) *After the Cosmopolitan? Multicultural Cities and the Future of Racism* (London: Routledge).

Kennedy, L. (2000) *Race and Urban Space in Contemporary American Culture* (Edinburgh: Edinburgh University Press).

Kinsmen, P. (1997) 'Renegotiating the Boundaries of Race and Citizenship: The Black Environment Network and Environmental and Conservation Bodies', in P. Milbourne (ed.), *Revealing Rural 'Others'* (London: Pinter).

Knowles, C. (2007) 'The Landscape of Post-Imperial Whiteness in Rural Britain'. *Ethnic and Racial Studies*, 31(1): 167–84.

Lasch, C. (1991) *The True and Only Heaven: Progress and its Critics* (New York: W. W. Norton).

Lawler, S. (1999) 'Getting Out and Getting Away: Women's Narratives of Class Mobility'. *Feminist Review*, 63: 2–24.

Leicester City Council (1991b) *Key Facts About Leicester: No. 3. The Economy*. (Leicester: Leicester City Council).
Leicester City Council (1991a) *Leicester Key Facts – City Profile 1991 Census* (Leicester: Leicester City Council).
Leicestershire County Council (2001b) *Census 2001 – Area Profile, Harborough District and Kibworth Ward* (Leicester: Leicestershire County Council).
Leicestershire County Council (2001a) *Ethnicity in Leicestershire – Key Results from 2001 Census* (Leicester: Leicestershire County Council).
Leicester Promotions (1997) *Dawn to Dusk: Incorporating Places to Visit Around Leicester* (Leicester: Leicester Promotions Ltd).
Low, S. M. (2003) 'The Edge and the Centre: Gated Communities and the Discourse of Urban Fear', in S. M. Low and D. Lawrence-Zuniga (eds), *The Anthropology of Space and Place: Locating Culture* (Oxford: Blackwell).
Mackenzie, J. (1986b) 'Introduction', in J. Mackenzie (ed.), *Imperialism and Popular Culture* (Manchester: Manchester University Press).
MacKenzie, J. (ed.) (1986a) *Imperialism and Popular Culture* (Manchester: Manchester University Press).
MacPherson, W. (1999) *The Stephen Lawrence Inquiry* (London: Stationary Office).
Malik, K. (2005) 'Born in Bradford'. *Prospect October*, 54–6.
Mckinney, K. D. (2005) *Being White, Stories of Race and Racism* (London: Routledge).
McIntosh, P. (2003) 'White Privilege and Male Privilege' in M. S. Kimmel and A. L. Ferber (eds), *Privilege: A Reader* (Boulder, CO: Westview Press).
Melucci, A. (1988) 'Social Movements and the Democratization of Everyday Life', in J. Keane (ed.), *Civil Society and the State: New European Perspectives* (London: Verso).
Morrison, T. (1992) *Playing in the Dark: Whiteness and the Literary Imagination* (Cambridge MA: Harvard University Press).
Murdoch, J. and Marsden, T. (1991) 'Reconstructing the Rural in an Urban Region: New Villages For Old?' *Countryside Change Working Paper 26*, University of Newcastle.
Nash, C. (2004) 'Genetic Kinship'. *Cultural Studies*, 18: 1–33.
Nash, C. (2002) 'Genealogical Identities'. *Environment and Planning D: Society and Space*, 20: 27–52.
Nayak, A. (2003) *Race, Place and Globalization: Youth Cultures in a Changing World* (Oxford: Berg).
Neal, S. (2009) *Rural Identities, Ethnicity and Community in the Contemporary English Countryside* (Farnham, Surrey: Ashgate).
Neal, S. (2002) 'Rural Landscapes, Representations and Racism: Examining Multicultural Citizenship and Policy Making in the English Countryside'. *Ethnic and Racial Studies*, 25(3): 442–61.
Neal, S. and Agyeman, J. (eds) (2006) *The New Countryside? Ethnicity, Nation and Exclusion in Contemporary Rural Britain* (Bristol: The Policy Press).
Ortner, S. (2002) 'Subjects and Capital: A Fragment of a Documentary Ethnography'. *Ethnos*, 67(1): 9–32.
Pahl, R. (1964) 'Urbs in Rure', *Geographical Papers* (London: London School of Economics).
Parham, A. A. (2008) 'Race, Memory and Family History'. *Social Identities*, 14(1): 13–32.

Parker, D. (2000) 'The Chinese Takeaway and the Diasporic Habitus: Space, Time and Power Geometries', in B. Hesse (ed.), *Unsettled Multiculturalisms: Diasporas, Entanglements, Transruptions* (London: Zed Books).
Parker, D. and Song, M. (2001) 'Introduction: Rethinking "Mixed Race"', in D. Parker and M. Song (eds), *Rethinking 'Mixed Race'* (London: Pluto Press).
Patterson, O. (1982) *Slavery and Social Death: A Comparative Study* (Cambridge, MA: Harvard University Press).
Phillips, M. (1993) 'Rural Gentrification and the Processes of Class Colonisation'. *Journal of Rural Studies*, 28(9): 123–40.
Puwar, N. (2004) *Space Invaders: Race, Gender and Bodies Out of Place* (Oxford: Berg).
Rapport, N. (1993) *Diverse Worldviews in an English Village* (Edinburgh: Edinburgh University Press).
Reary, D., Hollingworth, S., Williams, K., Crozier, G., Jamieson, F., James, D. and Beedell, P. (2007) '"A Darker Shade of Pale?" Whiteness, the Middle Classes and Multi-Ethnic Inner City Schooling'. *Sociology*, 41(6): 1041–60.
Richards, A. (1996) *Miners on Strike: Class Solidarity and Division in Britain* (Oxford: Berg).
Rhodes, J. (2011) '"It's Not Just Them, It's Whites as Well": Whiteness, Class and BNP support'. *Sociology*, 45(1): 102–17.
Rhodes, J. (2010) 'White Backlash, Unfairness and Justifications of British National Party (BNP) Support'. *Ethnicities*, 10(1): 77–99.
Said, E. W. (1978) *Orientalism: Western Conceptions of the Orient* (London: Penguin Press).
Savage, M. (2000) *Class Analysis and Social Transformation* (Buckingham: Open University Press).
Sayyid, S. (2006) 'BrASIANS: Postcolonial People, Ironic Citizens', in N. Ali, V. S. Kalra and S. Sayyid (eds), *A Postcolonial People: South Asians in Britain* (London: Hurst and Company).
Sayyid, S. (2004) 'Slippery People: The Immigrant Imaginary and the Grammar of Colour', in I. Law, D. Philips and L. Turney (eds), *Institutional Racism in Higher Education* (London: Trentham Books).
Sileby, D. (1995) *Geographies of Exclusion* (London: Routledge).
Skeggs, B. (2004) *Class, Self, Culture* (London: Routlege).
Skeggs, B. (1997) *Formations of Class and Gender* (London: Sage).
Smith, S. J. (1993) 'Residential Segregation and the Politics of Racialisation', in M. Cross and M. Keith (eds), *Racism, the City and the State* (London: Routledge).
Solomos, J. and Back, L. (1995) *Race, Politics and Social Change* (London: Routledge).
Steyn, M. and Conway, D. (2010) 'Introduction: Intersecting Whiteness, Interdisciplinary Debates'. *Ethnicities*, 10(3): 283–91.
Stoler, A. L. (1997) 'On Political and Psychological Essentialisms'. *Ethos*, 25(1): 101–6.
Stoler, A. L. (1995) *Race and the Education of Desire: Foucault's History of Sexuality and the Colonial Order of Things* (Durham, NC: Duke University Press).
Strathern, M. (1992) *After Nature: English Kinship in the Late Twentieth Century* (Cambridge: Cambridge University Press).
Strathern, M. (1982) 'The Village as an Idea: Constructs of Village-Ness in Elmdon, Essex', in A. P. Cohen (ed.), *Belonging: Identity and Social Organisation in British Rural Cultures* (Manchester: Manchester University Press).

Strathern, M. (1981) *Kinship at the Core: An Anthropology of Elmdon, a Village in North-West Essex, in the 1960s* (Cambridge: Cambridge University Press).
The Coalville Times (1997) 'Golden Days of Coal', p. 6, in *100 Years of the Coalville Times, Special Supplement*.
The Office for National Statistics (2005) *Neighbourhood Statistics, for wards in Leicester*.
Thompson, A. (2005) *The Empire Strikes Back? The Impact of Imperialism on Britain from the Mid-Nineteenth Century* (Edinburgh: Pearson Education).
Thompson, C. (2001) 'Strategic Naturalising: Kinship in an Infertility Clinic', in S. Franklin and S. Mckinnon (eds), *Relative Values: Reconfiguring Kinship Studies* (Durham, NC: Duke University Press).
Tutton, R. (2004) '"They Want to Know Where They Came From": Population Genetics, Identity, and Family Genealogy'. *New Genetics and Society*, 23: 105–20.
Twine, F. W. (2011) *A White Side of Black Britain: Interracial Literacy and Racial Literacy* (Durham, NC: Duke University Press).
Twine, F. W. (2010) 'White Like Who? The Value of Whiteness in British Interracial Families'. *Ethnicities*, 10(3): 292–312.
Twine, F. W. (2006) 'Visual Ethnography and Racial Theory: Family Photographs as Archives of Interracial Intimacies'. *Ethnic and Racial Studies*, 29(3): 487–511.
Twine, F. W. (2004) 'A White Side of Black Britain: The Concept of Racial Literacy'. *Ethnic and Racial Studies*, 25(6): 878–907.
Twine, F. W. (2000) 'Bearing Blackness in Britain: The Meaning of Racial Difference for White Birth Mothers of African Descent Children', in H. Ragone and F. W. Twine (eds), *Ideologies and Technologies of Motherhood: Race, Class, Sexuality, Nationalism* (London: Routledge).
Twine, F. W. and Gallagher, C. (2008) 'The Future of Whiteness: A Map of the "Third Wave"'. *Ethnic and Racial Studies* 31(1): 4–24.
Tyler, K. (2011) 'New Ethnicities and Old Classities: Respectability and Diaspora'. *Social Identities*, 17(4): 521–40.
Tyler, K. (2009) 'Whiteness Studies and Laypeople's Engagements with Race and Genetics'. *New Genetics and Society*, 28(1): 35–48.
Tyler, K. (2008) 'Ethnographic Approaches to Race, Genetics and Genealogy'. *Sociology Compass*, 2(5): 1860–77.
Tyler, K. (2007) 'Race, Genetics and Inheritance: Reflections upon the Birth of "Black" Twins to a "White" IVF mother', in P. Wade (ed.), *Race, Ethnicity and Nation: Perspectives from Kinship and Genetics* (Oxford: Berghahn Books).
Tyler, K. (2005) 'The Genealogical Imagination: The Inheritance of Interracial Identities'. *The Sociological Review*, 53(3): 475–94.
Vincent, C., Ball, S. J. and Kemp, S. (2004) 'The Social Geography of Childcare: Making Up a Middle-Class Child'. *British Journal of Sociology of Education*, 25(2): 229–44.
Wade, P. (2002) *Race, Nature and Culture: An Anthropological Perspective* (London: Pluto Press).
Ware, V. (2008) 'Towards a Sociology of Resentment: A Debate on Class and Whiteness'. *Sociological Research Online*, 13(5): 9 http://www.socresonline.org.uk/13/5/9.html.
Ware, V. (1997) 'Island Racism: Gender, Place and White Power', in R. Frankenberg (ed.), *Displacing Whiteness: Essays in Social and Cultural Criticism* (Durham, NC: Duke University Press).

Watt, P. (2006) 'Respectability, Roughness and "Race": Neighbourhood, Place Images and the Making of Working-Class Social Distinctions in London'. *International Journal of Urban and Regional Research*, 30(4): 776–97.

Wemyss, G. (2009) *The Invisible Empire: White Discourse, Tolerance and Belonging* (Farnham, Surrey: Ashgate).

Wemyss, G. (2008) 'White Memories, White Belonging: Competing Colonial Anniversaries in "Postcolonial" East London'. *Sociological Research Online*, 13(5): 8, http://www.socresonline.org.uk/13/5/8.html.

Werbner, P. (1991) 'Introduction II Black and Ethnic Leadership in Britain: A Theoretical Overview', in P. Werbner and M. Anwar (eds) *Black and Ethnic Leadership in Britain: The Cultural Dimensions of Political Action* (London: Routledge).

Westwood, S. (1991) 'Red Star Over Leicester: Racism, the Politics of Identity, and Black Youth in Britain', in P. Werbner and M. Anwar (eds) *Black and Ethnic Leadership in Britain: The Cultural Dimensions of Political Action* (London: Routledge).

Williams, R. (1973) *The Country and the City* (London: The Hogarth Press).

Wittgenstein, L. (1980) *Culture and Value* (Oxford: Blackwell).

Wood, M. (2010) *The Story of England* (London: Viking Press).

Wright, P. (1999) 'An Encroachment Too Far', in A. Barnett and R. Scruton (eds), *Town and Country* (London: Vintage).

Television programmes

BBC 1, 'Who Do You Think You Are?' series 8, screened August–September 2011. http://www.bbc.co.uk/programmes/b007t575.

BBC4, 'The Story of England', screened September 2010–October 2010.

BBC2, 'The White Season', screened 9 March–11 March 2008. http://www.bbc.co.uk/white/.

BBC2, 'Motherland: A Genetic Journey', screened 14 February 2003.

Websites

http://www.mayavisionint.com/English_Story/Episode_Guide.html. I. Accessed: August 2011.

http://www.independent.co.uk/opinion/commentators/matthew-norman/matthew-norman-implanting-a-black-face-in-midsomer-would-be-tokenism-2242713.html. Accessed: April 2011.

http://www.goleicestershire.com/food-and-drink/default.aspx/. Accessed: December 2010.

http://www.goleicestershire.com/explore/. Accessed: January 2006.

Index

African Caribbean slavery, 80, 87, 178
Agyeman, Julian, 41
Anglo-centricity, 40
anti-racist collective action
   Forum's legal action against the Council, 163–70
   Race Relations Amendment Act (2000)
   Residents' Association (RA) and the Forum, 151–6. *See* Residents' Association (RA) and the Forum in Streetville, 148–51
   White working-class backlash discourses against multiculturalism, 156–63

Back, Les, 24, 29–30, 32, 68–69, 158
Barbados sugar, 87
Beeson, John, 217
Belgrave, 82–3, 88
   perception of as a 'ghetto,' 98–101
   William's views, 96
Black Britons
   colonial relations to Britain, 80, 87
   personal testimonies, on interracial identity, 184–205
   slave histories, 179–80
Black people
   and denial of belonging to the English countryside, 41–2
BrAsian Bangladeshi organisation, 159–60
BrAsian(s), White perceptions of
   attitude towards women, 65–6
   class distinction, 61–7
   colonial relations to Britain, 80, 95
   and denial of belonging to the English countryside, 41–2
   and the perceived discourse of excess, 67–73
   economic success, 67
   as immigrants, 42
   perceptions of lifestyles, 100
   respectability, 61–7
   BrAsian shopkeepers and the White discourse of service, 55–61
   Streetville residents' point of view, 160–3
   urban culture and identity, 81
   wealthy, and the White discourse of BrAsians' excess, 67–73
   wealthy, inhabitants and the White discourse of BrAsians' 'social isolation,' 61–7
   White middle-class villagers attitudes, 42–3
   White residents' discourses on, 43–4
BrAsian women, 65
BrAsian women, education of, 66
British Chinese people, 113
British inner city neighbourhoods, 80
Bryne, Bridget, 21

Caribbean Rum, 87
class distinctions
   in Whites, 23
classed identities, 22
class positioning, 22
Coalville
   BrAsian and Chinese restaurants, 127–8, 127–30
   BrAsian-owned restaurants, 118
   convention and traditional values, 117, 128–31
   demography, 117
   ethnic composition, 118, 127–30
   local pride in the past, 125–6
   Memorial Square, 118
   Men's career paths, 122
   new businesses, 123–4
   NUM politics of strike, 122
   1898 pit disaster, 125
   postmining era, 123–4
   relationship between parents and children, 130–1

Coalville – *continued*
  socio-economic composition, 121–6
  unemployment, 122–3
  White co-conversationalists' critical reflections on racism, 130–42
The Coalville Times, 124
collective denial of Britain's colonial history, 79
colonial discourse of cultural differentiation, 42
coloniality, 74–8
Commission for Racial Equality (CRE), 168
cultural capital, 22

Dawn to Dusk, 83–5
Degnen, Cathrine, 49, 226n3

East India Company, 9–10
Edwards, Jeanette, 49, 179, 195
Electoral Commission, 146–7
empire, influence on everyday life, 11–12
English village community, 44–8
  spirit, 51–5
English village life, 40
ethnography, on Whiteness and social class
  in Leicester/shire, 211–14
  in terms of ethnicity and history, 214–19
  in the USA, 207–11
European Commission, 123
Evans, Gillian, 25–26, 30

Frankenberg, Ruth, 14–20, 33, 42, 61, 62, 66, 67, 73, 84, 90, 92, 99, 111, 117, 120, 138, 147, 209–211, 213

Gatson, Sarah, 220–1
Gilroy, Paul, 11–12, 19, 79, 100, 227n4
'Golden Mile,' 88–9
Greenville
  attitudes of Whites towards the minority of BrAsians, 40
  BrAsian shopkeepers and the White discourse of service, 55–61
  demography of, 48–50
  formation of White middle-class ethnicities, 51–5
  housing style in, 50–1
  immigrant imagery, 95–8
  in-depth interviews with White middle-class and working-class, 44–8
  Parish Council and, 45
  perceptions of White residents about the village, 44–8
  performance of coloniality, 74–8
  racial segregation, 92–5
  residents' perceptions of BrAsians, 159
  village community spirit, 51–5
  vs Streetville, 99
  wealthy BrAsian inhabitants and the White discourse of 'social isolation,' 61–7
  wealthy BrAsians and the White discourse of excess, 67–73
  wealthy BrAsians in, 43

Hartigan, John, 207–209, 211
Hall, Catherine, 1, 2, 10, 11, 30, 87
Hesse, Barnor, 3, 19, 20, 79, 80, 98, 180
Hill, Jane, 216– 218

Inner Area Programme (IAP), 149
interracial families' identities
  Clare's sense of ethnicity, 196–201
  Emily's account of her interracial family, 184–9
  influence of slave histories and ancestries in forming, 219–22
  John's account of histories of slavery, 189–92
  kinship ideologies, 179–81
  Sandra's sense of her interracial identity and family, 192–6
  Sophie's views: a White woman's views on slavery and genealogical identities, 202–5
  from Streetville, ethnographic study, 181–205
  Twine's ethnographic insights, 177–8

Knowles, Caroline, 16, 55, 61

Lawrence, Stephen, 168
Leicester BrAsians, 80. *See also* BrAsians
  and Belgrave, 89, 101–5
  perceived cultural differences with Whites, 95–6, 102
  Flo's account of BrAsians perceived cultural differences, 97–8
  food, 87–8
  as immigrants, 95–8
  perception of lifestyles, 100
  of Streetville, 90
  White portrait of, 103–4
  William's account of, 96–7
Leicester City Council, 81
Leicestershire, website and brochure promotions, 81–91
  Belgrave, 82–3, 88
  Black Britons' colonial relations to Britain, 80, 87
  BrAsian identities and culture in, 82, 102
  county's cheeses, 85
  county's pork pies, 85
  cuisines, 84–6
  of 'Golden Mile,' 89
  Melton hunt cake and pork pies, 85–7
  relationship between the city and the country, 82
  representation of rural English history, 83
  restaurants, 83
  significance of curry, 84–5
  Streetville, 90
  symbols of rurality, 82
Leicestershire County Council, 81

MacPherson report, 168
Midsomer Murders, 40–1
Motherland: A Genetic Journey, 203
multiculturalism, 15, 19, 25, 101, 105
  negotiating White working-class backlash against, 156–63
  representations of White working-class backlash against, 114–17, 136
multicultural politics, 150–1

multiethnic composition, 149–50, 157
muscovado sugar, 87

National Forest Company, 123
National Union of Mineworkers (NUM), 121–2
Neal, Sarah, 40, 41
negative racialised images of the city, 79
New kinship studies within anthropology, 117
Norman Conquest of Saxon England, 83

Ortner, Sherry B., 184

postcolonial English vernacular, 40
Powell, Enoch, 79
Purham, Angel, 221–2

Race Relations Amendment Act, 2000, 146, 167–8
racial distinctions
  in Whites, 23
racial hierarchy, 15, 19
racial segregation, between country and city, 105
  June's and Simon's views, 94–5
  Shelia's views, 92–3
Red Leicester cheese, 85, 87
Red Star's activism, 151–3, 155–6
Residents' Association (RA) and the Forum
  ethnographic research, 151–6
  Forum's legal action against the Council, 163–70
  functions of, 157–8
  key objectives, 149–50
  Malik's analysis of multicultural politics, 150–1
  multiethnic composition, 149–50, 157
  racialised views of members, 158–9
  residents' point of view of forums, 160–2, 166–7
  role in judicial review, 156–70

Sayyid, S., 3, 5, 19–20, 97
Scattered Belongings, 183

Skeggs, Beverley, 22
slave labour, 80
slave ancestries in formation of genealogical identities, 219–22
social capital, 22
Spooner, Rachel, 41
Stilton cheese, 85–6, 87
Strathern, Marilyn, 26, 49, 66, 130–131, 179, 203
The Story of England, 6–14, 83
Streetville
  anti-racist collective action in, 148–51
  BrAsian Bangladeshi organisation, 159–61
  demography, 148–9
  distinction between 'resentment' and 'racism'?, 158
  ethnic minority and religious organisations, 149
  funding initiatives and schemes for, 149
  as a 'ghetto,' 98–101
  interracial families' identities, ethnographic study, 181–205
  Residents' Association (RA) and the Forum, 149–50. *See also* Residents' Association (RA) and the Forum
  socio-economic composition, 148–9
Stuart Hall's 'new ethnicities,' 179–81

United States
  ethnography, on Whiteness and social class, 207–11
  mobilisation of slave ancestries in formation of genealogical identities, 219–22
  White amnesia of Native American histories within USA, 216–18

Wade, Peter, 179
Wemyss, Georgie, 8–10, 15, 16, 19, 107, 214, 215
Westwood's study of a Black youth project, 151–3, 155–6
White amnesia of the colonial past, 19–20, 43, 56, 67, 71, 74, 80, 91, 107, 112, 180, 189, 200–1
  of BrAsians' colonial relationships with the countryside, 95, 97, 142–3, 175, 213
  and denoting inner city as a 'ghetto,' 98
  in everyday constructions, 214–16
  in Leicester/shire, 218–19
  of Native American histories within USA, 216–18
White classed ethnicities, 21–7
White co-conversationalists, 81, 101, 165
  convention and traditional values, 117
  critical reflections on racism, 120, 130–42, 207
  on racialised constitution of Greenville, 91–101, 107, 160, 165, 219
  from Streetville, 177
  on Wealthy BrAsians, 89–90
White middle-class discourses, 26
White middle-class ethnicities, formation of, 51–5
White middle-class identities, 23–4
White middle-class villagers, 41–2
  attitudes towards BrAsians, 42–3
Whiteness studies through a postcolonial perspective, 14–21
White residents' discourses on BrAsians, 43–4. *See also* BrAsians
Whites
  attitude towards women, 65–6
  perceptions of BrAsians, 113
White working-class racisms in Britain
  perceptions of, 114–17
  BBC's *White Season*, 115–17
  Bonnett's arguments, 115
  in Coalville, 112, 117–21, 117–30
  perceptions of changing ethnic composition, 113–15, 128–9, 134, 136, 207
  racialised discourses of White BNP supporters, 116
  'White backlash' against multiculturalism, 115
women
  African Caribbean, 196–7
  Bangladeshi, 28

BrAsian, 65–6
BrAsian, education of, 66
portrayal of Indian, in poetry, 76
role in reproduction of the village
  community, 53–4
as a symbol of totality of cultural
  distinctions, 65

White middle-and working-class
  American, 16
White working-class, 114

Ye Olde Pork Pie Shoppe, 86, 88